THOMAS HARDY, O.M.
THE MAN, HIS WORKS AND THE LAND OF WESSEX

THOMAS HARDY, O.M.

From a photo by Clive Holland

THOMAS HARDY, O.M.

THE MAN, HIS WORKS AND THE LAND OF WESSEX

BY

CLIVE HOLLAND

ILLUSTRATED BY

DOUGLAS SNOWDEN

HASKELL HOUSE

Publishers of Scholarly Books

NEW YORK

1966

published by

HASKELL HOUSE
Publishers of Scholarly Books
30 East 10th Street • New York, N. Y. 10003

CONTENTS

ILLUSTRATIONS

THOMAS HARDY, O.M.

PREFACE

IT IS many years since I first met Thomas Hardy, and the recollection of the first meeting and chatting with him in the pleasant drawing-room at Max Gate, hung with interesting water-colours of Wessex scenery and originals of illustrations of his novels, which visit was to have many successors, remains vivid in my memory.

He proved, as I had anticipated, to be of rather less than average height, alert in his movements, of spare figure, with keen eyes, and on this occasion, as on many others, was dressed in a homespun or tweed knickerbocker suit.

He leaned back easily in the arm-chair, smiling as I asked questions as to the locale of some of his most important novels.

In reply to a leading question, he said : " It must not be taken for granted, however, that any given place is clearly indicated in any description in my books. Sometimes, indeed, I have blended one with another to provide the scene."

But some years later, when I cycled with him over a good deal of the ground in the district round about Dorchester and further afield, we visited villages and spots which, he admitted, might, with certain reservations, be considered as the places described in his books. Particularly was this the case with scenes in *Tess of the D'Urbervilles, Far from the Madding Crowd, The Trumpet Major, The Mayor of Casterbridge, The Return of the Native, The Well-Beloved,* and *Under the Greenwood Tree.*

On one of these occasions we had been riding up the lower slopes of the road which climbs up High Stoy, the scene of " The Lost Pyx " in *Poems of the Past and Present*. Hardy dismounted and leaned against the saddle of his bicycle, and with thoughtful gaze regarded the magnificent prospect of the Blackmoor Vale, which from this point in the road lay extended below us enveloped in a misty haze, through which the sunlight sent shafts of light, making it the more beautiful.

After a pause he said : " I am going to ask you a question. Will you answer it honestly ? "

" If it can be answered at all, it shall certainly be answered honestly," I replied.

" Well, then," he said, " if you had the choice of being born, would you have been ? "

What a simple and yet, on consideration, perplexing question ! One felt one ought to say " yes," but the speaker's solemnity, and even earnestness in putting the question, gave birth to a doubt.

In reply, I told Mr. Hardy that had he asked the question less abruptly, I should probably have said " yes " ; but that he had raised grave doubts in my mind. Then I asked him : " Would you ? "

After a pause the reply came : " No, surely not," followed by several reasons, which were weighty enough as the speaker stated them.

This, it should be noted, occurred at the time when he was at the height of his fame as a novelist—as near as I can remember—about two years before the publication of *Jude the Obscure* and Hardy's final abandonment of the novel as a means of literary expression.

A few years later and the pessimism or fatalism that permeates his books and most of his short stories, though lightened here and there by sly humour, as though he was silently amused at the sorrows, struggles and frailties of humans, was acknowledged in an interview that a distinguished critic had with him in the first year of the last century.

The critic was in a sense seeking to force upon Hardy

a robe of pessimism. He said to him : " I take it the pessimist holds that the principle of evil is the stronger."

To which Hardy replied : " No, I should not put it precisely in that way. For instance, people call me a pessimist ; and if it is pessimism to think with Sophocles, that ' not to be born is the best,' then I do not object to the designation."

Then, no doubt remembering the storm of criticism which had a few years before raged round his final novel, he went on to say : " I never could understand why the word ' pessimism ' is such a red rag to many worthy people, and I believe, indeed, that a good deal of the robustious, swaggering optimism of recent literature is at the bottom both cowardly and insincere. I do not see that we are likely to improve the world by asseverating, however loudly, that black is white, or at least that black is but a necessary contrast and foil, without which white would be white no longer."

On one occasion to the present writer Hardy claimed that his books were not " the gospel of pessimism " that one American critic had described them, " but as one continued plea against man's inhumanity to man—to woman—and the lower animals."

Somewhat strangely the conversation on another occasion took the turn of a discussion upon war which, as far as I remember, may have arisen from the strained relations then existing between this country and Germany over the Kaiser's famous or notorious telegram to President Kruger.

He said : " In my opinion war is doomed. It is doomed by the gradual growth of the introspective faculty of mankind, of their power of putting themselves in another's place and of taking and understanding a point of view that is not their own. In another aspect this might be called the growth of a sense of humour. Not to-day, nor to-morrow, but in the fullness of time, war will come to an end, not on account of moral reasons, but because of its absurdity."

Many who read this opinion, whether they agree or not

with the reason that Hardy advances for the ultimate ending of war, will pray that he may prove to have been a seer whose vision, to use his own words, " In the fullness of time," may come true.

Much has been written and said concerning the use by Hardy of many Anglo-Saxon words. He once stated that the use was deliberate and not merely fortuitous. He said, if I remember rightly : " My critics have sometimes taken me to task for the use of local Wessex words which they say have become obsolete. Whatever they may say or think, the words used are not obsolete down here in Wessex ; they are used and understood by educated people. So why, if they fill a gap in the language, and if they express an idea that cannot be otherwise so adequately or accurately expressed, why not use, and in a sense preserve them in the spoken or written language." Hardy continued to use these Wessex words to the end, not only because of their expressiveness and adequacy but also because, we think, he was impelled to use them by that vein of Anglo-Saxon character and love of by-gone things that were so marked in him.

But if he was a pessimist—from his own admission and the vein of gloom that runs through many of his novels and short stories and poems, who can deny but that he was ?—he was at the same time capable of the greatest kindliness, and had a charm that only those who got to know him well fully realized.

Hardy literally found his kingdom in Wessex, that ancient region which, before he touched it with the alchemy of genius, was a mere name, no longer existent upon the map. Now for tens of thousands of readers' he has made it familiar, and also its types, by-gone customs and " old crusted characters "—some of which even to-day in this sophisticated, mechanical age survive and may be met with in the remoter portions of the Hardy country—its breezy uplands, chalk cliffs, rocky coastline, peaceful hamlets and villages, life in its sleepy, historic capital, lovely vales, swelling downs, and gorse and heather-clad stretches of moorland.

No heath is more famous or widely known to readers than " Egdon " ; though some, Culloden Moor, for example, may be more historic.

Wellbridge Manor House, in which poor " Tess of the D'Urbervilles " passed her tragic honeymoon, has been visited by thousands, many of whom must have realized, while standing on the ancient Elizabethan bridge which spans the Frome, some at least of the atmosphere which Hardy was able to create as a background for one of his most poignant and memorable scenes.

And so true to life, though not photographically so, was Hardy in his character-drawing that one may occasionally, at least, even to-day, meet John Durbey-fields, Gabriel Oaks, Dick Dewys, Clym Yeobrights, Eustacia Vyes, Bathsheba Everdenes and Fanny Robins in the remoter parts of Dorset.

No other writer has so well depicted the whole of the countryside of any district as has Hardy that of Wessex, with its changes from hill to vale, its sharply defined divisions in the industrial pursuits of each locality, its old-world, still in many places, comparatively slowly moving life, and the ancient history bound up with it.

No other writer has successfully competed with him as a delineator of Wessex life and character. And none have rendered so subtly the half-conscious humour which often pervades the thoughts as well as the speech of Wessex folk.

Although the writing of this book had been contem-plated by me for many years it was the late Sir William Robertson Nicoll who, knowing the large amount of material I had gathered together, and the intercourse I had enjoyed with Hardy, urged that I should note every-thing connected with him for a book of the kind.

Naturally one has had to delve among masses of material : books, newspaper articles and cuttings, mag-azine articles, both British, Foreign and American, and letters. In addition to which I possessed the great advantage until recent years of living on the borders of Wessex, and of knowing what has become known as

" the Hardy Country " intimately. Many of the older inhabitants of Dorchester who knew Hardy as a boy I have conversed with, and much valuable material and many interesting details of his life have from time to time been given me by people who knew him well.

To the Editors and proprietors of the *Bookman*, *Bookman* (New York), *Critic* (New York), and many newspapers and magazines, too numerous to mention in detail, I am indebted for permission to quote from articles which, over a long period of years, I or other writers contributed to their pages dealing with Hardy, his books and Wessex. To the Editors of *The Times*, *Contemporary Review*, *Nineteenth Century and After*, *Athenæum*, and numerous papers in the area covered by the term Wessex, I am also indebted for information and the settling of dates which might have remained in dispute, and for facilities to consult their files. I am also grateful to Mr. J. Foster, of Dorchester, who many years ago kept a stationer's shop, and from whose library Hardy borrowed books as a boy, and in later years to the more recent proprietors of that shop ; to an artist friend, Mr. Fred Whitehead, and his wife, who knew Hardy well for many years, and whose caravan he used to visit when the artist was painting Wessex scenes ; to Editors of the *Dorset County Times* ; to the late Mr. Harry Pouncy, who knew Hardy well, and used to give Wessex lectures and recitations in dialect ; and to Dr. Batterbury, of Wimborne, and others at Oxford, Cambridge and other places I owe thanks for much interesting information of various kinds.

In some cases where in quoting the expressions " we are told " or " it is stated " the reference is to " The Early Life of Thomas Hardy " and " The Later Life of Thomas Hardy," by Mrs. Florence Emily Hardy.

I hope that this book may be the means of stimulating a wider interest in the great English novelist and poet, with whose life and works it deals, and to a more general reading of his novels and poetry.

THOMAS HARDY, O.M.

THE MAN, HIS WORKS AND THE LAND OF WESSEX

CHAPTER I

IT IS impossible to separate Thomas Hardy from that portion of England in which he was born, and afterwards made famous under the title of " Wessex," and the writer he became and the books and poetry that he wrote. But although many have considered that he was a writer with a somewhat limited field, and in a measure this criticism is true, it is nevertheless apparent to all those reading and studying his novels, poetry and dramas, how widely they apply to all that is most vital in human life, and how clearly they enable one to visualize the tragedy underlying existence wherever it be lived, north, east, south or west.

In reality it is a tribute to his genius that he should have found in the small county of Dorset and the few places beyond its borders which he described in his works, so much that is best and worst, richest and poorest in the minds and the actions of the characters which he put on paper. Certain it is that whatever Hardy's ultimate place may be in the Pantheon of English Literature— and we believe that it will always be very high and lasting—he certainly gives us a very complete picture of country life in South-Western England covering a period

of the mid-Victorian and late Victorian eras and in one
novel, and in what is admittedly his greatest poetic work,
a picture also of Georgian days.

Hardy must surely always remain even to those who
knew him best somewhat of a mystery. Indeed it is not
easy to trace in his immediate forebears anyone or any
circumstance that could have conduced to the ultimate
arrival upon the scene of life of a man of literary genius and
of a philosophical temperament such as Hardy's. There,
too, is nothing that is very striking to be recorded
regarding his " life " as the expression is generally interpreted.

There are probably few examples, and certainly none
since the late Victorian period, of an English writer even
approaching Hardy's distinction being so unknown to the
general public, and so little known in reality to those who
were privileged to reckon him as a friend or an acquaintance. There are probably several reasons for this. We
can easily mention two or three. Firstly, his introspective
and retiring nature—for he assuredly hated publicity of
any kind. Secondly, the fact that the most important
period of his life was lived before journalism had reached
the inexcusably intrusive heights that it has to-day. And
thirdly, that Hardy—we feel pretty convinced of this—
never realized that his actual personality was of importance to the public, or that they would be interested in
anything save his work.

Thus it was that he became first and foremost a writer
—always remained that rather than a society figure—
and most of the other things that he did had no very
important bearing on his life, though they had possibly
in some respects a definite bearing upon what he accomplished.

Another thing that probably drove Hardy into himself
was his great horror of cruelty of any kind and perhaps
especially of cruelty to animals. This in a hunting
county and a district surrounded by hunting counties to
a considerable extent cut him off from county society
which was interested chiefly in sport, and not in literature

Douglas Sheppon

Thomas Hardy's Birthplace.

" = Upper Bockhampton.

or intellectual pursuits. We remember several occasions on which he expressed his dislike of hunting of various types, and on one occasion when we were cycling in his company his horrified concern regarding a wounded bird we had come across by the roadside, and the earnestness he showed that we should at once " put it out of its misery." An act which he admitted he himself was loth to do.

It has been said over and over again that Hardy resented the coldness, or perhaps one should rather say indifference, with which he was, at least during the early period of his literary life, treated by people who should have recognized his great gifts and his genius. We hardly think that this fact troubled Hardy to the extent that some people were in the habit of believing ; but it is certain that, except on rare occasions, he never succeeded in throwing off the shyness and aloofness that was an early characteristic, and possibly, indeed, checked advances on the part of county and society people who could not be supposed to have any very great interest in literature or the subjects in which Hardy found his greatest pleasure.

Later in his life and after the publication of *Tess of the D'Urbervilles*, which brought to him fame, he could never have justly complained of either the lack of interest taken in him or his work, or any lack of appreciation. The very people who were supposed during his early struggles as a writer to have neglected Hardy, during the closing years of his life were many of them most anxious to know him, acclaim him, and to visit him and invite him to their houses.

Knowing Hardy as we did extending over a considerable period of years, we could well imagine the cynical humour with which he must have regarded the belated of advances made towards him.

Countless friends and acquaintances he had in his latter years, among distinguished men and women, who were only too anxious to admit his genius and possess his friendship ; but it cannot be said that the response made by Hardy, except in some very few instances, was at all marked.

On innumerable occasions, both in public speeches and in the Press, Hardy was referred to during his life as " a man of the people," and indeed critics in search of some explanation of his genius for disclosing in his novels and poems the often intricate and mysterious workings of the peasant mind, were in the habit of assuming that throughout all time his ancestry was only traceable through a long succession of peasant stocks.

We remember being shown on one occasion at Max Gate a very elaborate " family tree " of the Hardy family, which had been either prepared for or by Hardy himself. There, when one had mastered its intricacies, it was possible in its ramifications to trace that the Hardys of Dorset came from a French stock of landowners who had in the middle half of the 15th century settled in the Channel Islands at Jersey, having migrated there from the beautiful and romantic land of Normandy, the nearest port, Carteret, being separated from the Channel Islands by less than twenty miles of sea.

There is no doubt that Hardy was a little restive at the persistent endeavour of writers throughout his life to ascribe to him an entirely peasant or humble origin ; and perhaps it was one of the traits in his character which most amazed those of his friends, who, realizing his genius, considered that of prime importance, and his ancestry entirely a secondary consideration.

The curious may find in searching the records of the island of Jersey the history of one of the two Le Hardis who came to that island about the year 1360. This Le Hardi, or Le Hardy (whose Christian name was Clement) had married a sister of an islander, Sir William Lalague, otherwise known as Lulazin. It was this Clement who retained his Norman ancestral coat of arms, and was the founder of the central line of the Jersey Le Hardis or Hardys, descendants of which branch are found in the islands to-day.

The history of the Le Hardis in Jersey becomes somewhat

obscure after a period of a century, although it is known
that the office of Island Jurat, or magistrate, which had
been given to a Le Hardi in 1381, was handed down from
father to son for a long period without interruption.

During the period from 1404 almost to the end of the
15th century, the island of Jersey, and, indeed, the Channel
Islands generally, passed through a very troubled period
of existence.   Firstly, there was an attack by the French
in 1404, who had never admitted the sovereignty of
the English King over the islands, although the islanders
had sworn allegiance to King John.   The French were,
however, easily driven out ; but soon came the Wars of
the Roses and Margaret, queen consort of Henry VI,
scheming to win the support of the Comte de Maulevrier
for her husband promised the Comte the Channel Islands
as an inducement.   Maulevrier promptly attacked Jersey
and succeeded in capturing Mont Orgueil, the ancient
fortress which had been built where once stood a Roman
camp, and this he succeeded in holding with a portion
of the island from 1460–1465.*

Two years later the arrival of Sir Richard Harleston,
Vice-Admiral of England, led to Maulevrier's forces
being driven out of the island without much difficulty.
One is not surprised that the islanders, who were a
peaceable, hard-working race, objected to their islands
being made a battleground for the claimants of the
English crown.   They therefore appealed to King
Edward IV, who having defeated Henry VI had ascended
the throne, representing their point of view to the King.
Edward communicated this to Pope Sixtus IV, who
shortly afterwards endeavoured to satisfy the islanders
by issuing a bull directed against all who should in the
future attack the islands.   These remained in the status
of neutral territory until 1689.

During the period which immediately succeeded the
troubles we have referred to, the Le Hardi family had
succeeded in attaining considerable influence in Jersey,

* See *Things Seen in the Channel Islands*, by the author.

and another Clement Le Hardi, who was a great grandson of the first of that name, was evidently a man of
considerable character and enterprise. His house, situated in the parish of St. Martin, Jersey, towards the end
of the 15th century was undoubtedly one of the finest
on the island, and we are told that it was of the nature
of a fortified dwelling with its windows furnished with
iron gratings in order to defend it against the attacks,
which were at that period of frequent occurrence, of
bands of Norman freebooters, who in times of unrest
and war made descents upon the islanders. This house
was, we are also told, " fitted with double doors of great
thickness which were studded with iron nails." In the
early years of the last century, however, it was sold by
the then Sir Thomas Hardy and, unfortunately, pulled
down.

During the reign of Richard III, whose misgovernment
was the means of driving many representatives of English
noble families to the French shores, some of which passed
through Jersey, the Clement Le Hardi of that day seems
to have met some of these and probably formed his own
opinion regarding the stability of Richard's throne.
At any rate a few years later, when the Duke of Buckingham rose in rebellion against Richard, and Henry, Earl
of Richmond, afterwards Henry VII, decided to press
his claims and ascend the English throne, Clement Le
Hardi decided to espouse the cause of the Earl of Richmond, whose ship, driven out of its course and separated
from the fleet with which he intended to invade England,
had been forced to seek shelter in Jersey. The Earl
landed alone and went to Le Hardi's house at St.
Martin, and entreated him to afford him shelter until
he could return to France. Clement offered him hos-
pitality in spite of Richard's orders that the Earl should
be arrested and handed over to the authorities, which he
had issued when he had learned the Earl's presence in
Jersey. Le Hardi continued to give him shelter and
eventually took the Earl over to the Norman shore.

The somewhat legendary though romantic and

interesting story relating to this incident, recounts how the Earl of Richmond, when taking leave of Le Hardi on the beach in Normandy—possibly at Carteret or near Mont St. Michel—gave him his ring as a token of remembrance and of favours to come, with the words " Sic—donec " or " Thus—until." The words now form one of the mottoes of the arms of the Le Hardi family.

Two years later Henry, after landing at Milford Haven, defeated Richard III at Bosworth Field—where he was slain—and was afterwards crowned at Westminster in 1486. The new king did not forget his promise to Clement Le Hardi, and appointed him Lieutenant-Governor of the island, granting him the Seigneurie de Melache, and made him the chief magistrate, or bailiff of the island for life.

This Clement Le Hardi had a son named John who, perhaps tiring of the restricted opportunities afforded by the island, emigrated to England with his wife and children, and eventually is thought to have settled somewhere in the valley of the Frome a few miles from Dorchester. This event is of importance as establishing the Le Hardi family (afterwards to be known as the Hardy family) in Dorset.

The Jersey family meanwhile continued to carry on the traditions of its founders, and contributed in the ensuing centuries a considerable number of distinguished men to the service of the English monarchs.

The descendants of John, who, it is generally accepted, had settled in the valley of the Frome, became numerous, and one line contributed a long succession of distinguished men to the navy, including Rear-Admiral Sir Thomas Hardy, Kt., to whom a monument is to be found on the south side of the west door of Westminster Abbey.

Nelson's Hardy, afterwards Sir Thomas Masterman Hardy, Bart., who came of the Portisham branch of the Dorsetshire Hardys, is of course the most famous of the descendants of John Le Hardi. At the time of the Battle of Trafalgar, he was captain of Nelson's flagship, the Victory, and was at the Admiral's side when he fell to the deck shot through the spine by a rifleman in the main top of the French ship, *Redoubtable.*

The chief branch of the Hardy family, which had originally settled in Dorsetshire, eventually established itself in London, and had several distinguished members.

There have, however, always been descendants or at any rate connections of the original John Le Hardi living in Dorset, and mostly in the immediate vicinity of the Frome Valley.

It should be noted that towards the end of the 16th century and onwards, the name " Thomas " became a very frequent one in the family, and there was a Thomas Hardy living at Melcombe Regis, adjoining Weymouth, to the south-west of Dorchester, to the memory of whom there is a tablet in St. Peter's Church, Dorchester, of which town he was a benefactor in that he bequeathed a yearly sum of fifty pounds to be devoted to charitable purposes, and in 1569 founded the Grammar School known by his name.

The foregoing account of the Hardy family, which originated in the Le Hardis of Jersey, will serve the purpose of linking up the great novelist and poet with an ancestry of which we know, from what he once said to us, he was very proud, and of the authenticity of which there would seem to be very little doubt.

Indeed, one might not wrongly attribute the origin of *The Dynasts,* his greatest poetic work, the germ of which was conceived many years before the drama was written, to his pride of ancestry and the love of military pomp and grandeur to which that gave rise. There was also, it would seem, a poet in the Le Hardi family, centuries ago, who won some distinction. This consciousness, it may be noted, is also to be traced in his novel *The Trumpet Major.* In both of these works his kinsman, Nelson's Hardy, appears as one of the characters. The fact that this distinguished naval officer was a Dorset man was sufficient in itself to cause Hardy the poet, who was a distant connection, to give him such prominence. Indeed one of the finest scenes in *The Dynasts* is that depicting the death of Nelson, and the close association of the then Flag-Captain Thomas Hardy with that event.

A critical examination from a sociological outlook of Hardy's writings makes clear to one that master as he was in giving one life-like descriptions of the Dorset peasantry, their lives, thoughts and aspirations, he never in any way identifies himself with them, or appears to consider himself in any way actually related to them. Even in the notable and very valuable article he once wrote upon the Dorsetshire labourer, published in *Longman's Magazine*, July, 1883, one is conscious that he examines his subject from a very detached standpoint, and his analysis, though undoubtedly true and singularly subtle, is rather that of a sympathetic observer than of one writing with an inside knowledge of the class with which he was dealing.

It is quite certain that Hardy's mother was a woman of natural culture ; indeed, an old inhabitant of Dorchester who knew her, stressed this quality when describing and talking of her to the present writer. She undoubtedly encouraged him not only to read what are generally described as good and useful books—even the classics we are told—but also to set his face to an upward path as regards social advancement, rather than to identify himself too intimately with his peasant environment. Hardy himself, though undoubtedly proud of the ancestry that was traceable through the family tree of the Le Hardis, told us more than once that his own immediate ancestors had not been people of any considerable importance or social standing.

It was certain that his father's own particular branch of the family had during the century before Hardy's birth greatly declined from the position it once occupied, and it was this fact perhaps that has led several critics and writers to assume that the fate of the D'Urberville family in his most famous novel *Tess of the D'Urbervilles* was actually, or in part, drawn from that of some not far remote ancestor of Hardy himself. Probably there is no truth in the assumption, and indeed the novelist on

Hangman's Cottage
Dorchester.
"Casterbridge"

more than one occasion took pains to discount such a suggestion, and to warn writers against assuming that characters in any of his novels were drawn from life, or were actually friends or acquaintances. Also, it will be remembered that writers and others were accustomed to speak of Hardy's birthplace as a cottage. It was not so to be described, as, though a thatched house, it was of considerable size.

Hardy's well-known pessimism and mental attitude towards life, which was traceable not only in his books, and especially in the last few paragraphs of the tragic story of Tess, but in his conversation and even in his features, especially in his eyes, when in repose, was emphatically of an intellectual type, and not merely the pessimism which would have developed in a man who was unsuccessful or who had, through no fault of his own, fallen upon what are known as " evil times."

It is known, of course, that his father was a master builder in a comparatively small way, and this was the view of old people, who knew him well, with whom the present writer often conversed in former days. But at all events Thomas Hardy senior was able to afford considerable advantages of education for his son, the future novelist. What has been discoverable regarding Hardy's Norman ancestry goes to show that the ancestors on his father's side had gradually descended to the status of the West Country trading class, but his mother's people were the Swetmans and Childs, two families which were apparently small landowners, or farmers farming their own land, which often intermarried and lived in the neighbourhood of Melbury Osmund, a charming old village situated on the higher ground which connects the Frome Valley and the Vale of Blackmoor. So far as can be traced, his mother's forebears, both of the Swetman and Child families, figured during the Civil War between King and Parliament on the ultimately victorious side, while the Hardys, perhaps not unnaturally considering their descent, were Royalists.

Their house at Melbury Osmund, which is not far

from Evershot, is mentioned in Domesday, and the village takes the name Osmund from one of the early Bishops of Sarum or Salisbury, who in fact founded the new Cathedral there in the last years of the 11th century.

The place figures in Hardy's short story *The Duke's Reappearance*, which deals with the Monmouth Rebellion, where the novelist made use of a family tradition. The latter asserts that a Christopher Swetman was the owner of the house at the time of the Rebellion, and secretly espoused or at least sympathized with the ambitions of the Duke. After Sedgemoor, the story goes, a mud-bespattered horseman knocked at Swetman's door and declined to explain who he was. Swetman, however, gave him shelter, just as in former times another connection of the Hardy family, Clement Le Hardi, had sheltered Henry of Richmond, who had engaged in a somewhat similar undertaking. The story tells us that the Duke was discovered making violent love to one of Christopher Swetman's daughters in the garden, and her father, who had made the discovery, promptly ordered him to leave the house.*

Not long afterwards the news arrived of Monmouth's arrest in a ditch on Horton (or Shag) Heath near Wimborne, Dorset, and Swetman observed a mysterious figure removing the clothes of his late visitor, who had changed them for a disguise, from a cupboard. The tradition of this incident, according to Hardy, had been handed down from Swetman to Swetman for more than two centuries, although members of the Child family also lay claim to or have a similar or the same tradition.

Hardy's grandmother was born in 1772, lived to a good old age, and died in 1857, when the novelist was about seventeen years of age. People who knew the old lady, in speaking of her some years ago, told us that she was known as a remarkable character with an extraordinary memory for local stories, traditions and the events of the past. There is little doubt that Hardy

---

* There would appear little historical ground for this incident in the story. Probably the fugitive was one of the Duke's officers.

was most deeply indebted to her for many of the incidents which were afterwards woven into the fabric of his novels and short stories, and much of the local colour of past ages in Dorset which is so marked a feature both in his prose and poetry. There is no doubt that Hardy himself had a remarkable memory, and during our visits to him and excursions in his company in the villages surrounding Dorchester, he often chatted of long-ago incidents, slight in themselves, but which were of considerable importance in regard to the true understanding of peasant character and of past events.

How great an influence it had upon him and how useful a store was the knowledge that his grandmother imparted to him is made clear in the poem " One We Knew," which was published in 1902.

Edmund Gosse (afterwards knighted), one of Hardy's intimate friends, in an essay dealing with his lyrical poetry, which is included in his book *Some Diversions of a Man of Letters*, makes a distinct reference to the possibility of what he calls the poet's dangerous insight into the female heart having been acquired from his grandmother's tales to which Hardy in his childhood and adolescence undoubtedly listened.

It is, however, of course impossible to say how great an influence these and his grandmother's conversation may have had upon Hardy's temperament, or how far the subject matter of these stories was more or less responsible for his pessimistic outlook and the cynicism regarding women which in later life he was, as a writer, destined to exhibit.

Hardy's mother undoubtedly encouraged him, either intentionally or unintentionally, to translate his thoughts into concrete form, which were afterwards destined to take shape in his novels and poems.

She was, as we have already suggested, a naturally cultured woman, and undoubtedly added to the rather circumscribed experiences of life, which was her lot in the thatched home at Upper Bockhampton, by reading much that was best in the literature of the past.

Comparatively little, however, is known of her, who was a woman of rather less than average height, with grey eyes and brown hair, who nevertheless from her good carriage which she preserved till late in life, appeared taller than was actually the case.

Doubtless the fact that her life remains obscure is largely owing to the circumstance that she did not live to see her son at the height of his fame, when some reflected glory would surely have been shed upon her because of her son's achievements. But it is known that she read and induced her son also to read some of the Latin poets and those of Greece in translation, and had a liking for French romances and especially for tragedies.

It is therefore conceivable that the future novelist and poet was, as fate had it, to some extent brought up in an atmosphere directly conducive to a literary career, and one that undoubtedly exercised a great and lasting influence over his whole life.

How far the liking of Mrs. Hardy for the classics was strangely enough inborn and how far somewhat of a veneer upon her natural character it would be difficult for anyone to say.

Perhaps the earliest evidence of the influence of Hardy's mother upon his writing is to be found in one of his early novels, *The Hand of Ethelberta*, where one finds a picture quite in consonance with the undoubtedly liberal attitude towards class distinction which Mrs. Hardy is thought to have possessed, and was probably founded upon the knowledge of the needs and aspirations of the peasant classes which would naturally come to her through an ancestry such as that from which she derived her origin.

Hardy never minimized the debt he owed his mother in the upbringing she gave him, the sacrifices she made, and the influence she exercised on his receptive mind in his early youth by encouraging him to read books that were very unlikely to be the natural choice of a boy in his station.

It seems certain that Hardy's undoubted love of the

c

soil of the " Wessex," to use the term in its widest sense, which he created in English literature, of nature, his hatred of cruelty of all kinds, his artistic sense, and his stability and constructive gifts which appear in his novels, were chiefly inherited from his mother.

It is easy perhaps so to trace these characteristics of Hardy, and even to account for his ambition to make a name for himself in literature ; but there is much in his character and in his achievement, especially as a poet, which can only have had its remote origin in the French ancestry traceable on his father's side.

It is surely only the combination of these two lines of ancestry, with their very different and in some respects opposing characteristics, that can be accounted to explain Hardy at all. And like two rivers flowing to a common estuary were ultimately destined to produce one of the greatest novelist-poets of the Victorian age.

CHAPTER II

IT WAS at Upper Bockhampton, which lies some three miles north of Dorchester, in a large, secluded thatched cottage-like dwelling that on June 2nd, 1840, Thomas Hardy was born. We are told that he was a delicate baby who, but for the prescience and determination of the village midwife who attended Mrs. Hardy at his birth, would never have survived.

Indeed, he was thought by the doctor either to have been stillborn, or to have died immediately after birth. The midwife, however, thought otherwise, and by her skill and persistence undoubtedly saved for English literature a baby destined to become one of the stars in the mid-Victorian and late Victorian literary firmament.

At this time Upper Bockhampton, though comparatively near the county town of Dorset, was very isolated, and consisted of only a small handful of cottages with an inn of sorts. So small indeed was it that it had neither church nor school, nor even a sub-post office located in the village shop. It lies off the main road and to reach it in those days one had to travel along the ancient Roman highway, which Hardy himself has described in his poem " The Roman Road " to be found in *Time's Laughing Stocks*. He says of it :

> " The Roman road runs straight and bare,
> As the pale parting-line in hair,
> Across the heath. And thoughtful men
> Contrast its days of Now and Then,
> And delve and measure and compare.

Visioning on the vacant air
Helmed legionaries, who proudly rear
The Eagle as they pace again
The Roman Road."

Doubtless Hardy himself conjured up like visions when walking along it, as he often did in company with his mother. Even Dorchester at the time Hardy was born had no railway, and was very isolated, although it had spates of gaiety at fair time and on market days.

Bockhampton was, indeed, a remote place, and the wide stretch of Bockhampton Heath, which with Puddle-ton Heath forms the significant expanse to which Hardy gave the name of " Egdon," figures in several of his novels and short stories, and provided, as we well know, a ruminating place for him in his early days. Its low-thatched cottages, picturesque enough but very primitive, and dating back to " old ancient times," were a part of the landscape in keeping with the slowly moving and almost stagnant life of the little hamlet.

Hardy's home, fortunately still very much as when he passed his childhood and boyhood there, was one of the larger houses in the hamlet. Environed by the heath, which was gloomy and grim at times and at others beautiful, for example, in summer, with purple heather and golden gorse, it was undoubtedly the dominating Nature influence of Hardy's childhood and boyhood. It figures more than any other one natural feature or portion of Wessex in his writings, and those of us who believe in the influence of natural as well as intellectual environment in the fashioning of character can easily trace some of Hardy's grimness and fatalism to this ex-tensive stretch of heathland.

One gathers from what one has been able to learn from people who knew her that Mrs. Hardy possessed what may be best described as the conventional religiously inclined mind of those days, and that probably Hardy received in his boyhood that kind of religious instruction from her that was common in similar families at the time.

Stinsford Church. "Mellstock."

Thomas Snowdon.

We are told that occasionally the household went into Dorchester on Sunday mornings to attend service at the principal church of St. Peter's, which stands at the junction of Corn Hill and High East Street and West Street. Also occasionally visits were made to the county town on market days and at fair times. It was probably only on these occasions that the future novelist in his early childhood made his contacts with the world outside his native hamlet.

The Hardys, it is recorded, had been fond of music for several generations before the birth of the novelist, and his father was especially interested in church music. His own father (Hardy's grandparent) used as a young man to play the 'cello in the " quire " at Puddleton Church, where the Georgian gallery in which he sat is still to be seen. Other members of the family played for many years instruments in the Stinsford Church, which was the Parish Church also for Upper Bockhampton where they lived.

The fact that his father's business as a builder was at this period of a fairly prosperous nature, and his staff numbered half a score or more of workmen, served to make the elder Hardy a man of some standing, at least in Upper Bockhampton, and not entirely unknown in the circles and haunts of Dorchester business life. Indeed, in his quite considerable house the village choir with their varied instruments, references to which appear in several of Hardy's stories and novels, were accustomed to gather to rehearse not only sacred but also secular music, including dances and rounds, and on festal occasions the Hardy dwelling was the forgathering place where accredited neighbours were in the habit of meeting to celebrate passing events.

The fact that the house became a social centre of a kind must also have made considerable impression upon the infant and child mind of Hardy, who doubtless enjoyed the scraping of fiddles, rumbling of the bass viols and shrill screaming of the flutes, memories of which, indeed, are obvious to readers of his prose and poetry. Certainly from these gatherings and from the association which he had in early life with his father's workmen, the farm labourers and the serving maids that his father's prosperity permitted him to employ, made deep impressions upon his youthful mind which were never, indeed, entirely eradicated.

No one who either knew or conversed with Hardy in later years could fail to recognize the extraordinary memory which he possessed, especially of events relating to his early life and even childhood, which would with most people have passed into the limbo of forgotten things long before.

To students of Hardy there must always be a most fascinating ground of enquiry and of speculation regarding the life that he led of a semi-genteel character within his home, and the rougher, more peasant and more elemental life that he led when associating with the children and people of his native hamlet.

Many critics have noticed the conflict of two personalities in Hardy, and those who conversed with him occasionally could not fail to detect flashes of this warfare in his conversation, although it is true that the tendency he had to retire within himself, after perhaps a burst of unwonted confidence, seemed to erect a wall of partition between the companion of the time being and the real Hardy.

A very old inhabitant of Dorchester, who passed away only a few years before Hardy himself, and would had he lived till the time of Hardy's death have been six or seven years his senior, used to tell us how Hardy in early boyhood was, doubtless from this kind of double existence, rendered shy and retiring and became regarded by his inevitable companions, boys and girls of the hamlet, as rather " stuck-up " and even " queer." The latter undoubtedly from the fact that from a very early age he was undoubtedly introspective and rather inclined to isolation than to companionship. It is not difficult for the psychologist to imagine the ultimate effect of this loneliness, and spiritual and intellectual isolation of

the boy upon his ultimate character and achievements.

One cannot fail to realize that the nature of Hardy's
childhood, his environment, his friends, and associations
with older folk of the little Wessex hamlet where he dwelt,
had a very material influence upon a mind which in after
life developed a mental and analytical detachment regarding the peasantry of his native county which did not,
however, prevent a very sympathetic appreciation of their
struggles, vicissitudes and mental processes which appear
so clearly in his works.

One can gather little regarding any education, as the
term is generally interpreted, which Hardy received until
the age of eight years, when he became a pupil at a
private school kept by a man of rather exceptional
gifts.   It was to this that young Hardy travelled
along the high road through the meads for a period
at least of six years.   From data available it is made
clear that the education he received was of the rather
limited character prevailing in the country districts
at that period ; and, indeed, it is said that at one
time there were not half a dozen pupils attending the
school.   But there is little doubt that he owed a good
deal to his old schoolmaster, Mr. Isaac Glandfield
Last.

From the scanty material available and what one
learned years ago from Hardy's contemporaries it is
made fairly clear that he was not a particularly brilliant
pupil.   In fact, he was described by one who knew him
well as "rather indolent, not easily led, and always
seemed to be in search of something beyond the curricu-
lum to which he was subjected."   In a word, it may be
taken for granted that the boy gave evidence of being
rather of the student type than a mere schoolboy,
learning what he was obliged to learn, and taking things
very much as they came.

He certainly, in more senses than one, educated himself,
and his intellectual gifts were fostered by his mother, who
appears to have taken him in hand when he reached the

age of about twelve years and given him some personal attention and instruction.

A very old friend of Hardy's, who predeceased him by several years and who visited his home with some degree of frequency about this period, told us in relation to Hardy's ultimate fame as a writer that he, the speaker, thought much of the material the novelist used in his books and poems had been gathered by very careful, if unobservant, listening on Hardy's part to the conversation of his mother's serving maids, the villagers, and to the enlightening talk of his grandmother and her countless reminiscences and store of village gossip and tales.

There was, however, an opportunity for self-improvement in the shape of a "lending" library kept by a Mr. J. Foster in Cornhill, for many years, afterwards by the Misses Case, and we remember the proprietor telling us that Hardy as a youth and young man borrowed many books from him, including Dumas's historical novels. Hardy was also, in after years, a frequenter of the shop.

At the age of fourteen he finally left the school in Dorchester, to the educational system of which he certainly owed very little. Then two or three years were passed in an effort on the part of his mother to give him some sort of classical education and polish, which period was apparently spent very largely in a study of Latin writers in the original, and the reading of them in translation. Then came the time when the Hardys engaged for him a French governess, attached to the school his sisters were attending. How far the latter was able to impart much knowledge of her native tongue to her pupil it is impossible to say, although Hardy eventually became a fluent French scholar, and possibly through this nameless governess derived his liking for French literature.

Meanwhile Hardy was undoubtedly absorbing a great deal of special knowledge and of learning of a very varied kind, much as a sponge absorbs moisture with which it has been brought into direct contact.

Students of Hardy, possessing a knowledge of the rather elementary nature of his "schooling," estimated by present-day standards, can easily trace the effects of the self-education the future novelist and poet was undergoing during this period. Indeed he was obviously just one of those boys who learn most that is useful in life after the doors of the school, at which he was supposed to have been educated, had closed after him.

Certainly Hardy's keen and retentive mind during the period succeeding his leaving school, and before he went to London to follow the occupation of an architect, must have gathered a considerable amount of material relating to and knowledge of the peasantry and country life which was to serve him in such good stead in after years.

One of the most interesting sidelights upon his character is afforded by the circumstances to which Hardy himself in after life frequently referred, namely, that owing to his ability to write, and even at that early period to express himself fluently, many of the youths and maids of his native hamlet, and even of Dorchester itself, used to come to him and cajole him into writing their letters for them !

The mere fact that these boys and girls had not succeeded in acquiring the useful accomplishment of writing affords startling evidence of the elementary character of the education afforded the so-called lower classes even in the vicinity of a county town at that particular period. Hardy, we are told, perhaps even then with a cynical humour prompting him, agreed to act as the village yokels' and lasses' scribe, and as many of these epistles must undoubtedly have been of an amatory character, and as probably the majority of those who dictated them were of the female sex, this exercise of his art must have enabled him to come into contact with and study at first hand adolescent human nature and the emotions which stirred it under various circumstances.

At any rate this somewhat strange experience was destined to prove of the greatest use to the future novelist. Evidence is afforded in the amazingly beautiful, and particularly human, touch he imparted to the letter written by poor Tess to Angel Clare after he had deserted her, which appears in *Tess of the D'Urbervilles*.

One can imagine that the confidences which were thus entrusted to young Hardy were often given him under the impression, on the part of the confidant, that really he was scarcely old enough, and probably was too innocent, to quite understand the real meaning of the often impassioned sentences and intimate thoughts that he was entrusted to put down on paper.

Once, when referring to this strange employment of his youthful days, Hardy told the present writer that he considered that these love letters and other communications of which he was the scribe were of the greatest value, and, indeed, even in those early days, of great interest. They may undoubtedly sometimes have puzzled the young scribe, and they certainly must have started many trains of thought and given rise to many speculations quite in advance of his then knowledge of life.

Indeed, one can go to the pages of Hardy himself for evidence of this incident in what one might call his early sociological education, for in *The Mayor of Casterbridge* Mother Cuxsom, speaking to Richard Newson, says : "Love letters ? Then let's hear 'em, good soul. . . . Lord ! do ye mind, Richard, what fools we used to be when we were younger ? Getting a schoolboy to write 'em for us ; and giving him a penny, do ye mind, not to tell other folks what he'd put inside, do ye mind ? "

It was thus as an amanuensis for the boys and girls— principally girls—of his native hamlet that Hardy may be said to have graduated as a writer.

During the years from the time he left school to the time he entered an architect's office as pupil, the future novelist remained a retiring, abstracted and self-contained lad who was, as has been told, generally awkward and very shy in the presence of strangers and even of some of the neighbours. He probably learned much from Nature, which he studied closely, and the natural forces which he saw playing over the fields of Wessex, and the great stretch of dour, but beautiful moorland upon which he walked, and lay among the heather reading. And at the same time he was doubtless studying the human characteristics which in conflict went to the making of the lives of the people in his immediate environment.

When he was about sixteen years of age his father and mother seem to have awakened to a sense of the apparent futility and objectlessness of the life that their son was leading. Their means were not sufficient, had they even possessed the desire or ambition, to send him to a university for further education. Nor, indeed, did young Hardy evince any love for scholarship of the kind that a university might afford him.

Although Thomas Hardy senior had prospered to a certain extent, he had undoubtedly not made sufficient money to ensure that his son would be adequately provided for on his death. Probably his father, as appears from all one was able to learn years ago from his contemporaries, would have been satisfied for him to enter his own business, to take up farming, or to engage in some local industry or purely commercial pursuit. It was his mother who seems to have put an embargo upon any employment which would tend to lower the self-esteem and social position of the family ; or, perhaps one should say, not be likely to enhance the latter. Mrs. Hardy at any rate was possessed of sufficient ambition to wish for her son—as have mothers probably from time immemorial—opportunities or a position superior to that her husband had enjoyed or won.

After considerable deliberations, a way out of the difficulty was discovered in the person of a Mr. John Hicks, a Dorchester architect, who had at various times had business relations with Mr. Hardy. After several consultations, it was decided that young Hardy should be apprenticed, or, as we should refer to it nowadays, articled to Hicks ; the Hardys realizing that even a country architect was of a superior social position to a

Douglas Shorlaake

Dagberry Hill

builder, and that if their son were apprenticed to Hicks it would be at least a step up the social ladder for him.

As a matter of fact there was a revival of interest just about this period in the many country churches in Dorsetshire which had been allowed to fall into a state of disrepair, and efforts were being made in various parishes to raise funds for the necessary work of restoration. Luckily for his employer, and for young Hardy himself, quite a considerable number of commissions had recently come into the architect's office, which may perhaps have inclined him to realize the necessity for assistance in his work and to accept young Hardy as a possible help. Anyway, the latter readily fell in with the plans of his parents and entered the Dorchester office and was duly apprenticed. This not only was destined to provide Hardy with much additional experience, but was also to give him opportunities which were of great value later on.

Over and over again critics and students of Hardy's work have drawn attention to what may not inaptly be called the " architectural " structure of his novels, just as one can trace his interest in and love of architecture in the many detailed and accurate descriptions of buildings which one finds scattered throughout his pages.

Comparatively little is known of the John Hicks of Dorchester who was indirectly to exercise a very considerable influence upon the life and destiny of the young man who had entered his office. As luck would have it, the Fates had decided that this obscure country architect should live and be carrying on his work at a period when there was an extraordinary revival of interest taken in the condition of ecclesiastical buildings throughout the West Country.

During the earlier years of the century people's minds had been too much occupied by fears of invasion—and a state of unrest and mental tension existed, such as Hardy afterwards so vividly portrayed in the pages of his novel, *The Trumpet Major*—to devote much attention to the condition of their country churches. And immediately after the Napoleonic Wars there came periods of unrest and of social upheaval of a distracting character, including the riots in connection with the Corn Laws, and the violent opposition to the introduction of machinery on the part of agricultural labourers. All these circumstances doubtless led to the neglect of ecclesiastical property, with the result that many of the churches in country districts of Dorset, in common with those in other places, had suffered not only from considerable neglect, but in some cases were approaching a dangerous structural condition. Beetles had attacked the great oak beams of the roofs and belfries, and even in some cases where the stone used was soft in character this had actually begun to crumble.

The business of John Hicks of Dorchester experienced a considerable increase and demanded expansion. Unfortunately what provided grist to the architect's mill led to the destruction in many instances of beautiful architectural survivals or details of these, for not only was a campaign of restoration of a drastic nature initiated by the clergy, squires and other people concerned with or interested in church property, but in far too many cases towers and other portions of churches were pulled down and rebuilt, and even "furniture" was either injudiciously restored or replaced by modern substitutes, and little effort was made to preserve things of historical or other interest, or to carry out the work of restoration in character with the original building.

By all these works the Dorchester architect was kept very busy, his staff was enlarged, and assistants were sent out into the country districts to make preliminary surveys, measurements and estimates for contracts. Young Hardy was soon to be employed in this way, and some years ago there were preserved many sketches of his made about this time which showed considerable artistic gifts. Certain it was that the training he now received served him well in after life. Many of the drawings of buildings which he made and the details of windows and other portions of churches he had to copy so exactly, became extremely and historically valuable when these things were demolished in the orgy of destruction which prevailed in the middle half of the last century.

Hardy, himself, in after years gave a very accurate description of a young apprentice at work on this reconstruction. In it we see him taking his measurements with extreme punctiliousness, and even the contours of the columns and mouldings by means of a strip of lead known as a leaden tape, which was pressed into the hollows with his finger and thumb.

Hardy in later life more than once expressed his horror of the part he played in a movement which, ostensibly having for its purpose the preservation of the crumbling and decaying churches of his native county, was by reckless and ignorant enthusiasm the means of destroying much that was of historic and artistic interest and of course irreplaceable.

What he really thought about this deplorable and sacrilegious campaign of reconstruction is to be found by the curious in a report of the General Meeting of the Society for the Protection of Ancient Buildings held on June 20th, 1906.

Hardy, indeed, knew quite a number of instances of Dorset folk, who had migrated from the county, on their return expressing their horror at the vandalism which had destroyed so much of beauty and antiquarian interest.

In some cases family pews, used by their successive owners for centuries, had been removed bodily, and either done away with or placed in some other part of the church, and on more than one occasion members of the family, who returned to Dorset and visited the church of their ancestors, were shocked and even enraged to find this had been done. In some cases doubtless the general scheme of reconstruction or renovation rendered these acts almost imperative, but one can easily understand the amazement and annoyance created by such acts upon members of the family in search of ancient memorials.

Nor was this destructive campaign limited to the buildings themselves ; the churchyards, their tombstones and ancient monuments were also tidied up, and in some instances the first named were removed and placed over graves different to those they were intended to mark.

Hardy, himself, who regarded " this shuffling of tombstones with great disgust " told the tale of how a stone marking the grave of a misogynist vicar was placed over that of a notable actor and his wife, while their stone was removed to his grave.

But it was not only the removal and " shuffling " of the stones of the rich and the great, however, that caused Hardy most concern. And in this one detects his sympathy with the under-dog, and with the common folk in direct contact with whom he lived the greater part of his early life. In the address to which we have referred he expressed a deep regret that " It was oftenest the headstones of the poor inhabitants—purchased and erected in many cases out of scanty means—that suffered most. . . ."

His views are set out in a poem " The Levelled Churchyard " which is to be found in *Poems of the Past and the Present*, where he with mordant humour writes :

> " We late-lamented, resting here,
>   Are mixed to human jam.
> And each to each exclaims in fear
>   ' I know not what I am.'
>
> The wicked people have annexed
>   The verses on the good ;
> A roaring drunkard sports the text
>   Teetotal Tommy should !
>
>   .   .   .   .   .
>
> From restorations of Thy fane
>   From smoothings of Thy sward,
> From zealous Churchman's pick and plane
>   Deliver us O Lord !   Amen ! "

D

In the address from which we have quoted, and to which we have referred, Hardy, while emphasizing his dismay at the destruction of and removal of old memorials and of ancient portions of buildings, stresses the frequent necessity for work of restoration, but enters a plea for the careful preservation of the original form and details.

A keenly observant student of his character gains much knowledge from the argument he used in support of this view : " This is indeed the actual process of organic nature herself, which is one of continuous substitution. She is always discarding matter, while retaining the form."

Although it may not perhaps be generally known, keen as the young, would-be architect was in the early days of his apprenticeship, regarding his technical studies of Gothic art, he had already commenced to write poetry and to feel stirring within him that urge to literary expression which was afterwards to prove a victor over his technical training as an architect.

He wrote much verse during this period, and although some of it was incorporated in the various collections of poems which he published in later life, most of it was undoubtedly destroyed.   Certainly in some of the poems we have in mind the vividness of the descriptive passages, which have a definite relation to architectural work, must be traced to this period. We, however, believe that actually only one of these very early poems was ever printed, and that this was a set of verses composed and rewritten between 1857 and 1860 called *Domicilium.*

In April, 1916, Clement Shorter, then editor of the *Sphere*, and a great admirer and friend of Hardy, printed of the poem twenty-five copies in the form of a seven-page booklet, which were not for sale but for private distribution. Where these copies have disappeared to no one seems to know, but they must be classed as one of the rarest and probably most valuable of modern privately printed booklets.

Young Hardy at this period was also jotting down notes for essays, and even " skeletons " of tales ; but in this literary work the future novelist found no encouragement from either his father or his employer, and we are told that these ultimately, definitely informed him that he must devote himself diligently and successfully to his architectural studies on pain of dismissal and his father's high displeasure.

There is no doubt that, faced with the possibility of being thrown entirely on his own resources in the event of his disobedience, Hardy gave up his literary exercises until the end of his apprenticeship. During this period it is possible that he found some consolation for his abandoned literary experiments in his resumed studies of the classics. Certainly these had a considerable influence upon him, and this influence is traceable in his work.

He was fortunate, however, in not having to pursue his classical studies alone ; for one of Mr. Hicks's pupils, Barlow by name, of whom he had made a friend, proved to be of similar tastes to his own, and for a period of from two to three years they appear to have studied together, and as well as reading some of the classics, Homer and Virgil among these, studied also the Greek Testament. Hardy, the first Mrs. Hardy told the present writer, kept up his interest in the last named in later years by an almost daily reading.

From the period to which we have referred, for several years no biographer or writer about Hardy would be able definitely to state much regarding his mental development or his life. He had by this time reached manhood, and it is known he made several useful friendships, one of a literary character with a writer who visited Dorset, and others with several young students whose ambition it was to enter the Free Church ministry. With the latter, we are told, he studied the New Testament in Greek, and had many arguments regarding the relative merits of the Established Church and the Nonconformist Churches. There is, however,

very little known, and Hardy himself was always singularly silent concerning these years.

At the conclusion of his apprenticeship to Mr. Hicks,
instead of being absorbed in the business or entering that
of any other architect in his native town, he migrated
to London of which he knew very little. He had, however, while a small child, accompanied his mother on
a visit to a relative in Hertfordshire ; the return journey
was made through London, and they stayed for the
night at a famous Clerkenwell coaching inn.

He had also visited the metropolis with his father
in 1849 on a day trip from Dorchester, and afterwards
described the excursion, which was made in open railway
trucks, and how the excursionists arrived "blue-faced,
stiff-necked, sneezing, rain-beaten, chilled to the marrow,
many hatless as if in an open boat all night, and with
the men in a worse condition than the women, who had
turned their skirts over their heads for shelter."

On coming to London he made the acquaintance of
an architect, Mr. John Norton, who had an office in
Bond Street, and he proved a good friend and gave him
an introduction to Mr. Arthur Blomfield, afterwards
knighted. The latter was the fourth son of Bishop Blomfield, and became known for his church of St. Barnabas,
Oxford, that of St. Mary, Portsea, and his restoration
and rebuilding of St. Saviour's, Southwark. Blomfield
had devoted himself very largely to the restoration of
ecclesiastical buildings, and was a specialist in what was
then known as modern Gothic.

At the time of Hardy's first association with him,
Blomfield, although only thirty-two, was already President of the Architectural Association. Later on he was
appointed Official Architect to the Bank of England.
Hardy became his assistant, and, while receiving much
valuable instruction from him in London itself, travelled
about the country very considerably, superintending the
work of restoration of churches and other buildings
which his employer had in hand.

This famous architect proved a very congenial chief

Douglas Snowdon

The Barn
.Abbotsbury. "Abbotsea."

for young Hardy, because he was entirely opposed to the vandalism and destructive restoration work which was rather the fashion at that period, and had so shocked Hardy during his apprenticeship in Dorset.

The young architect, who was strangely enough, however, destined never seriously to follow the profession that he had adopted at the behest of his parents, while in London came under the influence of Sir Gilbert Scott, who was a contemporary of Blomfield. Hardy no doubt became a member of the class which Sir Gilbert formed for lectures of a then somewhat novel character, which consisted in visits to various ecclesiastical and other historical buildings of the metropolis accompanied by explanatory talks by Sir Gilbert Scott himself.

Although Hardy was almost a shut book regarding his London experiences of this time, there is no doubt that some of the incidents or at least the effects of mental influences which occurred during the five years he spent in London may be traced in the pages of his earlier novels.

As regards his architectural studies, it is quite possible that Hardy had a definite hand in the work carried out at St. Barnabas Church in Bell Street, Edgware Road, and the church in Addiscombe Road, Croydon ; buildings which were erected by his employer, Blomfield, during Hardy's service under him. There is no doubt in the minds of most people that he had a definite connection with All Saints, Windsor, and the Radcliffe Chapel at Oxford, for his work at the latter certainly provided him with local colour for *Jude the Obscure*, and he must have carefully noted the localities in which he afterwards placed some of the chief scenes of the novel.

With reference to Hardy's residence in London ! We know that it was in No. 16 Westbourne Park Villas, close to the Royal Oak station, and overlooking the Great Western Railway main line, that he took his first lodgings in London, and had his bachelor home from 1862–67. It was at 8 Adelphi Terrace, off the Strand, that he worked in Blomfield's office, which is still much as when he knew it, and he put on record that on one of his visits in after life to London, he saw again what he himself described as " the tall chimneys of Lambeth rising against the livid sky as though drawn in chalk on toned cardboard."

Another building more casually associated with Hardy is King's College in the Strand. Almost at the end of the period of his stay in London he seems to have felt that he had not received so thorough an educational training as he either needed or his ambitions prompted, and after some thought he entered himself as a student at King's College in the University of London, and attended evening classes for a considerable time, thereby acquiring valuable knowledge, and at the end of his studies might be said to have possessed more than a fair amount of scholarly endowment.

But all the while he was in London studying architecture there can be little doubt that he felt the urge towards literary expression which eventually was so entirely to detach him from the profession he had initially adopted, and of which he made so little use in after life. About this period he wrote many poems, some of which at least did not see the light of print for half a century after he had first conceived the ideas or put them on paper ; but these London years were not all occupied in architectural work and experimental writing, for Hardy himself used to recall his visits to the theatre, doubtless in the cheaper seats, which in those days were cheap enough to permit of frequent visits by even a boy with only slender resources.

It was about this time that he commenced to send his poems and some articles to various papers and magazines, but he met with no success, and he appears to have made it a practice not to send out what he had written a second time after rejection. Indeed he retained to the end of his life a very modest opinion regarding his work and, at a time when editors were only too willing to pay large sums for anything he wrote, would enclose stamps for return of any manuscript which he sent !

How deeply Hardy's experiences and studies in the Dorchester architect's office, and under Blomfield, were destined to affect his literary work is easily traced in his earlier novels, for it will not be forgotten that three of the principal characters in his first published work, *Desperate Remedies*, were architects, and the apprenticeship of Owen Gray at Budmouth might, without straining probabilities, have possibly been suggested by the author's experiences under Mr. Hicks at Dorchester. Then, of course, there is the steward, Aeneas Manston, who was a thorough-paced villain, an unusual type of character with Hardy, and the hero, Edward Springrove, who may have had something of Hardy himself and his own experiences woven into his character. We know, of course, that Hardy once denied that he had used his own personal experiences in this way in building up Springrove's character, but it is an admitted fact that most writers irresistibly put into their books fragments of experiences with which they have been connected and characteristics of people they have known, and students of Hardy will be inclined to believe that he was unconsciously using autographical material as well as that gained from another source. Certainly some of the descriptions of Springrove, his habits, preferences and mental predilections, seem to fit in with the Hardy that was known to his friends at the time the book was written.

Of course the London of Hardy's youth, as may easily be realized, was a very different place to the London of to-day. For one thing there was no Thames Embankment, and the foreshore of the Thames in front of Adelphi Terrace, in which Blomfield's office was situated, and where Hardy worked, was at times anything but savoury or pleasant to the olfactory nerves. Temple Bar, too, had not yet been removed, and the site now occupied by the huge block of buildings constituting the Law Courts, which were not commenced until the end of April, 1874, and not opened till December, 1882, was then a huddle of shops and business premises somewhat similar to the older buildings still remaining on the opposite side of the street, not far from the eastern end of notorious Holywell Street, or "Booksellers Row" which Hardy used, during his employment at Blomfield's office, frequently to visit in search of cheap books.

The "Coal Hole" (which still survives in name) in the Strand, and various other similar resorts, including several of the more ancient taverns of Fleet Street, were still existent, not much altered from what they had for a century or more been, and Hungerford Market still survived at the northern end of what is now Hungerford Bridge and where Charing Cross Station now stands. Hardy, it is said, often lunched at "coffee" houses near this spot, which was, of course, a very convenient one for the pupils at Adelphi Terrace.

Not only was there no ugly railway bridge across the bottom of Ludgate Hill, cutting off the very fine view there was in Hardy's day of St. Paul's on the crest of the rise, but Holborn Hill was very much steeper than it is to-day. The Underground Railway had only just been constructed, and was in its infancy.

Hardy seems to have gone now and then to Willis's Rooms, formerly the famous Almack's of the Regency period, in King Street, St. James's. In those days, of course, the most popular dances were Lancers, Caledonians and Quadrilles, and the frequenters of Willis's Rooms and other similar places would have opened their eyes very widely had even the "Kitchen" Lancers and Galops, popular later, been attempted, and doubtless would have been struck dumb with astonishment at the even more unconventional dances of the present day.

The Cremorne Gardens and the Argyle Rooms were also in full swing in those days, and Hardy seems to have frequented them occasionally, having heard of them from one of his fellow-pupils in Mr. Hicks's office at Dorchester.

In after years he referred to these experiences in several of his poems, and does so, indeed, in *Reminiscences of a Dancing Man* which was afterwards published. Hardy also said the experiences he gained in these resorts were some of them used in the " Society" incidents occurring in his ill-fated novel *The Poor Man and the Lady*.

These were days, too, when foreign opera was very popular, and the works of Verdi, Meyerbeer, Bellini, Rossini and others were being produced at Covent Garden and the old Her Majesty's Theatre, the site of which is now occupied by the Carlton Hotel ; and, as there was also an English Opera Company, Hardy used often to go to hear the works of Wallace and others.

Much of the London that Hardy knew in the Holborn district, and in the then narrow streets in the neighbour-hood of Lincoln's Inn Fields, Charing Cross and Trafalgar Square, has long passed away.

While in London the young architect visited many art museums and picture galleries, and the impressions and the valuable lessons that he gained on these visits he retained in after years.

It was about this period that he undoubtedly felt his limitations as an artist with a pencil or a paint brush, and to realize more and more clearly the possibilities that existed of making a name for himself in literature. It is even said that about this time he had the intention of obtaining employment as an art critic, and for this purpose he studied in the museums and art galleries the various schools of painting and sculpture which were represented in them.

Five and twenty years afterwards some of the dreamings that must have occupied his mind when visiting or study-ing in the various galleries he haunted appear in. his poem " The Vatican—Sala Delle Muse."

One might easily make many references to the use Hardy undoubtedly made in descriptive passages of his novels of the impressions of art which he received by these visits to various galleries and museums. For example, in a description of the members of the famous Mellstock (Stinsford) Choir appearing in *Under the Green-wood Tree*, one reads that " they advanced against the

Weymouth

"Budmouth Regis"

Douglas Snowdon.

sky in flat outline which suggested some processional design on Greek or Etruscan pottery." And in his early novel *A Pair of Blue Eyes* Hardy writes of the gas lights glaring over butchers' stalls as "illuminating the lumps of flesh to splotches of orange and vermilion like the wild colouring of Turner's later pictures."

There are many references to artists in his various works, and in *Desperate Remedies* we are told that one of the characters stretched out " a narrow bony hand that would have been an unparalleled delight to the pencil of Carlo Crivelli." Indeed, through all his works there runs this application of the knowledge of art acquired during his sojourn in London, enhanced by a natural gift of description, which serves to make Hardy's pictures of natural phenomena, as well as of people and of buildings, so life-like and vivid.

Although it may not be known to many of his readers and admirers, it is a fact that he never entirely abandoned the habit of sketching and painting which he had acquired in the architect's office, although this habit was continued merely for his own information and amusement. We remember his telling us on one of our visits, when he showed us some of his sketches, that he frequently found that ideas presented themselves to his mind in the first instance more in the guise of mental pictures than as subjects for writing down. It will be remembered, indeed, that quite a number of these sketches, pen and ink, or pencil drawings, were reproduced in the volume *Wessex Poems and Other Verses*, first published in 1898.

"Sketchy" as many of these drawings are, consisting of mere indications of the idea in the novelist's mind, they were in a number of cases extraordinarily striking, and in a measure adequate in conveying what he had at the back of his mind. One remembers among these the picture of "The Two Moths upon the Hour Glass," two people conversing in a Gothic cathedral ; the lights of a town shining strangely in a pitch dark night, and a French infantryman stalking along a narrow Dorset lane traversing a bleak country.

No one will deny, however, that of the many sketches and drawings that Hardy made, few would probably pass muster as works of art. Indeed they were more often than not in the nature of a pencil note of an idea, and were drawn without any great desire on the part of the artist for completeness or finish. They do, however, supply us with evidence of his artistic sense—if that were, indeed, necessary.

The year after Hardy came to London constitutes the period when he gave the most serious attention to the actual business of an architect. For some time, it is recorded, he thrust aside all temptations to deflect his energies into more attractive by-ways. And in 1863 he competed for one of the prizes offered by the Architectural Association for design, and was awarded the only prize. No doubt encouraged by this success, he afterwards wrote a technical paper and entered it in the competition for the medal and £10 prize which was offered by the Royal Institution of British Architects. He chose as his subject for the essay, " The Application of Coloured Bricks and Terra Cotta to Modern Architecture," and sent it in under a Latin nom de plume. Hardy was awarded the medal, but, no doubt to his disappointment, did not receive the monetary award, as the judge considered that the essay had scarcely dealt sufficiently in detail with the subject and " the portion referring to coloured and shaped bricks has scarcely been noticed."

This was destined to prove what may be described as Hardy's last serious attempt to make headway in his adopted profession. We find he gradually gave up his architectural studies, although for some time longer he continued to make visits with Blomfield to various buildings which were being restored or erected during several succeeding years, and he evidently was more and more inclined by his natural bent to pursue literature and especially poetry, than to go further in the profession for which he had studied.

He appears, too, about this time to have had some idea

of attempting play-writing ; and—this shows the thorough-ness which always distinguished him—had also the idea of going on the stage as a " super " for a short time to learn the technique of the theatre. Armed with an introduction given him by a well-known amateur actor of that day, he saw the stage-manager of the Haymarket Theatre with that object, but so far as we know nothing further came of the interview.

CHAPTER III

THE YEARS from 1862 onward while Hardy continued to live at No. 16 Westbourne Park Villas have a very important bearing upon his character, his ultimate intellectual development and attitude towards life. It was, as will be remembered, a very disturbed period politically, and was also one of very considerable storm and stress in the field of literary expression. The literary movement of the day undoubtedly had a considerable influence upon Hardy. Several of the great writers of the mid-Victorian age had either died or were drawing near their end. Charlotte Brontë had passed away, Thackeray and Mrs. Gaskell only survived her by a few years, and Dickens was then writing very little.

It is true there were several popular writers who held the literary stage : Charles Reade, the author of *The Cloister and the Hearth*, Wilkie Collins, who made a sensational success with *A Woman in White*, and Anthony Trollope, whose " Barchester " novels were just commencing to arouse public interest. Of these three probably only Trollope is destined to endure, a possibility which has been evidenced in quite recent times by the revival of interest in his works.

George Meredith was just commencing his literary career with *The Ordeal of Richard Feverel*, and not only was the world of politics and social ideals changing rapidly, but the social revolution which was to convert the England of the days of his father into a commercial, industrial and democratic nation had begun, and the process no doubt had a great effect upon the inquisitive and naturally philosophic mind of Hardy.

It was about 1864 that, having for some years toyed with poetry, very little of which ever saw the light of print, Hardy commenced to write prose, and sent an article entitled " How I Built Myself a House " to *Chambers's Journal*. Cast in the form of a personal experience, it fitted in with the policy of that old-established publication. That is to say, it was not only interesting, but was also instructive. It was published on March 18th, 1865, and told of the trials and satisfaction of a man in having a house designed and built according to his own plan, which in after years Hardy was, himself, destined to have done.

Strangely enough, Hardy's great contemporary, George Meredith, also made what is said to have been his first appearance in print in the same publication.

It was not until Hardy had won a distinct place in English literature that his verses became a marketable commodity. Fortunately he was able to retrieve, either by having kept copies or rewriting from notes or memory, some of the poems which he wrote in the 'sixties, and these were incorporated in the volumes of verse which were ultimately published, beginning with *The Wessex Poems* in 1898.

A few of these collected poems appeared before they were published in volume form, but by far the greater portion of Hardy's poetry was written many years before it saw the light of print.

He returned to Dorchester in the early summer of 1867, and went at Mr. Hicks's request back into his office as an assistant, where, however, he did not attend regularly, and thus was enabled to commence his first novel which ultimately bore the title of *The Poor Man and the Lady*, Hardy making use of the pseudonym "A Poor Man."

Before Hardy commenced to write this book, which he did in the intervals of his work in the architect's office, he probably had come to the conclusion that his knowledge of Wessex and of Wessex characters gained in his youth, and his experience as a student in London, would afford him sufficient material out of which to construct his projected novel.

Towards the end of October in 1867 he paid a visit to London to finally collect the books and other possessions which he had left behind him, and in January of the following year he began to make a fair copy of his story.

On July 25th, 1868, the copying finished, he despatched the manuscript of the novel to the well-known firm of Macmillan, who in after years became his publishers. He was not kept long ere receiving a reply, for on August 12th he had a very long letter regarding the manuscript, in which the following opinion on it was expressed. Mr. Alexander Macmillan, then head of the firm, *stated that he had read the novel carefully and " with much interest and admiration, but feeling at the same time that it has what seems to me drawbacks fatal to its success, and what I think, judging the writer from the book itself, you would feel even more strongly to its truthfulness and justice." The writer added that " much of the book seems admirable, and even full of power and insight." He, however, went into details of criticism, saying : " The utter heartlessness of *all* the conversations you give in drawing-rooms and ballrooms about the working-classes has some ground, I fear, and might justly be scourged as you aim at doing ; but your chastisement would fall harmless from its very excess."

It is interesting in view of Hardy's ultimate work to know that another person, John Morley, had seen the manuscript, and had come to a very similar opinion regarding it. He said in his report to Mr. Macmillan that it was " a very curious and original performance ; the opening pictures of the Christmas Eve in the tranter's house are really of good quality." The critic went on to say two very significant things regarding the possible

---

* *Letters of Alexander Macmillan.*

E

personality of the writer. One that some of the scenes in the novel read " like some clever lad's dream." Secondly, in conclusion : " If the man is young, he has stuff and purpose in him."

Hardy in the autumn of the same year did something towards rewriting a portion of the book, and in December he paid a visit to London and had an interview with the famous publisher. Macmillan was, however, quite definite in his decision that he could not publish the book, but he appears to have suggested to the young novelist that it was possible that a firm such as that of Chapman & Hall would do so, and, indeed, gave him an introduction to the head of the firm, upon whom Hardy called, probably on December 8th, with the manuscript, which he left with the publisher, afterwards returning to Dorchester.

Hardy did not appear to consider that the interview had been satisfactory, and in January of the following year, 1869, not having received any reply from Messrs. Chapman & Hall, he went to London again.

He stayed some little time there in lodgings, and visited the South Kensington Museum to study the pictures, and other places, until he at last received a letter from the publishers in response to which he called at their office in Piccadilly and saw Mr. Frederick Chapman, who pointed out another visitor who happened to be in the shop as Thomas Carlyle, who Hardy, with his usual particularity of observation, recorded was dressed in an Inverness cape and wore a slouch hat.

The outcome of this interview, which resulted in an experience common with many young writers not only of that period but of the present time, was that the publisher said he could not purchase the manuscript outright, but that he would publish it if Hardy would be prepared to pay twenty pounds towards expenses. Hardy agreed to do this, and the publishers promised to put the book in hand at once and the author thereupon returned to Dorchester and settled down to await the proof sheets.

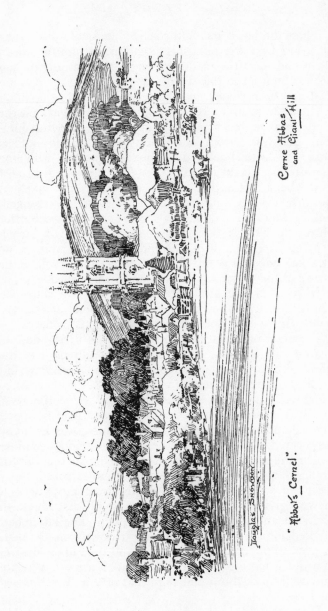

Douglas Snowdon.

"Abbot's Cernel".

Cerne Abbas and Giant Hill

These did not come, and after the lapse of a little time he heard from the publishers, who asked him to call on them and meet the reader to whom the manuscript had been submitted so that Hardy might receive the opinion that had been passed upon it.

Hardy went up to Town in March, and found that the reader was no less a person than George Meredith himself. He was shown into a dusty and untidy office, crammed with books, and found Meredith with the manuscript, who began to address Hardy upon the subject of the book. It appeared from what Meredith said that the firm were willing to publish the novel as arranged, but in Meredith's opinion it would be inadvisable for Hardy to publish the book as it stood, with its strong vein of Socialism, which would render it liable to be attacked vigorously by the reviewers, and possibly the future of the writer would be thereby imperilled.

In a word, we are told, the novel was a satire on country society and the nobility, London society, the foibles and failings of the middle classes, Christianity as it was then practised, and, in fact, ran atilt in addition against political and domestic morals, and most of the things an attack upon which the conventional reader would be likely to resent when so violently as Hardy had done. Moreover, the novel was described as " revolutionary," and was assumed by those who had read it to be based upon actual experience, which, of course, was in many ways ridiculous considering the age and the opportunities which the writer had enjoyed of mixing in the various grades of society which he described and satirized.

In the end Hardy took away the manuscript with a view to giving further consideration to all that Meredith had said and the points he had raised. The latter had advised him to rewrite it, toning it down considerably, or even to put it aside altogether, and start upon a novel of a much more conventional type with a more intricate and well worked-out plot than that of *The Poor Man and the Lady*.

It is not unlikely that Hardy himself was considerably

surprised that he should have written what had been characterized as a dangerous work of fiction, and one can well understand his amazement when one considers that up to that time he had been concerned with poetic expression and had not been conscious of any revolutionary predilections.

At any rate the novel eventually disappeared, except a few pages which were found in after years, and Hardy himself could never recollect exactly what had happened to it. It may have been sent to another firm of publishers and rejected ; or, on the other hand, he may have just put it away and forgotten it as he quite frequently did with his poems and other work.

While Hardy was still in London he had news of the death of his late employer, Mr. John Hicks, with whom he had recently been working. In the early spring he had a letter from a Mr. G. R. Crickmay of Weymouth, the purchaser of Mr. Hicks's business, asking him to come to the Dorsetshire watering-place to assist him in carrying out the church restorations that Hicks had begun, and some other contracts into which he had entered.

Hardy went down to Weymouth, called on the architect and ultimately agreed to work with him for a time. This he did, working in Hicks's old Dorchester office on the completion of church buildings which he had already begun under his late employer's directions. At the end of the short term arranged, Hardy agreed to work at Mr. Crickmay's Weymouth office for a period of three months, which was afterwards extended. He now resided regularly at Weymouth, and did a good deal of rowing in the bay and bathing, as he was an expert swimmer. He remained there some time, and it was while residing at this popular Wessex seaside resort that he turned his attention seriously to literary work.

He carried with him, however, to the sea memories at least of the London with whose life he had been brought in contact for a time. Surely there is an echo of his memories of London when he speaks of the local architecture of the older portion of Weymouth as " A Soho or Bloomsbury street transplanted to the seashore, drawing only a smile from the modern tourist who has no eye for solidity of beauty."

During this period of his residence at Weymouth, there is little doubt that Hardy was keenly observant of the life going on around him, and of the various character-istics of the people who visited the popular resort, even in those days. Of his friends and the people who knew him well while he resided at Weymouth, practically nothing is discoverable, although many years ago we came across an elderly man whose father knew him, and of whom he hired boats, but his early works tell the student how keen an observer he must have become, and how natural a gift for analysis of character and human limitations he must, even in those days, have pos-sessed.

There are certainly memories of Weymouth in the poem entitled " At a Seaside Town in 1869," which appears in the collection *Moments of Vision*.   There we have a picture of the chalk cliffs of Osmington Mills and onwards to Lulworth or "Lulstead" Cove, as Hardy named it, and of the breezy greetings of and the haltings for talks with the fishermen of Weymouth, described by Hardy as " keen sea salts," and even a mention of the town band !

In August or September, 1869, there came to the drawing office in Weymouth a young man with whom Hardy struck up an acquaintance, and with whom later Hardy attended a quadrille or dancing class, which was a source of much social amusement and interest to them both. This acquaintance was destined to figure after-wards in the new novel which Hardy was then just commencing, in the character of Edward Springrove.

Early in the winter Hardy had finished all the drawings for the church restoration that he had engaged to do, but he continued to live at Weymouth in lodgings, and applied himself closely to writing *Desperate Remedies*, which was, as a work of art, probably far below in interest his rejected *The Poor Man and the Lady*. In February following Hardy left Weymouth and went back to his home, as he evidently felt that he could work much more rapidly if he cut himself off from the gaieties of the seaside town.

There is a poem of his called " The Dawn after the Dance," dated from Weymouth, which probably contains some of his experiences at the quadrille class.

In February of the following year Hardy, while at his mother's house, received a letter from Mr. Crickmay, asking him to go into Cornwall to obtain particulars of a church that he had engaged to rebuild. He wrote and refused the offer of work, as he was very busy upon *Desperate Remedies*. But in March, when the architect again approached him, having finished writing all except three or four chapters of the novel, he agreed to go.

He finished the story, and sent it off to Mr. Alexander Macmillan, and on the following Monday he left for St. Juliot, near Boscastle, in Cornwall, where the church was situated that Mr. Crickmay had agreed to restore or rebuild.

Unimportant as this architectural job may have seemed to Hardy, compared with getting on with his literary work, it was nevertheless destined to have an unlooked-for influence on his life, for in the rectory of St. Juliot he met a lady, Miss Emma Lavinia Gifford, the younger daughter of Mr. J. Attersoll Gifford, a solicitor, who was also a niece of an Archdeacon Gifford of London. She was the sister-in-law of the then rector of the parish, the Rev. Caddell Holder, M.A., who was a son of a Barbados judge. Miss Gifford's presence in her brother-in-law's household was owing to the fact that her sister required her help in the parish, which, we are told, had been much neglected by the previous rector.

In her own memoirs, the first Mrs. Hardy recounts how interested everyone in the rectory, and even many in the parish itself, were at the thought of the restoration of the old church, and in the arrival of the architect's assistant, who was to do the preliminary work of investigation and measurements. In these recollections she gives us a description of Hardy's arrival in the following words :

" I had to receive him alone, and felt a curious, uneasy embarrassment at receiving anyone, especially so necessary a person as the architect. I was immediately arrested by his familiar appearance as if I had seen him in a dream—his slightly different accent, his soft voice ; also I noticed a blue paper sticking out of his pocket. . . . So I met my husband." (And here follows an interesting picture of Hardy, as he appeared to his future wife.) " I thought him much older than he was. He had a beard and a rather shabby greatcoat, and had quite a business appearance. Afterwards he seemed younger, and by daylight especially so. . . . The blue paper proved to be the MS. of a poem, and not a plan of a church, he informed me to my surprise.

" After this, our first meeting, there had to be many visits to the church, and these visits, of deep interest to both, merged in those of further acquaintance and affection to end in marriage, but not till after four years."

Hardy paid several visits to St. Juliot, and on these occasions the future Mrs. Hardy records riding her horse on the cliffs and along the roads with him walking at her side. They also sketched and talked of books, and walked to Boscastle Harbour, and to other places of interest in the neighbourhood.

A correspondence was also kept up between Miss Gifford and Hardy. When the time for the event came, neither the latter nor his employer, strangely enough, were present at the opening of the church, which took place with some considerable ceremony, and aroused a great deal of interest in the neighbourhood. Hardy, however, after this, still continued to pay visits to St. Juliot's Rectory.

On many occasions in later years attempts have been

made in the Press to connect the characters of Hardy's romance *A Pair of Blue Eyes*, which appeared soon after the completion of his visits to Cornwall, as well as some of the scenes which are laid in the Duchy, with himself and his experiences while visiting at the house of his future wife (these presumably may in some measure represent or at least be reminiscent of St. Juliot). Hardy himself on several occasions, and once to the present writer, repudiated the idea that he figured in the story at all, or that any part of it, other than scenery, could be considered inspired by his experiences at the Cornish rectory. The chief male character, he more than once said, was, both as regards appearance and mental as well as physical characteristics, in part a sketch of a nephew of Mr. Hicks, his first employer, with whom he had been associated while working in that architect's office.

It has been suggested, however, more than once that Henry Knight, the reviewer in the novel, and Elfride's second lover was in some measure a sketch of the novelist. Close students of Hardy, however, and of the facts relative to the first Mrs. Hardy, still cling to the belief that in some measure the character of Elfride was that of Miss Gifford, possibly as Hardy imagined she was before he married her.

It was on his return to Weymouth, to carry on the work of making the drawings for the restoration of the church, that he received another disappointment in his would-be literary career, for in April, 1870, Messrs. Macmillan wrote saying they were sorry to find themselves unable to publish his novel *Desperate Remedies*, most probably on account of some of the incidents it contained. The young novelist, perhaps sensing that a publishing house of the standing and tradition of that of Macmillan was probably not the most likely to issue books of the kind, sent off the manuscript again ; this time to Messrs. Tinsley, who were publishing novels at that time of a general character, and more like those which Hardy was seeking to write.

The book was not actually complete, a synopsis only

of the last two chapters having been sent, but, notwithstanding this, Messrs. Tinsley very promptly wrote,
making the author an offer for publication of the book.
Perhaps encouraged by this he left the employment of
Mr. Crickmay and went again to London.

It would appear that Hardy, during the period of his
connection with the restoration of St. Juliot's Church
and work in the Weymouth architect's office, had reached
a point in his life when he came to regard architecture
only as a means of employment until he should establish
himself by his literary work.

He remained some time in Town, and appears at this
time to have written verses which afterwards appeared
in the collection *Wessex Poems and Other Verses*, inscribed
with the initials of Miss Gifford.

He did a small amount of work while in London,
helping his old employer, Arthur (afterwards Sir Arthur)
Blomfield, and also another architect, a Mr. Raphael
Brandon, who was interested in Gothic architecture.

In view of the publishers' offer for *Desperate Remedies*,
he asked for the return of the manuscript from them, and
we are told his future wife was engaged during the
autumn of 1870 in making a fair copy of the original
manuscript, and of the final chapters which Hardy
finished about the same time.

When completed, the book was sent off again to Tinsley
at the end of the year, and in due course Hardy heard
from the publishers again, but for some unknown reason
the terms stated were at variance with those offered in
the first communication with Tinsley. As has been the
case with so many young authors the publishers demanded
the payment of a sum—seventy-five pounds in this case—
towards the cost of production, which sum was to be
returned to Hardy if the book covered expenses, and should
it more than pay expenses Hardy was to share equally
with the publishers whatever profits there might be.

In the following month Hardy came up to London
and paid Tinsley the seventy-five pounds that had been
demanded ; and then returned to Dorset to await the

DOUGLAS S. SNOWDON.

"Havenpool"

Poole Harbour

proofs, and fill in his spare time with writing down notes of old country customs and folk-lore that he was able to gather from the old people at Upper Bockhampton and the vicinity.

On March 25th, Messrs. Tinsley published *Desperate Remedies* in three volumes. Hardy's name did not, however, appear on the title-page. A few days later the book was reviewed very favourably in the *Athenæum*, which spoke of it as being a powerful novel, and this was followed on April 13th by a very favourable notice in the literary columns of the *Morning Post*. A few days later, however, the *Spectator* attacked the book vigorously, apparently chiefly on account of Hardy having made an unmarried lady, who was the owner of an estate, the mother of an illegitimate child. The whole review was written in the extraordinarily self-righteous and highly conventional style then prevailing with some reviewers.

Hardy afterwards spoke of how he had sat down upon a stile, leading to a field that he had to cross on his way back from Dorchester to Bockhampton, to read the review in the *Spectator*, and the bitterness of hearing of the " heat " that his novel had generated in literary circles.

He also recalled that on returning from a visit to Cornwall in the following June he saw in Messrs. Smith & Sons' " Catalogue of Surplus Books " his three-volume novel advertised for sale at half a crown. This was additional evidence that the book had been killed, probably by the review in the *Spectator*, and that he was very unlikely to see the return of any part of the seventy-five pounds that he had paid the publishers as an advance against expenses.

As a matter of fact a year after the book had been published Hardy received an account from Messrs. Tinsley Bros. which showed that they had sold 370 sets out of a printing of 500, and that Hardy's loss after the accounts had been balanced was only a matter of fifteen pounds. On the whole a sale of 370 sets of a book, which was so different to the usual run of novels popular at that time, was not altogether unsatisfactory in the case of a new author.

Hardy's next novel, which was destined to establish him as a writer of unusual gifts, was called *Under the Greenwood Tree*. The original title of it, however, was *The Mellstock Quire*, with a sub-title of " A Rural Painting of the Dutch School." He again first sent the manuscript to Macmillans, and by a misreading of their letter with regard to the novel, wrote and asked for its return. The firm sent it back. In fact they had been willing to publish it. He had completed it soon after the publication of *Desperate Remedies*, and with his usual carelessness, if not indifference, after its return to him by Macmillans, put it aside.

When Tinsley, who admired Hardy's work, and probably saw a coming novelist in him, asked him a little later for another book, Hardy mentioned that he had a manuscript, but that he could not for the moment recall where it was. Tinsley was insistent on seeing it, and Hardy wrote down to his home at Bockhampton asking his mother to have a look for it and to send it on to him if found.

Some time in April the mislaid manuscript of *Under the Greenwood Tree* reached Hardy, who was still in London, and he sent it on to the publisher without even looking through it. Eventually Tinsley agreed to give the novelist thirty pounds for the entire copyright, which offer was accepted. Eventually Hardy received a further ten pounds, for the book had received the distinction of being also published in the famous Tauchnitz library, and Tinsley sent the author half the amount received from the German firm.

All this time Hardy was still dabbling with architecture, doing competition drawings for schools and occasionally work for Arthur Blomfield in Adelphi Terrace, with whom he always remained on very friendly terms.

Under the Greenwood Tree, published in May, 1872, was well received, and as a result Tinsley, who was at that time running a rather famous magazine named after the firm, to which a number of popular writers during its existence contributed, asked Hardy if he would write him a serial story to run throughout the yearly volume. Before agreeing to Tinsley's terms Hardy seems to have gone into the question of the law of copyright, and eventually told the publisher that he was not prepared to sell all rights for the sum suggested. Finally he accepted the amount for the serial rights and those in a three-volume edition of the story.

This novel, *A Pair of Blue Eyes*, was written with great rapidity, and, indeed, the first chapter or two with extraordinary speed. Hardy, however, had no experience of serial writing, and, we are told, had not plotted the whole of the novel before he sat down to commence it. Having done the first instalment he decided to take a holiday, and sailed on August 7th on board one of the boats of the Irish Mail Packet Company from London for Cornwall.

He went on with the writing of this story, and on his return to London found that it did not progress satisfactorily, and on this account went down to his home and worked hard at it. The action of the story, it will be remembered, takes place on the coast of Cornwall not far from Tintagel, and no doubt many of the excursions that Hardy had made while on his various visits to St. Juliot's Rectory provided him with the local colour and perhaps even with outlines of some of the characters.

It was in 1872 that Hardy was approached by Leslie Stephen, then the editor of *Cornhill*, and a well-known figure of literary society of that day, asking whether Hardy could write a serial story for the magazine. He said he had read *Under the Greenwood Tree*, and expressed a high opinion of it, and added that a story of that particular type would probably interest and be successful with the readers of *Cornhill*.

Upon how slender a thread had hung the possibility of Leslie Stephen getting into touch with Hardy, and of the commencement of an association which was so materially to advance the novelist in his career, has often been told.

In those days the postal arrangements in country districts, and apparently especially in Hardy's neighbourhood, were of a most primitive character, and there was no regular delivery of letters to Bockhampton. It was apparently the custom of the postmaster at Dorchester to rely upon any letter reaching the Hardys by the hand of some neighbour. As a matter of fact Leslie Stephen's letter had been dropped in a lane by one of the school children to whom it had been entrusted for delivery, and had it not been picked up by a labourer and brought to Hardy's house, might never have reached him. One can easily imagine the man walking up the narrow path leading to the thatched cottage, unconscious how important on Hardy's future was to prove the letter he had picked up and bore in his hand.

The novel *A Pair of Blue Eyes* met with very considerable success, and as a result Hardy was encouraged immediately to set about writing a successor to it, and commenced *Far from the Madding Crowd*.

At the end of September, Leslie Stephen received as much of the manuscript of the story as Hardy had then written, and a few days later the novelist received a letter saying that the story was just what had been required, so far as could be seen, and although it was the editor's usual practice not finally to accept a story until he had it in his possession, and had the opportunity of reading the whole of the manuscript, he had decided to purchase *Far from the Madding Crowd* on what had been submitted to him.

As to Hardy's method of working, he once recalled how, when wandering about the countryside, ideas often came into his head when he had not a scrap of paper upon him. Under such conditions he said that he would pick up large dead leaves, chips of wood left by the woodmen, or pieces of slate, and jot down rapidly upon these unusual materials the ideas which came into his head.

There are many entries to be found in Hardy's diaries which show how closely he kept in touch with and studied not only Nature, but also the various types with which he came in contact. There is also evidence, from their fragmentary character, that these notes were made on the spot.

It was usual for the novels in the *Cornhill* to be illustrated, and Hardy seems to have had some misgivings as to whether the artist likely to be employed would have sufficient knowledge of the dress, appearance and general character of the types depicted in the story to enable him to draw satisfactory illustrations, for he wrote to the editor of *Cornhill*, telling him that if necessary he could supply some rough sketches likely to be of use to the artist.

Hardy's habit of "calling a spade a spade" in relation to the fate of Fanny Robin, one of the characters, proved likely to get him into trouble, for Leslie Stephen wrote him warning him that he must deal with such subjects in "a gingerly fashion." This warning was apparently issued in consequence of readers having taken exception to a passage in the instalment which had appeared.

Hardy always found his inspiration most active when in the country, and indeed all his best work was done amidst the scenes and in close touch with types of character he described. As soon, therefore, as the story had well started on its publication in *Cornhill*, he retired again to Bockhampton to finish the other instalments.

Somehow or other one does not associate the finished style and "architectural" character and beauty of Hardy's prose with rapid production, but at any rate his first serial story was written at a very considerable speed, and much more rapidly than Hardy himself had at one time considered possible.

It was during a visit to London in the winter, when the story was drawing to a conclusion, that Hardy entered into society through his friendship with the editor of *Cornhill*, whose intellectual gifts had a great

influence upon his own.   At the house of Leslie Stephen
he met a number of interesting people.

In August Hardy finished the manuscript of the story
and sent it in, and on the 17th of the following month
he married Miss Emma Lavinia Gifford at St. Peter's,
Elgin Avenue, Paddington.   Her uncle, Dr. E. Hamilton
Gifford, who was at that time Canon of Worcester, and
afterwards became Archdeacon of London, officiated.

CHAPTER IV

A FEW MONTHS later, during the autumn publishing season, *Far from the Madding Crowd* appeared in two-volume form.

On his honeymoon Hardy paid his first visit to the Continent. Such visits were more frequent during the ensuing years than generally supposed. Mr. and Mrs. Hardy visited Rouen among other places, and, on their return, the young married pair settled for a time at Surbiton.

Naturally the success of *Far from the Madding Crowd* brought a suggestion from both the editor and publishers of the *Cornhill* for another serial, and Hardy, who agreed to write it, took rather a risk in breaking for him almost entirely new ground in the novel *The Hand of Ethelberta; a Comedy in Chapters*, the scene of which is chiefly laid in the Isle of Purbeck, and was quite a different type of story to the one which had just achieved such success.

Hardy, who eventually became President of the Authors' Society, very early evinced his interest in the subject of copyright law, and in May, 1875, we are told, he formed one of a deputation to Mr. Disraeli, afterwards the Earl of Beaconsfield, in support of a motion for the appointment of a select committee to enquire into the state of the law relating to copyright. It was this year that the idea of a poetic work dealing with the Napoleonic Wars (evidently the germ of the drama which afterwards saw the light as *The Dynasts*) came into his head. As was the case with much that Hardy wrote, the idea lay dormant for many years before fruition.

In the summer of 1875, Mr. and Mrs. Hardy went to Bournemouth, and visited Swanage, then a small fishing village, afterwards destined to develop into a popular seaside resort, where they took lodgings at the house of an owner of fishing-boats, and settled down for the autumn and winter, during which *The Hand of Ethelberta* was finished, amidst the environment in which some of the chief scenes of the story were laid.

During the time he was at Swanage one of his poems, a ballad called " The Fire at Tranter Sweatley's," which he had written while employed by Blomfield in Adelphi Terrace, London, was published in the November number of the *Gentleman's Magazine*, 1875, and afterwards appeared in his volume *Wessex Poems*.

It was also while at Swanage, and during talks with their landlord, who told Hardy stories of his seafaring life, some of them of the smuggling days, that the novelist doubtless obtained material for the one or two short stories which he wrote with a smuggling incident as the plot.   Possibly that of *The Distracted Preacher*.

Everyone who has gone mackerel fishing, which the writer has done many times in Swanage Bay, knows how voracious these fish are, and that the bait may be anything from a piece of red flannel to a tiny piece of shining tin.

Hardy used to tell a story, based upon what his land-lord sea captain had told him, of some smugglers who were once waiting to meet a French lugger half-way across the Channel, and, when surprised by a revenue cutter some miles off the Bill of Portland, pretended they were fishing for mackerel, but having no suitable bait on board broke up the clay pipes they were smoking, and fastened pieces of them above the fish hooks, and, much to their surprise, found they had caught mackerel !

On discovering that the smugglers were at least ostensibly fishing, the revenue officers sailed away, and doubtless the cargo was " run " according to plan.

While at Swanage, Hardy was busy making entries in his voluminous note-books, or, when they were not at hand, on odd scraps of paper, mostly of incidents and thoughts some of which he afterwards doubtless used in his novels and stories in some form or another. In these notes, some of which were afterwards published, one traces Hardy's keen appreciation and interest in various phases of natural phenomena, such as sunsets, the songs of birds, and the motion and roaring of the sea which, while he was at Swanage, formed one of his delights to see and listen to.

While there, Hardy must have been very pleased with an appreciative article which appeared in the French *Revue des Deux Mondes* dealing with his novel *Far from the Madding Crowd* under the title of " Le Roman Pastoral en Angleterre."

About this time he was writing a good deal of verse, and throughout his life poetry was undoubtedly his favourite means of literary expression. Those who knew him are agreed that his great desire was to become a poet, and this was never modified or altered by the great success he won as a novelist. Indeed Hardy on more than one occasion rather pathetically explained that he was a novelist only because of the necessity to earn a living !

About this time, too, Leslie Stephen, who had become one of Hardy's greatest and most useful friends, and Hardy often engaged in controversy regarding theological subjects, and those dealing with the origin of species. Such discussions were undoubtedly quite in keeping with Hardy's temperament, and the particular type of philosophy that, as a thinking man, was inevitably evolved out of that.

After *The Hand of Ethelberta* was finished in January, 1876, and the manuscript sent to the publishers, Mr. and Mrs. Hardy removed in the March to Yeovil with the view of searching that part of the country for a permanent home.

Leslie Stephen was by no means pleased to receive for publication in his magazine something so different from the last work ; but, perhaps because of Hardy's growing

Robert Swain

Grey's Bridge
Dorchester. "Casterbridge"
.

Fordington Church

reputation, the story was accepted, and commenced in the *Cornhill*.

The Hardys were, however, unsuccessful in finding a home on the Somersetshire-Dorsetshire border, and, almost immediately after the publication of the first instalment in the *Cornhill*, the Hardys set out in May on a tour of Holland and the Rhine, and went to quite a number of interesting places in both. Hardy afterwards recorded his disappointment with the character of the Gothic in the cathedral at Cologne, from which city they proceeded down the Rhine to Bonn, Coblenz, Ehrenbreitstein, and Mainz. A tour in those days of some adventure, which has since become so commonplace and popular with holiday-makers.

Afterwards they went to Baden, the Black Forest, and Strasbourg, returning to England by way of Metz and Brussels. Hardy made many notes of this tour and in such vivid phrases as " The Rhine glared like a ribbon of blood, as if it serpentined through the atmosphere above the earth's surface." This peculiar impression of the river was created upon Hardy's mind by the mist which enveloped the landscape—which it frequently does— and through which the sun shone, creating the appearance that he noted.

While at Brussels, perhaps even with the idea for *The Dynasts* already actively germinating in his mind, he visited the Field of Waterloo, and undertook several investigations in trying to trace the exact locale of the famous ball of the Duchess of Richmond. He returned to London by way of Antwerp.

While in London Hardy appears to have visited Chelsea Hospital, and heard accounts of the battle in a room of The Turk's Head near-by, given to him by a few pensioners who had taken part in the campaign.

He returned to Yeovil with his wife and resumed their enquiries, which had been interrupted by their continental tour, for a cottage in which to take up their residence. In the end their search for a home was once more transferred from the borderland into what may be almost called the central Dorset region, and eventually they discovered a house overlooking the Stour at Sturminster Newton, called " Riverside Villa," of which they became tenants at midsummer and furnished after a shopping expedition to Bristol ! This little town, afterwards appearing in Hardy's pages as " Stourcastle," was their first actual place of residence, and though the house was small they undoubtedly spent very happy days there during their two years' tenancy of the house, and several of Hardy's poems commemorate these.

The Hardys seem to have passed their time in country walks, in rowing on the river, and in the ordinary occupations of life in a small town, and from all we have been able to gather kept rather to themselves, and do not appear to have had many friends. Indeed, one old lady who knew them then spoke of them as " gentlefolk keeping very much to themselves."

As exhibiting Hardy's methods of work, one may mention an entry which he made in his diaries, in which he says, while at Sturminster Newton: "A story has been told me of a doctor who attended a woman unable to pay him. In settlement of the debt he said he would take the baby, which had died. This he did, and it was kept on his mantelpiece in a large glass jar in spirits. On the doctor afterwards marrying, he treated his wife badly, and still persisted in keeping the dead baby on his mantelpiece."

So far as we are aware Hardy, however, made no use of this incident in any way, as he may originally have intended. It would have provided him with a grim subject for a Wessex tale!

His novel *A Pair of Blue Eyes* was very favourably criticized in the *Revue des Deux Mondes* early in 1877, and the story was evidently of the kind favoured by French readers. Hardy himself evidently liked the book, which was perhaps not unnatural, as it most probably recorded incidents and described scenes which were at all events related to his experiences at St. Juliot, and his courtship of the rector's sister-in-law, who was now Mrs. Hardy.

He approached the publishers with a view to a new edition, and the latter at once said that they would publish one, although for some untraceable reason the firm did not carry out this arrangement, and it was ultimately republished by Henry S. King & Co. in one volume.

All the while that Hardy was residing at Sturminster Newton he was busily engaged in making notes which would prove of use to him as the basis of future work, or at least could be used as incidents to be woven into future novels, stories and poems.

In conversation with various business people as well as with country folk he was constantly acquiring knowledge of incidents which had taken place in the county, some of them of such tragic or dramatic possibilities for use as that he recorded of the two soldiers of the York Hussars, who were shot in the first year of the 19th century on the top of Bincombe Down for desertion. This incident was afterwards used by Hardy as the dramatic germ of his tragic story *The Melancholy Hussar*, and the real names of the unfortunate men were used.

It was about this period, too, that Hardy got into touch with a Mrs. Chatteris, who was the daughter of Admiral Sir Thomas Hardy, with special reference to some of the incidents in the life of his famous namesake. Probably the information he thus obtained was ultimately woven into the fabric of *The Dynasts*.

It was while residing at "Riverside Villa" that he started the writing of *The Return of the Native*, in many ways one of the best and most characteristic of the Wessex novels. The story was sent in instalments to Messrs. Chatto & Windus, and was first published in the pages of *Belgravia*, a monthly magazine then popular, commencing January 1878, and running through four volumes, and was illustrated by Arthur Hopkins. The scenes of *The Return of the Native* have entirely to do with "Egdon" Heath, that stretch of wild moorland lying between Wool, the "Wellbridge" of *Tess of the D'Urbervilles*, and Hardy's home at Upper Bockhampton, and not with

the particular part of the country in which he was residing
at the time he wrote the novel.

Near the end of December of this year Hardy attended
an inquest, which was held at the village of Stourton
Caundell, on the body of a boy who was presumed to
have been poisoned. It is not quite clear why Hardy
was present at the post-mortem though we know that he
was, but he records how he and a Dr. Leach, the coroner,
went to a cottage, and in an upstairs room found the
body on a box covered with a sheet. While the autopsy
was being made by a Mr. Long, it appears Hardy and
the policeman present each held a candle ! The enquiry
itself was held at the village inn. Doubtless Hardy's
object in attending this gruesome event was the thirst for
first-hand information and new experiences so characteristic of him, and the possibility of using the incident at
some future date.

In the following year, 1878, Hardy became impressed
with the idea that it would be better for his literary
work—or at least the financial side of it—if he were to
settle in or nearer London, and in pursuance of this idea,
early in the year he and Mrs. Hardy went to Town to
look for a house, and in the end found one that suited
them at Upper Tooting, near Wandsworth Common.

In after years Hardy expressed himself as being doubtful whether this move to London had been entirely a
wise step.

In March of this year their tenancy of the cottage at
Sturminster Newton ended, and with it what Hardy
himself expressed as having been " a very happy time,"
and one which was certainly fruitful of a considerable
amount of poetry, some of which afterwards appeared in
his volume of poems called *Moments of Vision and Miscellaneous Verses.*

The house Hardy occupied near Wandsworth Common
was at that time known as 1 Arundel Terrace, Trinity
Road.

While living here Hardy threw himself with some zest
into London society, and was, in the middle of the year

in which the Hardys came to London, elected a member of the Savile Club.   He met a good many interesting people, among them Professor Huxley, for whom he developed a great liking, and Huxley's views undoubtedly had a considerable influence upon him.

In August and September of this year the novelist was again in Dorset paying calls, mixing with the country folk, going into Dorchester on market days and chatting with the types which he depicted in *Far from the Madding Crowd* and afterwards in *Tess of the D'Urbervilles*, and doubtless storing up incidents for future use.

He returned to London towards the end of September, and agreed with Messrs. Smith Elder for the publication in three volumes of *The Return of the Native*.   In regard to this book Hardy made an interesting suggestion.   He wished a sketch map that he had drawn, covering the scenes in which the novel was laid, to be put as a frontis-piece to the first volume.   However, even then Hardy guarded himself against the too close identification of the scenes appearing in the story with actual places, for he, in his suggestion to his publishers, used the words " Supposed scene in which *The Return of the Native* is laid."

In connection with this it may be noted that Hardy throughout his writings never used the word Dorset, but refers to the area covered by his novels and poems under the generic name of " Wessex," which descriptive name appears for the first time in the novel *Far from the Madding Crowd*.

As an instance of Hardy's desire for accuracy of informa-tion the first Mrs. Hardy used to tell a story of how on one occasion while resident in London her husband hurriedly left his study, where he was engaged in writing, on hearing a tune played upon a street barrel-organ somewhere near at hand.   It was a tune which he had heard whistled by a friend employed with him in the architect's office at Dorchester, who had told Hardy many years before that it was one to which he had danced either at the Cremorne Gardens in London or the then famous

Douglas Snowdon

The road to Shaftesbury.

"Shaston."

Argyle Rooms. Hardy had, however, never known or had forgotten the name of the tune, and on hearing it played that summer morning outside his house in Arundel Terrace had promptly left his writing and hastily sought the organ-grinder for information. Unfortunately Hardy did not get much satisfaction, as all the tune was named on the list in front of the organ was " Quadrille," which of course conveyed nothing, and was merely a description of a dance.

As a matter of fact, Hardy never discovered the real name of the tune which had haunted and so intrigued him.

In November *The Return of the Native* was published in three volumes by Messrs. Smith Elder, and *The Times* review, which was favourable, remarked *inter alia* that the novelist had laid his scenes " further from the madding crowd than even before."

In consequence of a letter from his father on the last day of the year, telling him that his mother was in poor health and suggesting that he should pay a visit to them, Hardy on February 1st went down to Dorset, and arrived there, as he records, on a very tempestuous day of rain and sleet.

During his stay at Upper Bockhampton he visited both Weymouth and Portland, and especially Chesil Beach, and doubtless some of the material that he gathered was afterwards incorporated in that most stirring romance of the Napoleonic period, *The Trumpet Major*.

There is a strange tradition current in the so-called Isle of Portland, or, as Hardy named it, " the Isle of Slingers "—which, by the way, is not an island at all but a peninsula—that the violence of the waves and tides in " Deadman's Bay," which is an indentation on its western side, strips all the drowned sailors of their clothing.

In the middle of February he returned to London, and in June he was present at an International Literary Congress held in the rooms of the Society of Arts. A few days later he also attended a Soirée Musicale at the Hanover Square Club, at which were gathered the members of the Congress and of the company of the Comédie Française. Hardy evidently felt on this occasion as on many others, when he found himself more or less a stranger in large companies of people, " a fish out of water," for he himself says in an entry of his diary : " I was a total stranger and wondered why I was there."

Hardy always noted carefully and with interest the characteristics of people with whom he was brought in contact in buses, other conveyances, or when on foot, and in portions of his diaries which have been published one can discover many graphic " thumb-nail " sketches of types—especially those of girls and women—which may have formed the basis of the descriptions he afterwards applied to various characters in his novels.

In the early part of this year Hardy's story " The Distracted Young Preacher " appeared in the *New Quarterly Magazine*, occupying some fifty pages.

In the middle of 1879 Leslie Stephen opened negotiations with Hardy, with a view to his contributing another serial to the *Cornhill Magazine*. Hardy, it appears, had just about then commenced writing *The Trumpet Major*, and informed his editor that the book in hand was a story dealing with the reign of George III and the Napoleonic period. The idea does not seem to have struck Leslie Stephen very favourably ; he did not feel very enthusiastic about a historical novel for his publication.

It was eventually published in 1880 as a serial in *Good Words*, a magazine then belonging to Isbister & Co., Ltd., and ran throughout the year.

Possibly to assist him with the local colour, we find that in the latter part of August, Hardy was visiting his parents, and was joined by his wife shortly afterwards, when they went to Weymouth and took lodgings overlooking the harbour.

Doubtless Hardy explored Portland and the downs which lay to the north-east of Weymouth while there, and also neighbouring villages with a view to accurate descriptions of the scenery for use in *The Trumpet Major*, the principal scenes of which, as is well known, are laid at Weymouth and the immediate neighbourhood.

During the winter of this year the Hardys were again in London, and he attended several public and other functions, among which was the Inaugural Dinner of the Rabelais Club, founded by another writer, Sir Walter Besant, and held at the Tavistock Hotel. Hardy was asked to join this club in recognition of the fact that he was the author of the most virile works of fiction then being published.

About this period Hardy was brought in contact with quite a number of interesting men, both writers and others, and met among the former Henry James, the American novelist, and Richard Jefferies, the latter of whom had already attracted some attention with his *The Gamekeeper at Home*, and who, one would imagine from his love of country life, must have made some appeal to Hardy himself, and have had something in common.

Hardy also got to know Browning through Mrs. Procter, who was the widow of " Barry Cornwall," and the acquaintance thus begun with Mrs. Procter extended over many years and led to a close friendship.

Hardy also met Tennyson about this time at a house he had temporarily taken in Belgrave Square.

It is interesting to note that Tennyson, who seemed on that occasion to have been in a genial humour, telling amusing stories and asking Mrs. Procter riddles, said that his personal preference was for Hardy's *A Pair of Blue Eyes*. Although Tennyson pressed Hardy to visit him at his home at Aldworth House, near Haslemere, he never appears to have done so.

It was in July that he arranged for the publication in three-volume form of *The Trumpet Major* with Messrs. Smith Elder, after it had run its course as a serial, and it was during the summer of the same year that he paid a visit to France with Mrs. Hardy. After seeing Amiens and the cathedral, in which Hardy was much interested, they went on to Etretat, where, we are told, they bathed every day, and that Hardy was accustomed to remain in the water too long, with the result that in the autumn of the same year he fell seriously ill.

They returned in due course to London, going down in the early autumn to Dorset. Later in the year they paid a visit to Cambridge, and were shown the usual things worth seeing. It was while at Cambridge that Hardy first felt premonitions of the serious illness with which he was to be struck down.

By a somewhat strange coincidence they returned to London on the same day, October 23rd, on which *The Trumpet Major* was published.

On the Sunday following he was evidently seriously ill, and a neighbouring surgeon was called in and pronounced him suffering from an internal complaint accompanied with hæmorrhage. Naturally Mrs. Hardy was very alarmed, and in her distress applied for advice to their great friends the Macmillans. Alexander Macmillan sent his own doctor to see Hardy, and he agreed with the diagnosis made by the surgeon and forbade the patient to make any attempt to get up. It was thought that a serious operation would become necessary, but this might possibly be avoided if Hardy could be persuaded to remain in bed for a very considerable period.

Hardy was naturally troubled at this verdict because he had already commenced a new story for *Harper's Magazine* called " A Laodicean," which was to begin publication in the following month. The first part had already been printed, and the story naturally when once started could not well be interrupted. An additional worry was the fact that *Harper's Magazine* was issuing an English edition for the first time and, of course, great importance was attached to the presence in it of a story by Hardy. The nature of his illness necessitated his lying in bed with his legs actually higher than his head. Of course, under such circumstances, to write the book himself was impossible, and so he tried to complete the story by dictating it to Mrs. Hardy. By the end of May the rough draft of the book was finished.

About this time there was an entry in his diary, or on some scrap of paper, of the following thought which also holds good at the present time when there is distinctly a tendency in fiction towards romanticism. Hardy wrote : " Romanticism will exist in human nature as long as human nature itself exists. The point is (in imaginative literature) to adopt that form of romanticism which is the mood of the age."

Writers of to-day will doubtless be in agreement with the opinion that is wrapped up in the last few words of Hardy's statement. Namely, that to win at all events monetary success as a writer, it is necessary to fall in with " the mood of the age " to a very large extent, and the demands of the reading public.

All the time of his illness Hardy was doubtless turning over in his mind many ideas and thoughts which were ultimately used in succeeding novels and volumes of verse. Indeed most writers, we fancy, often find their brain most active when their bodies are weakest, and the period of recovery from an illness one of unusual mental activity.

A very interesting incident occurred which shows how Hardy was in the habit of sometimes using the most trivial matters, of a novel kind, in his work. During March one of the Miss Macmillans called on the Hardys and sat in the window watching an unusually beautiful sunset, and Hardy subsequently made a note of the fact that so he might enjoy the beauty of the sun the idea occurred to her of reflecting the sun on to his face by a looking-glass. It will be remembered that this was exactly the plan adopted by Sue in *Jude the Obscure* during Richard Phillotson's illness.

It was six months after he had been laid aside before he was strong enough to go for a walk alone, although on several occasions before then he had been out for carriage drives. He recalls how he went one sunny morning,

Douglas Snowden.

Evershot. "Evershead."

towards the end of spring, for a walk on Wandsworth
Common, and how he stood reciting to himself the verses
from Gray's "Ode on a Vicissitude" which were in a
measure singularly appropriate, and ran :

> " See the wretch, that long has tost
>   On the thorny bed of pain
> At length repair his vigour lost
>   And breathe and walk again ;
>
> The meanest flow'ret in the vale,
> The simplest note that swells the gale,
> The common sun, the air, the skies,
> To him are opening paradise."

Before Hardy had recovered from his illness the three
years' lease of the house at Upper Tooting, where he had
lain ill, had run out, and an extension had to be granted
to them.

They decided to return to Dorset, and departed at the
end of May for Dorchester, with a view to finding some
dwelling which would enable them to live in the country,
which it was now deemed desirable for Hardy to do.
Eventually they found an unpretentious house with a
conservatory, called " Llanerne," situated in The Avenue
at Wimborne, appearing in a photo which we have as a
pleasant but unpretentious villa, and they entered into
possession of this on June 25th. Hardy delighted in the
garden, which was full of all sorts of old-fashioned flowers,
and fruit.

During the August of that year he and his wife visited
Scotland, and after a lengthy tour finished up with a
visit to the Lakes and Chester, and then returned
home.

It was during the autumn of this year that Hardy was
engaged in correcting his story " A Laodicean "—which
had nearly come to an end in *Harper's* as a serial and
had been illustrated by the well-known artist, George
du Maurier, the author of the famous novel *Trilby*—for

publication in three-volume form. He found a new publisher for it in the firm of Sampson Low, Marston, Searle & Rivington, in the autumn of 1881.

The Hardys' life at Wimborne, though quiet, was not without interest, as they made a number of acquaintances, and took part in a form of entertainment then very popular in the little Dorset town, namely, Shakespeare readings at each other's houses.

Hardy soon became acquainted with a well-known Wimborne resident, one of the last of the Serjeants-at-law, who was a County Court judge by the name of Tindal-Atkinson, and visited him very frequently. It was the judge who had persuaded Hardy to join the Shakespearean Society of which a Dr. George H. Batterbury was at that time the secretary.

Dr. Batterbury, who is still living, in a letter recently received by the present writer says : " We used to meet at one another's houses and read a play of Shakespeare, each taking a part arranged beforehand. . . . The Hardys went very little into the society the town afforded, and, indeed, Hardy himself was very reticent, and did not seem to wish to mix with the people of the town. . . . All people who knew Mr. and Mrs. Hardy liked them ; but very few did. I used, however, on my rounds, to sometimes meet him evidently deep in thought, walking in the country on the outskirts of the town. When he was not too absorbed to notice me he usually smiled and passed the time of day. So far as I am aware the Hardys took no part in the public life of the town."

Hardy was able to go to London in December to make arrangements for the publication of a novel that he had sketched out, which was ultimately published as *Two on a Tower*. It first appeared serially in the *Atlantic Monthly* in January of the following year, and ran throughout 1882. In the British Museum, it is interesting to note, are some portions of this story bound up and called Part I, Part IV, and Part V, evidently only prepared to secure the copyright.

To show the thoroughness of Hardy's documentation in

his novels, it is interesting to note that he sought permission to visit Greenwich Observatory, because Swithin St. Cleeve, one of the principal characters in his contemplated story, was an amateur astronomer. This permission was granted, and no doubt his visit assisted him later on in the astronomical details.

In January and February of this year Hardy appears to have taken part in several Shakespearean readings in Wimborne, and to have been considerably amused at some of the performances of his fellow-readers, especially the head of the house where one of these readings took place. This gentleman appears to have distinguished himself by the way in which he insisted on duplicating some of the parts. There was also an old general, known to us and to relatives who lived in the town, who amused Hardy immensely by the care with which he endeavoured to avoid in his reading any words or expressions of Shakespeare which might in that mid-Victorian age be deemed to savour of impropriety.

One of the most interesting events in Hardy's life in 1882 must undoubtedly have been the production in March of J. Comyns Carr's adaptation of *Far from the Madding Crowd* at the Prince of Wales Theatre, Liverpool, to see which the Hardys went to the Merseyside city. Hardy was disappointed with the " freedom " with which the story had been treated by the dramatist, but with Miss Marion Terry, then very popular, in the part of Bathsheba Everdene, the heroine, the play was well received, and was ultimately brought to London and produced in the following month at the Globe Theatre.

It is believed that the production of the play brought no profit to Hardy or to the adapter, although it ran for a considerable time.

In the autumn of 1882 Hardy was in the west of England gathering material for his work, visiting places which appear in his novels under thin disguises, Lyme Regis, Charmouth, Bridport, Salisbury and Axminster, and before returning home he and Mrs. Hardy went to Dorchester, and he called on the Rev. William Barnes, the Dorset poet, who was rector at Winterborne Came, situated a little to the south of Dorchester, during the last quarter of a century of his life. It is interesting to note that there are many Winterbornes clustered together, and they take their name from the little streams that almost invariably dry up in summer.

CHAPTER V

IT WAS in the autumn of this year that the Hardys paid a visit, via Weymouth and Cherbourg, to Paris, where they took a small flat on the left bank of the Seine for several weeks and explored the city, visiting the principal picture galleries and Versailles, all the while housekeeping in the truly Parisian style, going to the open-air markets in the early morning for their vegetables, taking their chief meals in restaurants, and apparently thoroughly enjoying themselves. Comparatively little evidence is discoverable in any of his novels or poems of the visits he paid abroad, and Hardy appears to have made the Paris trip merely one of pleasure and not productive of the usual voluminous notes on men and things which he almost invariably set down.

In the autumn Mrs. Hardy's brother-in-law, the Rev. Caddell Holder, Vicar of St. Juliot, died, and Hardy felt the loss as he had become genuinely attached to him. He realized that the pleasant visits he had been accustomed occasionally to pay the rectory had thus come to an end. In one of the poems appearing in *Moments of Vision and Miscellaneous Verses*, called " Quid Hic Agis," he evidently refers to the circumstance that he had occasionally read the lessons in the church that he had helped to restore, when his brother-in-law was not equal to the task of that and also of preaching.

In 1883 Hardy contributed a long short story, by no means one of his best, called " The Romantic Adventures of a Milkmaid" to the summer number of the *Graphic*. This has not been reprinted, we believe, in England, though it was by George Munro the following year in New York.

An illuminating glimpse of the mental attitude and independence of view which characterized Hardy all his life, is afforded by what he wrote down about this time, which is as follows : " In future I am not going to praise things because the accumulated remarks of ages say they are great and good, if these accumulated remarks are not based upon observation ; and I am not going to condemn things because a pile of stupid views raked together of tradition and acquired by instalment say antecedently that they are bad."

Hardy and his wife visited London several times in 1883, and there he, at the house of Lord Houghton, met Robert Browning again, and also Rhoda Broughton, who was becoming one of the popular women novelists of the day. One would, indeed, have liked to know what Hardy thought of the kind of novels that this popular lady wrote for a considerable period of years, most of them bearing such sentimental titles as *Dr. Cupid, Good-bye Sweetheart*, and *Red as a Rose is She*.

It was towards the end of June, 1883, that the Hardys left Wimborne to go to Dorchester.

The Hardys' search for a house in Dorchester itself in the middle half of 1883 was destined to be unsuccessful, for they could find nothing that suited their ideas of what their future home should be.   Ultimately Hardy was successful in obtaining by purchase a plot of land belonging to the Duchy of Cornwall, situated about a mile outside the town itself on the Dorchester to Wareham road.

Everyone knows that this site proved ultimately to be that of a Roman camp or of a Roman villa, for on setting out to sink the well, which had to form the water supply in those days, the diggers had only got to a depth of about three feet ere they came upon Roman-British remains of pottery and also skeletons.

At first Hardy and his wife, both, as he once told us, after this discovery felt that the spot was not a very promising one for a home, " where Roman soldiers slept," but ultimately they not only decided to go on with the excavations of the foundations of the house, but also to " put up with any ghosts which might haunt the neighbourhood."

Quite a lot of Roman remains were unearthed in the process of getting out the foundations, and afterwards in laying out the garden which surrounded the house. These were carefully collected together, and the best examples of the treasure-trove were in after years to be seen in cabinets in the drawing-room at Max Gate, though, we believe, Hardy gave some to the Dorchester Museum.

In the " Proceedings " of the Dorset Field Club is to be found an account of the Roman-British remains which were found upon the site of the house. These " Proceedings " were the paper that he had read six years previously at a meeting of the Field Club held in Dorchester.

At the very beginning of the following year Hardy was busy planting trees and planning the garden at Max Gate, which was the name that he had decided to bestow upon his home outside Dorchester, which he had himself designed.

He went to London in January, 1884, and it is interesting to note that he met Lawrence Alma-Tadema, R.A., the artist, who had become famous for his classical pictures of Roman and Greek baths, life at the classical period and similar subjects, and afterwards was knighted. The artist evinced a great interest in the particulars Hardy was able to give him of the result of the excavations at Max Gate.

In March of this year Hardy made a note of his intention to write a novel which provisionally he called *Time Against Two*. The germ idea was probably used, though only incidentally, in the rather fantastic story he ultimately wrote called *The Well-Beloved*.

Hardy, who had used a knowledge of circuses—for which, indeed, he appears to have had a liking all his life —so effectively for scenes in his novel *Far from the Madding Crowd*, placed on record that he attended in June, 1884, a

Gateway Poxwell Hall

"Oxwell Hall."

performance of Tayleure's Circus, which had drawn up in a field at Fordington. There he was the witness of an incident which appears to have dwelt in his mind, and was perhaps incorporated in a poem, published many years afterwards, entitled "Circus Rider to Ring Master," which appeared in the volume of poems *Human Shows, Far Fantasies, Songs and Trifles*, published by Macmillans in 1925.

In August, 1884, a company of strolling players arrived in Dorchester, and took up their abode in the Market field. Hardy attended a performance of *Othello*, which he described in his diary with his usual vivid touch and extraordinary picturesqueness, and one can only wish that he had given us a novel, the principal characters of which were strolling players such as those that evidently interested him so intensely on that and other occasions.

During August Hardy went off to the Channel Islands by the Weymouth route with his brother. They visited the three chief islands, and Hardy, in a note, made friendly fun of the manners of the guests at the hotels at which they stayed, who were apparently chiefly commercial travellers.

It was about this time that on his return to Dorchester he started to write *The Mayor of Casterbridge*, and he had also before leaving London, which he visited, promised to write for *Macmillan's Magazine* a story, afterwards to be called *The Woodlanders*, which appeared two years later, from May, 1886, to April, 1887.

Very little is known of Hardy's sister, Mary, but that she was a woman of observant character is made manifest by a remark of hers which Hardy records in the year 1884, when she declared to him that the women of the past generation had then (when she spoke) faces out of fashion, facial expressions having their fashions like those of clothes.

It would seem from this that the Hardy family as a whole were rather remarkable for keenness of observation, and certainly in many of their sayings recorded by Hardy himself, and some of them repeated to us, evidence can be deduced in support of this supposition.

In the early part of January of the following year Hardy visited Eggesford, at the invitation of Lady Portsmouth, where he was told he should have full liberty to work quietly on the book he was then writing, the library having for this purpose been put at his disposal. One gathers, however, that the house party assembled there contained people who proved more interesting to the novelist than his work, and certainly little of the latter was done. Hardy described his host as " a farmer-like man with a broad Devon accent," and also records that in walking round the estate, the Earl had shown him a bridge over which, he stated, illegitimate children had, in then quite recent times, been thrown, so that they might be drowned. One wonders, indeed, when Hardy made this note, whether he had not some idea of using the circumstance for a dramatic short story or as an incident in a novel.

It was in the late spring that the last chapters of *The Mayor of Casterbridge*, which had occupied Hardy a year in writing, were finished.

A day or two after this event, Hardy makes a note in the following words : " The business of the poet and novelist is to see the sorriness underlying the grandest things, and the grandeur underlying the sorriest things."

A little valuable and interesting insight is thrown upon the political rancour of this period by an account that Hardy gave of an evening party they attended. He said that a well-known Conservative peeress, who had lately become acquainted with him, came up to him and said : " I am ashamed of my party ! They are actually all hoping that General Gordon is murdered, in order that it may ruin Gladstone ! "

The rumour of Gordon's death at Khartoum had just that evening reached London, and although it was not generally credited, it proved to be quite true, as was known a few days later.

A week or two after the party which we have mentioned, Hardy went down into Dorset to superintend the furnishing of his house which had just been completed. It had taken nearly eighteen months to build, and Hardy constantly superintended the work.   The ground on which the house stands is bounded on one side by the Wareham high road, and was originally one and a half acres in extent, but eventually another half-acre was added.   An interesting fact in connection with this is that Hardy was the first freeholder under the Crown for many generations, for the ground belonged, as we have said, to the Duchy of Cornwall, and was the property, therefore, of the Prince of Wales of the time, and had been sold, one may imagine, as a special concession because of Hardy's eminence in literature.

The house had a very different appearance at the time Hardy entered into occupation than it has at the present time.   It was then, of course, entirely devoid of creepers, the garden was, in places, little more than a rough field, and the view from the windows was, of course, quite unobstructed by the trees which afterwards grew up and shut it in from observation from the high road.   Away to the left of the front door, across a field near the centre, could be seen a mound with trees, possibly a tumulus. From the windows of the house in those days one could see Conygar Hill, a portion of the Came Plantation, and the outstanding landmark known as Culliver's or Culliford Tree.

The drawing-room into which visitors were usually first shown lay on the right of the front door, while the dining-room was on the opposite side of the small hall.

When first Hardy went to Max Gate, he had made his study the room above the drawing-room, overlooking the drive which leads from the high road to the house. Afterwards he changed the room, and his study was for some years situated at the back of the house, facing west.

It was in this room, lined with many books, and the mantelpiece laden with photographs, that on one of our visits, we photographed him at his desk, the only photograph, we believe, of that kind that was ever taken.   The last room that he used for his workroom was one added much later, and built over a new kitchen, and it was this room that was identified with the later years of Hardy's literary life. It had a large window facing towards the sea.

It is interesting to note that *The Woodlanders* was written soon after the Hardys settled at Max Gate, while *Tess of the D'Urbervilles* was written in the second study that he had, and *The Dynasts* and his later poems and literary work was accomplished in the third of his studies.

An event of considerable interest to the present writer was the early visit of Robert Louis Stevenson to the Hardys in their new home. Stevenson, who was personally known to us, and with whom we corresponded after he went to Vailima, Samoa, was living at the time at Bournemouth in a house a short distance away from our own, pleasantly situated at the top of one of the then wild, heather- and gorse-clad chines at Westbourne. The house was named Skerryvore, after the great lighthouse that Stevenson's father and uncle had built in 1844 on a rock of the Inner Hebrides off the Scotch coast.

Stevenson wrote merely announcing that he would call on the Hardys, and appeared a few days after with his wife, his stepson and another relative. The Scotch novelist had become famous for his romance of pirates, originally called *The Sea Cook*, which first ran as a serial in *Young Folk's Paper*, a weekly publication long since dead, and was afterwards published in book form as *Treasure Island*. The Stevensons were on their way to spend a time on Dartmoor, the pure air of which had been recommended to Stevenson by his Bournemouth doctor, Mr. Thomas Bodley Scott, as likely to benefit his health, which was poor at the time. They never, however, got as far as Dartmoor, for Stevenson fell ill at Exeter, and had to go back to Bournemouth.

Hardy was, at this period, hard at work, notwithstanding his long periods of meditation and rambling about the countryside, when his poems may be said to have been germinating in his mind, and an entry made in November, 1885, shows how hard on occasion he worked, for he spoke of writing from half-past ten in the morning till midnight upon *The Woodlanders*, the plot of which, it appeared, he altered more than once.

One of his most dramatic stories, *The Mayor of Caster-bridge*, which is a favourite with many readers, commenced running in the *Graphic* newspaper, and also in America in a weekly publication of Harper Brothers. This story exhibited quite a new phase of Hardy's genius, and we think may be rightly described as owing its origin to both Biblical and classical influences. The chief character in the story is that of a simple man, of an obstinate and determined nature, who was no one's enemy but his own, and seems to have been pursued to his end by the Fates or a Nemesis which dominates several of Hardy's stories.

He states about this time of his own work that its object was to " intensify the expression of things, as is done by Crivelli, Bellini, etc., so that the heart and inner meaning is made vividly visible."

About this period the Hardys paid occasional visits to London, and in the spring and summer of 1885 were settled in Bloomsbury, so that Hardy might the more easily reach the reading-room of the Museum in which he spent a good deal of his time in research, and the reading of books otherwise unavailable to him.

Hardy throughout his life took very little part in politics, but while in London at this time he was present at a Home Rule debate in the House of Commons and heard a number of the then prominent political figures, including Gladstone, speak.

Towards the end of May of this year (1886) *The Mayor of Casterbridge* was published in two volumes, by Smith Elder and Co., and in after years, we have heard, Hardy expressed the view that he had injured this story more than any other when it appeared serially. As is the case to-day, editors demanded in a serial that it should have a " curtain " in each instalment, and to fall in with this suggestion Hardy said that he added events to the narrative which had no particular *raison d'être*. Of the power and drama of the story, however, there is no question.

Evidence that from almost the very first days of his literary life he was really a poet rather than a novelist is afforded by Hardy himself, as he used to say that his novel-writing was mere journey-work in which he was not really interested seriously.

Stevenson, who read *The Mayor of Casterbridge* when it appeared in volume form, wrote to Hardy saying how much he had enjoyed it, and that he considered the chief character of outstanding interest, seems to have had some idea at the time of his letter of attempting to dramatize it. Whether Hardy replied to this letter with its tentative offer is not known, and a search of the several " Lives " of Stevenson which have been published has not revealed any reference to negotiations of any sort. It is just possible, therefore, that Hardy did not take the suggestion seriously, or was not sufficiently interested in it to reply to Stevenson's letter.

About this time Hardy met many famous people, and among these Dr. Oliver Wendell Holmes, the American essayist and poet, who had become known in this country as the author of *The Autocrat of the Breakfast Table* ; Whistler, the artist ; Linley Sambourne, the famous *Punch* artist and cartoonist ; Bret Harte, the American novelist, and a number of others. Hardy also met Lady Camperdown about this time, then an old lady, and, as was often his custom on meeting new acquaintances, he jotted down his impression of her in a very vivid phrase, and, doubtless recalling the origin of the title, said that while sitting next to her he " could not get rid of the feeling that I was close to a great naval engagement."

One very interesting fellow-novelist that he met about this time, whose work, indeed, although dealing chiefly with the life in towns, had something of the character of Hardy's own in its frank realism and underlying pessimism, was George Gissing, who had written a novel that had excited considerable interest called *The Unclassed*. In writing to Hardy with reference to this book, Gissing expressed the opinion that Hardy himself must also have held, namely that " when writing for English people one may not be thorough ; reticences and superficialities have to be found to fill places where one is willing to put in honest work.''

Even so far in advance of the actual writing, not to say the publication of *The Dynasts*, Hardy was spending time in the British Museum delving for material for his *magnum opus*. At the end of the summer, when he returned to Max Gate, he got to work on *The Woodlanders*, in performance of his promise made to the Macmillans.

In October of this year Hardy lost a great friend by the death of William Barnes, the Dorset poet, whom he had known ever since Barnes had had a school in Dorchester, next door to the office of John Hicks, the architect. After Barnes retired on his appointment to the living of Winter-borne Came, the rectory of which is but a short distance from Max Gate, the novelist saw a good deal of his friend, and used to walk across the fields to visit him. Ultimately, as is well known, Hardy made a selection of Barnes's poems, which were issued in volume form as *Poems of Rural Life in the Dorset Dialect*.

The life at Max Gate appears at this period to have been very uneventful, and, indeed, it could hardly be otherwise, considering the isolation of the house and its immediate surroundings.

In the February of 1887 Hardy entered in his diary with great accuracy that he finished *The Woodlanders* at 8.20 p.m. He evidently experienced much the same feelings as do many other writers regarding the completion of a work. He expected to feel delighted at its accomplishment, but apparently felt only the relief that comes from the completion of most mental work of a strenuous or continuous nature.

It was difficult to obtain from Hardy, which we endeavoured to do in after years on several occasions, an expression of what was actually his favourite novel, or which he considered contained his best work ; but we heard from an intimate friend that on one occasion at least he had expressed satisfaction on the whole with *The Woodlanders*.

Cerne Abbas
"Abbots-Cornel."

Douglas Snowdon.

Nowadays, as then, one finds among readers various opinions regarding what is Hardy's best novel. On the whole probably *Tess of the D'Urbervilles* remains the favourite, with *Jude the Obscure* close up, notwithstanding the depressing nature of the story ; while those who like drama are inclined to vote for *The Mayor of Casterbridge*, leaving the more rural tales, such as *Under the Greenwood Tree*, *The Woodlanders*, *Far from the Madding Crowd*, and *The Return of the Native* to readers for whom the quiet countryside and its characters and descriptions of Nature have most attraction.

It was in March of this year that the Hardys started for a tour in Italy, which included visits to Aix-les-Bains, Turin and Genoa, which last named place inspired the novelist to write at a later period verses entitled " Genoa and the Mediterranean."

What must give rise to curiosity on the part of students of Hardy, remembering his quite considerable experiences of foreign travel, is the fact how little use he made in his prose works of his experiences, and of scenery which would have afforded excellent backgrounds for novels or stories. Only in fugitive verses are references to be found to the tours which he took abroad, especially in the middle half of his life.

It was not, however, that Hardy did not make considerable notes while travelling.

He visited, also in company with Mrs. Hardy, Pisa and ascended the leaning tower ; Florence, where they found settled a Mrs. Baxter, daughter of the poet Barnes, who was a writer then known to readers as " Leader-Scott." From Florence they went on to Rome, and among the other places visited was the house in which Keats died. Hardy made numerous notes of this visit to the Holy City, which certainly impressed him in a very definite way.

Out of the visit came the sonnet which he called " Building a New Street in the Ancient Quarter," which certainly was based upon his observations of the then practice of building new edifices upon ancient foundations. Hardy, himself, admitted that he was far more interested in pagan than in Christian Rome, and had a distinct preference for the buildings or churches in which he could discover traces in the architecture of ancient temples.

One gathers from notes, which have survived in Hardy's diaries, that he was an inveterate and almost tireless sightseer, and one can, therefore, easily realize that on leaving Rome he was apparently suffering from a state of mental indigestion as well as possibly physical fatigue.

The Hardys returned to Florence, and made an excursion to Fiesole in company with Mrs. Baxter. Unfortunately the excursion was marred by an accident which might have ended in a serious catastrophe. When they arrived at the foot of the hill on which Fiesole is situated they found an omnibus waiting to take people to the town. They entered this conveyance, to which only one of the two horses intended to draw it had been harnessed. The animal almost immediately took fright, and set off at a furious pace back towards Florence along the road which was in a dangerous state owing to repairs then being carried out. Fortunately just before a collision, which appeared inevitable, with a steam tram which ran between Florence and Fiesole, could take place, the horse was stopped by some workmen, and the occupants of the omnibus escaped.

Hardy afterwards crystallized this visit to this ancient town in a sonnet which he called " In the Old Theatre."

While at Florence the Hardys also visited the graves of Shelley and Keats, and that of Mrs. Browning, and the scene of Browning's poem "The Statue and the Bust," which is supposed to have been placed in the Piazza dell' Annunziata.

Hardy, in a letter a copy of which we have, afterwards wrote of this Florence visit and association with " Leader-Scott " as follows :

" During our stay in Florence in 1887 my wife and I saw her almost every day ; and we made pilgrimages together to many spots of interest, she being, of course, as a long resident in Italy, an invaluable guide. Among these was the grave of Mrs. Browning, who to Mrs. Baxter's ('Leader-Scott's') regret had died shortly before the latter's arrival in Florence. It was in Mrs. Baxter's company also that I stood in the Piazza dell' Annunziata and gazed at the statue of the Grand-Duke Ferdinand I, opposite the Palazzo Riccardi-Menelli, we having been led there by the famous lines :

'There's a Palace in Florence the world knows well,
And a statue watches it from the Square.'

which opens the story told in 'The Statue and the Bust.'

"In making this inspection an incident occurred which may be worth recalling. Having seen the statue we looked for the bust, but were informed by an obliging waiter standing in a door hard by that it had unfortunately been taken down from a particular spot in the palace façade which he pointed out. He added luminous details and I gave him a lira for his information.

"On the first Sunday after my return to London I met Browning, and he was interested to hear of the incident. 'But that waiter,' he added with a hearty laugh. 'Why, I invented the bust.' It is, of course, just possible, though not likely, that Browning's memory was at fault, and that the friendly waiter did not lie. Curiously enough, Mrs. Baxter inclined to the opinion that there had been a bust, and that the waiter spoke the truth."

A visit was also paid to Venice and, of course, Hardy proved greatly interested in the architecture, and, indeed, seems to have derived more pleasure from his Venetian experiences than from any others in Italy during the tour.

From Venice the Hardys apparently went direct to Milan, and possibly Hardy profited during the visit by the local colour he obtained for the Milan Cathedral scene afterwards used in *The Dynasts*.

While in the historic Lombardian city, famous for its *Duomo*, Hardy was possessed with the idea of obtaining data regarding the Battle of Lodi. He was not very successful, but he made a casual acquaintance of a young officer of a Scotch regiment of foot, who happened to be staying at the Grand Hotel de Milan, where the Hardys had taken up their quarters, and who afterwards visited Lodi in Hardy's company. One may easily imagine how Hardy and his Scotch companion (as they sat upon the bridge which spanned the little river Adda) discussed the military traditions regarding the battle, and the surprise defeat of the Austrians by Napoleon.

On the return of the Hardys to London in April, 1887, they looked about for accommodation, and lived for some little time in a house in Campden Hill Road. Hardy appears, during the few months of the London season, to have gone out a great deal, and to have met with some very interesting people, including Lady Carnarvon.

This was the year, of course, of Queen Victoria's Jubilee, and Mr. and Mrs. Hardy saw the procession passing along Piccadilly from the Savile Club. It is well known that during Queen Victoria's reign the Arts were not very highly esteemed by the monarch, who, indeed, is known not to have possessed any great appreciation of these. On this account the Court officials, who were responsible for issuing the tickets admitting to Westminster Abbey, appear to have made many blunders, for not only was Robert Browning, already admittedly a great poet, omitted from the list, but large numbers of other distinguished people connected with literature, art and science were not invited to be present.

At the end of the London season the Hardys returned to Max Gate.

As evidence of Hardy's persistent " hankering " to shine as a poet, an entry from his diary may be quoted. He says of the year that had just passed (1887) that he had been able to hold his own in fiction by the completion of his story *The Woodlanders*, adding : " Whatever that may be worth."

Hardy was always an omnivorous reader, and the books that he had either perused or glanced through this year were, as was often the case, a strange mixture of classics and romance, poetry and prose, but comparatively few modern books or works of fiction figure in his lists.

There was always a good deal of controversy during Hardy's lifetime, especially in the middle years, regarding the " colour " of his political opinions.   On more than one occasion Hardy mentioned this to us, and also on an occasion, when we were on a cycling expedition which took us to High Stoy, overlooking the beautiful Blackmoor Vale, and back to Dorchester through Minterne Magna and Cerne Abbas, he expressed opinions which showed—as one might readily expect—a breadth of view that would have placed him unintentionally or otherwise, and certainly unannouncedly on his part, at that time in the ranks of Liberalism.

An entry to be found in a diary, made towards the end of January, says: " I find that my politics really are neither Tory nor Radical.   I might be called an Intrinsicalist.   I am against privilege derived through accident of any kind, and am therefore equally opposed to aristocratic privilege and democratic privilege (by the latter I mean the arrogant assumption that the only labour is hand labour—a worse arrogance than that of the aristocrat), the taxing of the worthy to help those masses of the population who will not help themselves when they may, etc."

He goes on to argue that although there should be equal opportunity for all, those who would not avail themselves of it should merely be cared for, and not allowed to become a burden upon the shoulders of those who have made good use of their opportunities, a view held by many.

In January and February of this year there appeared in *Murray's Magazine* a long short story, "The Waiting Supper," which, we believe, has not been reprinted in England, and in March there appeared an interesting article by Hardy on "The Profitable Reading of Fiction" in the *Forum*, New York, also not reprinted.

Hardy was essentially a countryman, and many times he expressed a horror of town life, as compared with the quietude, peace and interest of that of the country. On more than one occasion there is an expression of this view to be-found in his diaries, where one finds the following note : " The fiendish precision or mechanism of town life is what makes it so intolerable to the sick and infirm." One may well imagine—Hardy is speaking of the late 'eighties when he wrote this—what he would have thought of the mechanical precision and noise of town life of the present day.

The student of Hardy, and those who knew him, must wonder at the persistence with which his mind followed an idea that sometimes did not materialize in the shape of a story, poem or novel till years afterwards. It was in April, 1887, that one finds Hardy again making notes, far in advance of the date when they were likely to take material shape or literary form, for at that time there is an indication that he was turning over in his mind what eventually in all probability was the germ of his last novel, *Jude the Obscure*. At that time he apparently regarded the idea merely as a plot for a short story, telling of the struggles, ultimate failure, and suicide of a young man, who, possessing great ambition, had in early life been afforded few opportunities.

In the middle of the year the Hardys were once more in Paris, and as always seemed to be the case went about a great deal, visiting picture galleries and other exhibitions, including the Salon, where one of Gabriel Guay's most notable pictures, " The Death of Jezebel," of which we possess a reproduction, was hung, and aroused, apparently, a greater interest in Hardy than did any other picture.

They returned towards the middle of June to London, and took up lodgings at Upper Phillimore Place, Kensington, where they remained until the end of July.

Hardy's sympathy with all animals, whether suffering or those in the lives of which, in his imagination, there might exist the possibility of suffering, is shown by an entry made in July of this year, when he had evidently been studying the horses in the carts which passed their lodgings heavily laden in the early mornings on their way to Covent Garden, for he asks : " What was on the faces of those horses ? Resignation. Their eyes looked at me, haunted me. The absoluteness of their resignation was terrible. When afterwards I heard their tramp as I lay in bed, the ghosts of their eyes came in to me saying ' Where is your justice, O man and ruler ? ' "

The value of Hardy's notes, not only to him but to future students and historians of social manners, as throwing a light on customs which were, in those days, singular, but afterwards became general, and were even deemed at the date of which Hardy writes to be non-existent, is shown by an entry which speaks of a dinner party held at Walter Pater's, the author of *Marius the Epicurean*, at which there was a handsome girl, one of the guests, whom Hardy describes as " smoking and the possessor of a cruel small mouth, and in a class of interesting women that one would be afraid to marry." A forerunner, evidently—as smoking by women was almost unknown—of the women of a later age he lived long enough to see.

Early in August he sent a story that he had written to Harry Quilter, the editor of the *Universal Review*, a wonderful monthly publication de luxe, which had gathered to itself many of the leading writers of the day as contributors, that must have cost an immense amount of money to run. The story was called "A Tragedy of Two Ambitions," telling of the lives of Joshua and Cornelius Harborough, the sons of a village millwright, who had worked hard with the idea of entering a university and being ordained. Their mother, who was anxious for them to do this, had gathered together a sum of nearly one thousand pounds for the purpose. On her death, however, it passed into their father's hands, who was a drunkard, and was squandered in drink. In after years, after serving a sentence in gaol at " Fountall," the cathedral city of Wells, their father, who had married a gipsy woman, and had gone about the country with her, proposed to settle down again at " Narrobourne " (East Coker).

The brothers set out to intercept him on his release from

Douglas Snowdon.

Beaminster.

"Emminster."

the gaol, so that they might persuade him not to return to the place where they themselves were living. After a quarrel he left them, and a few moments later they heard him fall into a near-by stream, and like a flash the thought entered their minds that this would prove a solution of their difficulty. They stood discussing the question as to whether they should go in search of him until it was too late, and he had been swept away and drowned. As the body was not discovered for some considerable time afterwards, it was unidentifiable and, therefore, no one ever learned of the share of the brothers in the tragedy.

Here, as in many of his stories, Hardy seizes upon a tragic and sensational idea and works it out to its inevitable end without any incident to lighten the sombreness of the main plot.

Hardy was in the habit of jotting down in his diary the descriptive names which he afterwards gave to various districts, such as " The Valley of the Great Dairies," that is to say, the valley of the Frome ; " The Valley of the Little Dairies," Blackmoor Vale ; " Green Hill," Woodbury Hill, near Bere Regis ; " Talbothays Farm," Norris Hill Farm, near Dorchester, owned at one time by his family ; and the " Street of Wells," Fortunes Well, Portland.

It was in September of 1888 that Hardy made one of his frequent excursions into the countryside, partly by train and partly afoot, visiting the Vale of Blackmoor and Evershot, and several places connected with the Hardy family history. At one time the Hardys possessed quite a considerable amount of landed property at Woolcombe, Frome St. Quentin, and round about.

Hardy had, of course, many letters with reference to his stories and novels, and soon after the story " A Tragedy of Two Ambitions " was published in the *Universal Review* in 1889, he received a letter from Edmund Gosse, thanking him for it, in which the writer said he thought it was one of the most dramatic and complete stories Hardy had written.

It was in February of the same year that Hardy seems to have again played with the idea which was ultimately to be carried out in his fantastic and elusive story *The Well-Beloved*, for he apparently had been tracing the facial resemblance in several generations of a certain family, and makes a note that the idea of a face and characteristics persisting in three generations or more would make a fine novel.

Hardy's notes upon people that he casually met while on his visits to London in buses, on the Underground Railway, or at people's houses were often illuminating, and doubtless provided him with material for the descriptions of characters in his novels and stories, as suggested by such a note as the following, made after meeting a girl in an omnibus. Hardy wrote down : " That girl in the omnibus had one of those faces of marvellous beauty which are seen casually in the streets but never among one's friends. It was perfect in its softened classicality—a Greek face translated into English. Moreover, she was fair, and her hair pale chestnut. Where do these women come from ? And who marries them ? "

It was about the middle of 1889 that J. T. Grein, the well-known dramatic critic and writer upon the stage, who founded, in 1923, " The People's Theatre," Whitechapel, wrote to Hardy asking whether he would give him permission for the adaptation of *The Woodlanders* as a stage play. In his reply to Mr. Grein, Hardy stated that the ending of the story—as all readers are, of course, aware—turned upon the unhappy life of a wife doomed to be cursed with an inconstant husband. Hardy went on to say : " I couldn't accentuate this (fact) strongly enough in the book by reason of the conventions of the libraries, etc.," adding : " Since the story was written, however, truth to character is not considered quite such a crime in literature as it was formerly ; and it is therefore a question for you whether you will accent this ending, or prefer to obscure it."

It is of interest to note that in March of the following year he took part in a " symposium," having for its subject " Candour in English Fiction " (in which also Walter Besant and Mrs. E. Lynn Linton took part) in the pages of the *Eclectic Magazine*, New York.

One cannot quite see that, even in the experienced hands of the adapter who had proposed the turning of Hardy's novel into a play, *The Woodlanders* would have been very suitable for stage production.   Anyway, nothing was done in the matter of production, although we believe that Mr. Grein actually made an adaptation of the novel. Of course in those days English managers, doubtless largely on account of financial reasons, were not prepared to flout the censor, or the susceptibilities of the public, to the extent of producing a play of the type that a faithful adaptation of *The Woodlanders* must inevitably have been.

One now reaches in Hardy's life a period of great importance, for it was in the middle of 1889 that Hardy, on his return to Dorchester, proceeded to get down to the writing of what was destined to prove his most popular and, in the opinion of many, possibly greatest prose work— *Tess of the D'Urbervilles.*

We are told that he worked steadily day by day at it. For this story Hardy had a number of offers for the serial use directly it became rumoured that he was engaged on a new novel.

Ultimately in the autumn of the year, the first chapters had been completed, and were offered to Edward Arnold, then the editor of *Murray's Magazine*, who had been the first to write to him regarding the possibility of obtaining the serial rights.   In less than a month the instalments were returned to him, as was explained, owing to the frankness with which Tess's relations with Alec D'Urberville had been treated.

The manuscript was promptly sent on to Mowbray Morris, the second applicant appearing on Hardy's list, who was the editor of *Macmillan's Magazine*, and very promptly was declined for much the same reason.

Naturally Hardy was disturbed by these refusals, for at that time he was by no means too comfortably off, and, to put it frankly, needed the money that the story would have produced.

We are told that he contemplated finishing the novel and bringing it out in volume form, forgoing what would have been derived from the serial rights, but for financial reasons abandoned this idea. Owing to his failure to place it with the two magazines we have named, and prevented from publishing it in volume form for the reasons we have given, he proceeded to make concessions to conventionality by cutting out portions of some chapters and also by modifying some incidents. The portions of the story which he deleted temporarily were restored later on when it appeared in volume form. His practice was, we are told, to write the modified passages in coloured ink, so that the original sentences or paragraphs could easily be restored.

One can well imagine the cynical humour with which Hardy undertook these " sacrifices to the conventions " ; but, nevertheless, he had done a wise thing, for the emasculated version of the story was ultimately accepted by the editor of the *Graphic*, who had originally been, we believe, the third to write to Hardy asking for the serial rights of the story, and it was arranged that it should be commenced in that paper in July, 1891.

Hardy was also busy about this time in writing poetry, and doubtless some of the poems ultimately appeared in volume form, and in one of them entitled " At Middle-Field Gate in February," there appear quite a number of young women as field workers with whom Hardy had been acquainted in his childhood and boyhood.

Hardy's religious beliefs—which the first Mrs. Hardy always took great pains to explain to visitors were in reality quite orthodox—have been questioned and discussed by those who knew him, and in the Press. Personally, we should rather describe his views about middle life, and during the period of some twenty years when we knew him, as having a distinctly agnostic bias, whatever they may have in later life become, and an entry in his diary dated January 29th of the year 1890, rather bears out this view, for there he says : " I have been looking for God fifty years, and I think that if he had existed I should have discovered him." All his life, undoubtedly, Hardy was much troubled by questionings of the existence of good and evil, and how it should be that evil was permitted by a Deity, who could presumably have so easily checked the evil, and in doing so provided poor humanity with a much happier and better world in which to live.

We, ourselves, recall that her husband's religious views evidently caused Mrs. Hardy some disquietude. This was perhaps natural when one remembers her ancestry, and her connections with very orthodox Church people. On several occasions on which we were at Max Gate, she endeavoured to " tone down " the interesting conversation in which Hardy was giving free expression to his " doubts," evidence of which is indicated by the quotation from his diary just made.

It may here be remarked, perhaps appropriately, that Mrs. Hardy was a gracious, kindly woman naturally hospitable, and of a very conventional type that would have fitted her to play to perfection the part of a lady of the manor concerned with kind and charitable acts, or of a country clergyman's wife devoted to his parish. One of her great interests in life was her very beautiful cats, which visitors were shown with pride and seldom failed to admire.

One gained the impression, however, that " Thomas " occasionally found her " tiresome," and that in reality there could not be much intellectual understanding between them, Hardy's introspective and brooding nature being entirely opposite to hers, and, contrary to the old—and too often accepted—saying, opposites do not invariably or of necessity form the desired complement, the one of the other.

Mrs. Hardy herself, too, had " literary leanings," concerning which she more than once spoke to the present writer. It is known, of course, that she from time to time contributed poems—mostly, if memory serves, concerned with her pets—to the columns or " Poet's Corner " of the local paper. Once Hardy referred to these poetic efforts of his wife with a rather wry smile flickering about at the corners of his mouth.

What may not be so well known is that Mrs. Hardy had

written novels—or at least stories of considerable length—which on one occasion she told us her husband would not let her publish, adding that they were in a box somewhere at the top of the house.

Mrs. Hardy's excursions into verse were not of a much higher standard than the poems that usually find gratuitous acceptance with local papers. One would much have liked to have known what those stories (or novels) of which she spoke were like, and how they dealt with the characters concerned. Anyway, one can be reasonably sure that they would not have shocked the "general reader" as some of the novels of her husband had done.

Mrs. Hardy was much liked in Dorchester, and we remember an old inhabitant telling us, a week or two after her death, that she would be "sadly missed." In what particular way was not, we think, specified.

In March of the following year the Hardys were in London, and from May onwards were paying their usual visits to their many friends and going out a good deal into society. In May Hardy sent the manuscript of his short stories *A Group of Noble Dames* to the *Graphic*, and these were published in the *Graphic* Christmas Number for 1890. These short stories were : "Barbara, daughter of Sir John Grebe" ; "The Lady Caroline, afterwards Marchioness of Stonehenge" ; "Anna, Lady Baxby" ; "The Lady Icenway" ; "Squire Petterick's Lady" ; and "Lady Mottisfont," most of which, some under slightly altered titles, are to be found in the collection, *A Group of Noble Dames*, in company with "The First Countess of Wessex" published in *Harper's Magazine* (December, 1889), and illustrated by Alfred Parsons and C. S. Reinhart ; and "The Lady Penelope," which was published in *Longman's Magazine* (January, 1890).

In the *Graphic* version the tales were ascribed to various persons, e.g., "By the Old Surgeon," "By the Rural Dean," "By the Churchwarden," etc., and the tales were somewhat altered and revised for publication in volume form.

In the middle of June of this year there was trouble over the stories that he had sent to the editor of the *Graphic*, for, although Arthur Locker himself liked them, his directors took exception to some of the incidents in several. We believe that after a consultation, Hardy made certain modifications, and the stories appeared, as we have already said, in a Christmas number of the *Graphic*.

In August the Hardys went to Weymouth, and had lunch at the old " Royal Hotel " where George III and his daughters danced during his memorable visit to that fashionable watering-place, and where he bathed, which incident Hardy incorporated in his novel *The Trumpet Major*. While the town assemblies were open to the public the place where the royal party disported themselves was always roped off by a red cord, and at the time of the Hardys' visit, the holes in the floor for the uprights carrying the cord were still to be seen.

Towards the later part of the year Hardy finished writing *Tess of the D'Urbervilles*, having made the deletions which had been insisted upon for serial use.

In the January of the following year Hardy was busily engaged at Max Gate choosing the short stories for publication in volume form which afterwards appeared under the title of *A Group of Noble Dames*. Then he went to London and found it under snow.

In February the Hardys were back in Dorset, and he erected in the border of the lawn in the garden a large stone, which he afterwards named " The Druid's Stone," that had been found buried about a yard deep in the soil.

Some few years later we took a photo of Hardy standing by the stone for which he, indeed, seemed to have a great regard. He was clad on that occasion very characteristically in tweed coat, cycling knickerbockers, and thick woollen stockings.

He once told us, while standing by it, that he believed it was at least two thousand years old, and had proved a heavy task even for the seven or eight men employed to get it out of the hole which had been dug around it.

Sherborne

"Sherton Abbas"

I

Charred bones and ashes were found surrounding the stone.

In the April while the Hardys were in London, seeking for accommodation in which to settle during their usual spring visit to Town, Hardy had the honour of being elected a member of the Athenæum Club.

While in London this time, he was taken down to the then rather noted training college for schoolmistresses at Whitelands, and recorded his impressions in the following terms : " A community of women, especially young women, inspires not reverence but protective tenderness in the breast of one who views them. Their belief in circumstances, in convention, in the rightness of things, which you know to be not only wrong but damnably wrong, makes the heart ache."

He was evidently affected by the visit, which he afterwards said he would not have missed for anything, and contrasted the strenuous and purposeful life he had witnessed at this institution with scenes at a fashionable party he had attended a few nights before, and much to the disadvantage of the latter.

About this time he appears to have devoted considerable attention to what may be called educational matters and social studies, for he not only visited in May a large private lunatic asylum, where he only intended to stay a very short time and stayed the greater part of the day, but he also visited the Training College at Stockwell for girls.

It was in August of this year that the Hardys returned to Dorset after a very busy social season, during which Hardy had met many distinguished people, including Lord Wynford (who, when Hardy was lunching at Grosvenor Square, told him that he would not live in Dorset for fifty thousand pounds a year), Lady Milnes-Gaskell and G. F. Watts.

He now started on correcting *Tess of the D'Urbervilles* for publication in volume form, and restored to their places the paragraphs and chapters of the original manuscript that had been left out at the request of the proprietors of the *Graphic* on its serial publication. The name " Talbothays," which Hardy gave to the dairy, was derived from a farm belonging to his father which, however, at that time had no dwelling upon it.

Once, however, some time after the volume publication of the story, when on a cycling expedition with Hardy, he told the present writer that there was a farm near Moreton in the Frome Valley which, as regards appearance, he had had in his mind when describing " Talbothays " of the novel. Indeed we visited the farm, and we remember Hardy leaning over the rickety gate, and discoursing on the hard life of the farm labourer, and upon the disrepair into which some of the farm buildings had been permitted to fall.

In September the Hardys were once more in Scotland, this time on a visit to Springwood Park, the home of his friend, Sir George Douglas, the Scotch writer, some time lecturer in Scottish literature at Glasgow University, and the author of quite a number of books dealing with the Scotch Border and Scotch poetry. They finished their autumn tour by returning down the East Coast, visiting Durham, Whitby, Scarborough, York, Peterborough, and other places, and naturally the cathedral towns afforded great pleasure to Hardy.

An illuminating light is thrown upon the study of the susceptibilities of serial fiction readers of the day by the objection of the editor of the *Graphic* to the incident in *Tess of the D'Urbervilles*, where Angel Clare carries Tess and her dairymaid companions in his arms across the flooded lane. Arthur Locker suggested that it would be more in keeping with the pages of a newspaper intended for family reading if Hardy described the girls as being conveyed across the lane in a wheelbarrow, and this in the serial version of *Tess* was done ! A whole chapter, too, dealing with the christening of Tess's baby, was tabooed, although it afterwards appeared in the story when published in volume form.

William Ernest Henley, however, whom Hardy had met some little time before at the Savile Club, who was editing a weekly review called the *National Observer*, expressed himself willing to publish this chapter, and it appeared in that paper on November 14th, 1891. The *Fortnightly Review* in May, 1891, and the *Eclectic Review*, New York, in June published the offending episode as "The Midnight Christening ; A Study in Christianity."

On November 30th *Tess of the D'Urbervilles; a Pure Woman Faithfully Presented*, was published, which became Hardy's most popular novel. As will be remembered, it aroused quite a storm of protest in the Press, from private individuals, and from subscribers to circulating libraries, which doubtless astonished no one more than Hardy himself.

CHAPTER VI

IT was about this time that we saw a good deal of Hardy, visiting Max Gate on several occasions, and going on cycling excursions with him. It was quite evident to us that Hardy was not only distressed by the hostility that had been aroused in the Press regarding a book which was admittedly his finest prose work up to that period; but, being a very sensitive artist, he was pained by the lack of insight which such criticism indicated.

Of this there is no doubt, and Hardy on one of the occasions we have mentioned told us so, that he had been very worried by the work necessitated in hacking to pieces the story for serial publication in the *Graphic*, and by that entailed in restoring the passages that had been deleted so that they might be included in the volume form.

After its publication he was literally " snowed under " by letters addressed to him, criticizing the book, praising or attacking it. Moreover, the numbers and length of the reviews which the book received, and the correspondence in the Press, entirely distracted his attention for the time being from any work such as he had planned.

Since Hardy had come into the public eye as a writer, the curious had always been questioning the character of his religious opinions. The publication of *Tess*, with the curious conclusion of the story, where he says : " After the black flag had been run up on the staff fixed upon the cornice of the tower of Winchester Gaol, notifying that Tess had been hanged, ' Justice ' was done, and the President of the Immortals (in Æschylean phrase) had ended his sport with Tess. And the D'Urberville knights and dames slept on in their tombs unknowing," revived this curiosity, and it was definitely stated in several quarters that Hardy was an agnostic, or at all events a fatalist.

One is unable to discover that he took any steps to combat this view until very late in life, when a critic, dealing with his work generally in an article, wrote saying that he creates " an all-powerful being endowed with the baser human passions, who turns everything to evil and rejoices in the mischief he has wrought."

To this critic and several others it is believed that Hardy intended to reply, and the draft of a letter exists in which he combats the theories regarding his opinions that had been advanced.

Among the many letters Hardy received immediately after the publication of his most famous story were those from strangers of both sexes recounting experiences similar to that of Angel Clare and of Tess, many asking his advice. Some of the feminine correspondents were people of position, judging from the letters themselves and the addresses from which they were sent, although in the case of quite a number of communications he was requested, if he sent any replies, to do so to post offices under initials.

Hardy often wondered why these people trusted him with their secrets to the extent that they did. But they need not have feared to trust him, as he destroyed all their letters, and no one ever heard their names mentioned. Some of them, we are told, not only asked his advice, but suggested that he should meet them and hear the details of their story, possibly thinking that they might prove interesting to him, and useful in his future work.

Rather perplexed as to what he should do under the circumstances, Hardy consulted his friend, the famous judge of the Divorce Court, Sir Francis Jeune. The latter strongly advised him not to meet any of the writers privately, in case it should lead to trouble and complications, and Hardy never did.

One effect of the notoriety which the publication of the

"Max Gate"
Dorchester

Douglas Snowdon

novel brought Hardy was a shower of invitations from people in all classes of society. The book, indeed, provided conversation for weeks at dinner tables, both in London and the provinces, and often, we are told, the discussions which it provoked became very heated, and the guests definitely split up into two distinct groups, " For " and " Against."

There was a review of the book in the *Edinburgh Quarterly*, which Hardy afterwards characterized as " a smart and amusing article," adding, however : " It is easy to be smart and amusing if a man will forego veracity and sincerity." This extract from his note-book (or diary) is interesting because he goes on to say : " How strange that one may write a book without knowing what one puts into it—or rather the reader reads into it." And then he adds : " Well, if this sort of thing continues, no more novel-writing for me. A man must be a fool to deliberately stand up to be shot at."

The writer remembers how Hardy said very much the same sort of thing when discussing *Tess of the D'Urbervilles* with him, and the storm that it had raised, on an excursion to the high land above the Blackmoor Vale. Certain it is that Hardy about this period may be said to have definitely conceived the idea of abandoning fiction for poetry.

Of course, the effect of all the diverse and other criticism, the discussions round the dinner tables of the great, and the humble, was to arouse a universal interest in the book, resulting in large sales in America and the Colonies, and translations being issued in other languages.

It was about this time that Hardy heard of his father's failure of health, and went to see him.

Although he visited his father constantly he was not present when the old man died on July 20th, in the house in which they both had been born.

In August Hardy had the pleasure of receiving his former chief, Sir Arthur Blomfield, at Max Gate. The latter had taken a house in Dorset for a month or two. During his visit to Hardy he expressed his liking of the design of the house, which is said rather to have surprised the architect. Hardy took him over to Puddletown Church, so that the famous architect could inspect the interesting features of that quaint church, which has a Transitional Norman tower with perpendicular additions, and the Athelhampton chapel, containing altar tombs with effigies of the Martin family, the most ancient of which dates as far back as 1250 ; and also a fine Jacobean gallery.

While in London in the early autumn Hardy paid a visit to Fawley Magna, Berkshire, which was to figure in *Jude the Obscure*, as "Marygreen."

A little later in the same month he was present at Tennyson's funeral in Westminster Abbey, and afterwards met his friends Edmund Gosse, Austin Dobson, the essayist, and the two poets Theodore Watts-Dunton and William Watson.

A sidelight is thrown on Hardy's preference for well-developed women and girls by an entry made in December while in London. After a visit to The Empire in Leicester Square, then one of the most popular music-halls, he wrote : "The dancing girls are nearly all skeletons. They should be penned and fattened for a month to round out their bodies."

In January, 1893, he finished writing, and sent to Scribners, in New York, a short story, "The Fiddler of the Reels," which afterwards appeared in their magazine in the May number.

About this time Hardy made a very significant entry with regard to fiction which certainly can be said to apply to many of his own prose works: "The whole secret of fiction and the drama—in the constructional part—lies in the adjustment of things unusual to things eternal and universal. The writer who knows exactly how exceptional and how non-exceptional his events should be made, possesses the key to the art." A dictum of great service to all who would excel in that art.

The Hardys, in the spring of this year, paid their usual visit to London, and took a whole house at 70 Hamilton Terrace, Regent's Park, and bringing up their own staff, found themselves much more comfortable and at home than they had ever been in Town before. Hardy, of course, had become not only the great writer he always was, but a popular novelist, and this visit to London was full of lunches, dinners and parties, where they met not only many people they knew already but many others, including the Duke and Duchess of Teck and their daughter Princess Mary, the present queen.

As an indication of the popularity of *Tess*, it is interesting to note from an old Academy catalogue of 1893, which we have, that there were several pictures of Wessex scenes, and of places mentioned in the novel, amongst them one entitled " Tess of the D'Urbervilles' Ancestral Home," in reality one of the picturesque Manor House at Wool, in the valley of the Frome, and also a picture called " In Hardy's Country, Egdon Heath."

In the spring of the same year Mr. and Mrs. Hardy paid a visit to Ireland, being the guests of Lord Houghton, the then Lord-Lieutenant, and Hardy recalls going with Henry Lucy, afterwards Sir Henry Lucy, a famous Victorian journalist and humorist, who for many years wrote a running commentary in *Punch* called " Essence of Parliament " under the signature of " Toby, M.P.," to see the scene of the Phœnix Park murders which had ten years before shocked the world. Hardy, who was always keenly interested in the dramatic or the tragic, also visited the rooms in which the bodies of Lord Frederick Cavendish and his fellow-victim, Mr. Thomas Henry Burke, had been placed, and made a note that the room had not been cleaned out since the time of the murders.

Soon after the return of the Hardys from Ireland to London, after having visited Killarney and other beauty spots, Hardy's one-act play called *The Three Wayfarers* was put in rehearsal at Terry's Theatre. It was actually a dramatization of his story *The Three Strangers* which he had renamed.

As will be remembered, the story turns upon the fraternizing, at a christening party given at Higher Crowstairs on the downs, of three strangers who had come to the door and craved admission. One of these was a hangman—

unknown at the time—on his way to Dorchester (Caster-bridge) to execute a man on the following morning for sheep-stealing. The second stranger who came to the door was, by one of those grim touches by which much of Hardy's work is marked, the escaped, condemned criminal. The two of them fraternized and sat drinking mead together until the third stranger came to the door and craved admission. On entering he " became a picture of abject terror," and hastily closing the door, fled.

A minute or two afterwards the sound of a gun was heard, and the company present knew that it signalled the escape of a prisoner from the Dorchester gaol. They also con-cluded that the man who had so hurriedly left them was the escaped convict. As a matter of fact he was the brother of the man who was due to be hanged on the following morning, and it was his amazement at seeing his brother he thought to be in gaol, sitting drinking in the cottage, which caused him to take to his heels. The hangman revealed himself to the company, and called upon those present to go in pursuit of the supposed criminal.

In the story the escaped prisoner was never recaptured. Hardy had dramatized the story at the suggestion of his friend, James Matthew Barrie (now Sir James Barrie, Bart., O.M.), and on the 3rd June, 1893, the play was acted with one or two other short plays and well received. The Hardys saw it in company with Lady Jeune and a party of friends.

In connection with this it is interesting to note that two years previously Hardy had contributed to a symposium initiated by the *Pall Mall Gazette* on the subject of " Why I don't write Plays." This has not been reprinted.

Soon afterwards he met Mrs. Pearl Mary Teresa Craigie, who had created something of a sensation about that time by her three novelettes, *Some Emotions and a Moral*, *A Study in Temptations* and *The Sinner's Comedy*, in the then well-known Pseudonym Library published by T. Fisher Unwin, a series in reality of long short stories in tiny volumes with

mustard-coloured wrappers, which were then immensely
popular. Mrs. Craigie, whom we also knew was a very
charming woman, the daughter of a very wealthy proprietor of a popular patent medicine, who wrote under
the masculine pseudonym of "John Oliver Hobbes," a
practice then rather popular with women writers. There
were also a "George" Egerton, and a "George" Paston,
women novelists, and to-day we have a "George"
Preedy, the thin disguise of Marjorie Bowen.

Hardy in the summer of this year paid another visit to
Oxford, this time incognito, as he wished to attend the
various social functions then taking place and see what was
to be seen unrecognized.

About this time a Parisian paper called *L'Ermitage* was
conducting a symposium regarding the opinions of prominent people upon the existing social system. Hardy's
reply to the editor's question was a very original one, for
he put in a plea that society instead of conforming to a
set of rules or conditions which were meant to apply to
all types of individuals should properly be divided into two
groups comprising individual temperaments with a "different code of observances for each group."

The remaining portion of the year till October appears
to have been without any outstanding incident and consisted chiefly in visits to friends and to various places,
including one to the Milnes-Gaskells' seat at Wenlock
Abbey, and later to Sir Francis and Lady Jeune at Arling-
ton Manor, where there was, as Hardy records, a very
interesting and lively house party.

Towards the end of the year he was writing poetry
again, including a poem called "The Glass-Stainer," and
in December was at work on an abandoned short story,
"An Imaginative Woman," published in the *Pall Mall
Magazine* in April, 1894, and afterwards in the collection
Wessex Tales.

About this time also Hardy was collaborating with the
Hon. Mrs. Arthur Henniker, herself a novelist, in a story
called "A Spectre of the Real," which we believe was afterwards published in a popular newspaper or magazine.

To the Christmas number of the *English Illustrated Magazine* he contributed an article "Ancient Earthworks at Casterbridge," with illustrations from photographs by W. Pouncy.

Christmas at Max Gate was enlivened—as was the usual custom—by the visit of carol singers, which event always seemed to have delighted Hardy and of which occasion he left one of his " thumbnail " and vivid sketches in words.

Early in the following year (April, 1894) Hardy seems to have been troubled regarding an agreement into which he had entered to supply a serial story for *Harper's Magazine*, and wrote asking the American publishers to allow him to cancel it.   The story that was involved was afterwards published as *Jude the Obscure,* the reception accorded to which by both the Press and the public was the direct cause of Hardy definitely abandoning fiction.

In the middle of April the Hardys returned to London and took up their quarters in a house in South Kensington, and at the end of April he went to see George Meredith at his home near Dorking.

In view of the fact that the George Meredith of biographers and writers has always been pictured as a reserved and rather pompous individual, whose great obsession was to deflect attention from the fact that his father was a tailor, Hardy's verdict upon him is significant, for he stated that on the occasion of the visit he paid his fellow-novelist, which was evidently very interesting, Meredith appeared " a shade artificial in manner at first, but not unpleasantly so, and he soon forgets to maintain it, so that it goes off quite."

About this time there was produced in a London theatre (the Adelphi) a melodrama which was thought to have been based upon Hardy's *Tess of the D'Urbervilles*, to dramatize which or to permit of its dramatization, indeed, he had received many requests, but hesitated either to grant permission for this to be done or to tackle the dramatization himself, on account of the reluctance of London actor-managers to risk anything with a play likely to arouse the

same kind of adverse criticism and comment as productions
of Ibsen's dramas had done not long previously.

Hardy went to the Adelphi to see the play but there
is no record, so far as we know, of what he thought
of it.

Notwithstanding the fact that he had given up all idea of
producing a dramatization of his famous story, Hardy still
continued to receive letters from many famous actresses—
among whom were Ellen Terry, Sarah Bernhardt, and
Mrs. Patrick Campbell, who was then making a name—
asking that they might be allowed to play the name part
if the play were written.

At the end of July the Hardys returned to Dorchester.
Hardy, who had been left behind at the house in South
Kensington to see it locked up and bring along some odds
and ends of luggage, met with a slight accident when
dragging one of the portmanteaux downstairs, from which
he suffered for some time.

He returned to London in October to discuss the question
of the serial for *Harper's Magazine*. Eventually an
altered version, with some passages to which exception
had been taken by the editor deleted, was agreed to.

In the March of the next year (1895) Hardy spent a
good deal of time in the neighbourhood of Dorchester
and other places in Wessex with Macbeth Raeburn,
the artist, who was to do frontispieces for the "Wessex"
edition of his novels. Raeburn had gone down to Dorchester so that he might make sketches upon the spot,
and have at the same time the assistance and advice
of the novelist in making the best possible selections of
subjects.

Hardy went to many of the places with Raeburn, but he
could not always do so, and records the difficulties which
the artist experienced in entering Charborough Park,
which was the scene of *Two on a Tower*, to make a sketch
of the tower on which the young astronomer, Swithin St.
Cleeve, carried out his observations. Hardy tells how,
when Raeburn came to the house to ask permission to
sketch it, the butler warned him off, saying : " You had

Affpuddle

"East Egdon"

better be off before the missis sees you, or the bailiff comes
across you."

Nothing daunted, we are told, Raeburn tried to make
a sketch from behind a tree, but while engaged in his work
the bailiff turned up and ordered him out of the park.

The artist was, of course, a Scotchman ; and thinking he
detected in the accent of the bailiff a fellow-countryman,
asked him if that were so.   They discovered then that,
strangely enough, they came from the same village, and all
difficulty was at an end, for the bailiff told the artist to
draw what he liked, only to be careful not to let the old
lady see him.

One of the great events of June of that year was the laying
of the foundation stone of the Catholic Cathedral at Westminster, at which Hardy was present ; and later on he went
to St. Saviour's, Southwark, in which he was interested on
account of the restoration work which was then in progress
under the direction of his old employer, now Sir Arthur
Blomfield.

Hardy and Meredith dined together at the Burford Bridge
Hotel, near Dorking, with the Omar Khayyám Club.
Both of them made speeches on what is thought to be the
only occasion they either of them did so in public, though
this is not so.

It was in August of this year, when back at their home near
Dorchester, that Hardy was busy upon arranging *Jude the
Obscure* for publication in volume form, and restoring passages which had to be deleted to enable it to be published
in *Harper's Magazine*.   The first instalment of the story was
called *The Simpletons*, and had appeared in the previous
December, while the title had in the next number (January,
1895) been altered to *Hearts Insurgent*, and a note was
printed explaining the reason of the alteration.   It was
stated in the magazine that " the author's attention having
been drawn to the resemblance between the title, *The
Simpletons*, and that of another English novel, he had decided
to revert to the title originally selected, viz., *Hearts Insurgent*, which will therefore be used in future parts of the
story."

"Marygreen" approximates to Great Fawley, N. Wantage
"Alfredston" _____ Wantage
"Brown House & Barn" — Red House & Barn, on road
                                    top of hill between Wantage
                                    & Fawley
Jude's entry into Christm.— Down the hill by Wantage Rd.
"Christminster":—
   "Beersheba" — the purlieu called Jericho
   "St Silas" — St Barnabas
   "Chief St" — High St
   "Fourways" — Carfax
Meeting place of Jude } — Cross in pavement Broad St.
 & Sue _____
"Crozier Coll:" Oriel?
"Old Time Street". Oriel Lane?
"Rubric Coll" — Bresenose?
"Cardinal Coll" — Christ Ch. Coll
"The Cathedral" — Christ Ch
"Cardinal Street" — St. Aldate's St.
Ch. with Italian Porch. St Mary's
"Theatre of Wren" — Sheldonian
The octagonal chamber (p. 141) Cupola of Sheldonian
   Oldgate Coll: New Coll.
The riverside path" — The Towing path

LIST OF PLACES, IN THOMAS HARDY'S HANDWRITING, MENTIONED IN
"JUDE THE OBSCURE," SUPPLIED TO THE AUTHOR.

This revision work to which we have referred was always detested by Hardy, and in the case of *Jude the Obscure* he said that owing to " the labour of altering the story to suit the magazine, and then having to alter it back, I have lost energy for revising and improving the original as I meant to do."

It will be gathered from what has already been said that Hardy was exceedingly fond of dancing and it is therefore not without interest that one is able to record the last occasion on which he is known to have indulged in this pastime. He was about fifty-five at the time and when he attended the annual sports at The Larmer Tree (while paying a visit to General and Mrs. Pitt-Rivers at their seat at Rushmore), he took part in the dancing. The original tree was a wych elm, once marking the boundary of Wilts and Dorset, but now replaced by an oak tree planted in the centre of the former tree's shell.

The Hardys returned to Max Gate after this visit, and on November 1st what was to prove so important an event in Hardy's literary life occurred, the publication of *Jude the Obscure* by Osgood McIlvaine & Co., in one volume, containing a preface and an etching of Oxford, the " Christminster " of the story, by H. Macbeth Raeburn, and also a sketch map of Wessex. The book was dated 1896.

Hardy was in for a terrific storm of criticism, for the attack upon the novel which was made in many of the papers and reviews was extremely bitter and vitriolic, and was backed up by anonymous letters and post cards. The wave of protest spread not only to America, but even as far afield as Australia, and it is recorded that, if a certain writer can be believed whose letter contained a packet of ashes said to be those of *Jude the Obscure*, the book was even burned by some people.

Much of the vituperation which the book received took the form of personal attacks upon and abuse of the author, and although Hardy, who possessed a sardonic sense of humour, was at the time less disturbed than might have been expected by all the abuse that was heaped upon his

K

head, there is no doubt that it served to confirm him in his determination to write no more novels.

A memorable sentence of Hardy's was jotted down which runs as follows : "I cannot help thinking that the real trouble has been what people with nasty minds have read into my book rather than what anyone has actually discovered that I have written."

There were, however, numbers of people of discrimination who recognized in *Jude the Obscure* a masterpiece, and what, except for the general gloom and inevitable tragedy of the story, might have ranked as Hardy's most popular and greatest work in prose. Among those who appreciated the novel was Swinburne, whose *Poems and Ballads*, published thirty years or more before, had met with a very similar storm of criticism and protest.

About the same time a review was published, which we have been unable to trace, of an appreciative character, and one would imagine from Hardy's letter to the reviewer, which we are about to quote, that the notice of the book pleased him on account of its appreciation of the story as a work of art. He says in this letter, which was written at Dorchester on November 10th, 1895 : "Your review is the most discriminating that has yet appeared. It required an artist to see that the plot is almost geometrically constructed—I ought not to say *constructed* for, beyond a certain point, the characters necessitated it and I merely let it come. As for the story itself, it is really sent out to those into whose souls the iron has entered, and has entered deeply at some time of their lives, but one cannot choose one's readers." Hardy goes on to say in depreciation of his work, and he never seems to have valued his fiction very highly : "You have hardly an idea how poor and feeble the book seems to me, as executed, beside the idea of it that I had formed in prospect."

It is evident that some critics had referred to the story as "grimy," for in a postscript, Hardy says in explanation of its sombreness : "The grimy features of the story go to show the contrast between the ideal life a man wished to lead, and the squalid real life he was fated to lead. . . . But

I must have lamentably failed, as I feel I have, if this requires explanation and is not self-evident. The idea was meant to run all through the novel. It is, in fact, to be dis-covered in *everybody's* life, though it lies less on the surface perhaps than it does in my poor puppet's."

In another letter written from Max Gate about this time, Hardy says that " there was nothing perverted or depraved in Sue's nature." And he goes on to say that she was a type of woman which had always an attraction for him, but that he had not hitherto dealt with the type owing to the difficulty he felt that there would be in doing so.

We know from what he told us that he was distressed at the storm of criticism that raged around *Jude the Obscure*—much of which he considered unjust and even stupid—but underlying it all there was undoubtedly a feeling in Hardy's mind that in some way he had failed with the book, to which he refers as being " a mass of imperfections."

In December the Hardys went up to London. They returned during the same month to Dorchester, and Hardy was confronted not only with an avalanche of reviews, which were added to every week, but also with Press cut-tings of paragraphs, in some of which the writers had the temerity to state that the book was largely autobiographical. Hardy made no reply to these ridiculous suggestions and statements, but many years later, in answer to a corre-spondent who wrote to him as to whether there was any truth in what had been suggested, he replied that there was " less of his own life in *Jude the Obscure* than in any of his other books." To the present writer Hardy wrote : " There is more of autobiographical interest—if you care about such matters—in my poems than in the whole of my novels."

It is, however, known that some of the incidents had occurred in real life, and were known to him, or that he had heard of them, and, as showing the amazing character of his memory, Hardy mentioned that " Jude " was suggested to him by a youth that he had once met while on his way to school, which event must have occurred a half-century before. It will be remembered that " Jude " drove a baker's cart, and was in the habit of reading books at the same time, at no small risk to pedestrians and drivers of other vehicles in the narrow lanes of the countryside with their sharp turnings.

Owing to the storm of criticism in the Press and the very extravagant and abusive nature of some of the criticisms, Hardy seems to have had a doubt as to whether when he went to London he would be received by friends and acquaintances quite as cordially as had always previously been the case.   In the country there was no doubt that the attack upon " Jude " on the score of morality, and because of the " realism " of some of the scenes in it, had a decided effect upon the hitherto cordial relations existing between him and some of his friends.   However, he need not have troubled, for he had by that time attained an eminence that assaults on him by the Press could not injure, and the Hardys found themselves just as much in request as they had formerly been, and went into society a great deal.

They this year again occupied the house in South Kensington of two years previously, and Hardy unfortunately contracted a chill and was laid up for some time with rheumatism, and had to go for a change to Brighton.   It was while recuperating by the sea that he was asked by members of the Glasgow University Liberal Club to stand for election as Lord Rector.   For some reason or other he decided to decline the invitation, and gave no reasons other than that they were personal ones in his reply to the honorary secretary, which was sent from Brighton on May 16th, 1896.

The controversy regarding *Jude the Obscure* still continued to rage, and soon after the Hardys' return to London in the middle of the season, and at a time when they were going out again very frequently, the first Bishop of Wakefield, the Rev. W. W. How, who was suffragan of Bedford, wrote to the papers stating that he had put Hardy's novel on the fire !

It is recorded that Hardy was somewhat sceptical regarding this statement of the Bishop's, remembering that fires were not easily available in summer, and the undoubted difficulty of burning a thick novel like *Jude the Obscure*. He, however, took no notice of the Bishop's action, and indeed this act of intolerance sensibly affected the man in the street favourably respecting any judgment he had formed regarding the book.

At any rate Hardy could have comforted himself by the fact that the books of quite a number of great writers, from early times onward, including early translations of the Scriptures, had been burned in this way by intolerant and misguided individuals.

One injury that the Bishop did undoubtedly do at any rate to Hardy's pocket was brought about by means of a letter he addressed to the head of W. H. Smith & Sons, the great newsagents and book distributors, " exposing the evil tendency of the book." As a result the book was quietly withdrawn from the circulating libraries, and from sale on the bookstalls, and an assurance was given the Bishop that " any other books by the same author would be carefully examined before they were allowed to be circulated."

The attack on the novel was almost world-wide, and the *New York World*, which in later years became rather notorious for its sensationalism and " muck-rake " stories of crime and scandalous society doings, attacked the book in the very strongest terms. The critic proved to be a maiden lady, who referred to the book as being " one of coarseness which is beyond belief," and went on to say that she " opened the windows after reading it to let in fresh air."

This critic was a Miss Jeannette L. Gilder, and it is not unnatural that Hardy was greatly astonished in July to receive a request from her, when she happened to be over in London, that she should be permitted to interview him and give what she called " his side of the argument."

Hardy's reply, although it is true there was an underlying vein of irony, shows very clearly the kindly and conciliatory nature of the man, and in the concluding paragraph he treats his correspondent with a great deal more gentleness than she deserved, for he says (while refusing to grant the interview) : " At the same time I cannot but be touched by your kindly wish to set right any misapprehension you may have caused about the story. Such a wish will always be cherished in my recollections, and [he added] it removes from my vision of you some obviously unjust character-istics I had given it in my mind."

It is only fair to say that Miss Gilder's reply, by return of post, was one that did her credit, for she wrote from her hotel :

DEAR MR. HARDY,

I knew you were a great man but I did not appreciate your goodness until I received your letter this morning.

Hardy was destined, a short while afterwards, although he did not know it at the time, to meet Miss Gilder at the house of an American lady who had invited him to an evening party. He noticed that while he was conversing with his hostess another lady drew near to them and appar-ently listened closely to the conversation. Afterwards he heard who she was.

In this year the Hardys, after returning to Dorchester to see his mother, went for a holiday to Malvern, and while there visited Worcester to see the cathedral and china works, from whence they proceeded to Warwick and Kenilworth, and naturally saw the ruins of the famous castle associated with memories of Queen Elizabeth and her favourite, Robert Dudley, Earl of Leicester. Strat-ford-on-Avon was also visited.

In the middle of September of this year the Hardys went to Belgium, and the architecture of the railway station at Bruges so struck Hardy that he afterwards said that the latter was the only town with a station which satisfied him as to its architectural design.

Visits were paid to Brussels and then they went on into

"Christminster."

the beautiful valley of the Meuse, seeing Namur and Dinant. In those days there was a casino, and high gambling went on at the last-named place, and Hardy records that he had a conversation with one of the players who believed he possessed a system, on the reliability of which, however, Hardy expressed his doubts of its infallibility. That these were justified was a day or two later evidenced by the fact that the gambler left Dinant almost without a penny.

They also visited Spa, that delightful and picturesque summer resort, and then on returning to Brussels Hardy went out to Waterloo, and made studies of the ground over which the battle was fought, and visited the chief places, such as La Belle Alliance, Le Ferme de Mont St. Jean, and Hougoumont, associated with the battle, obtaining material which doubtless was later incorporated in *The Dynasts* to which he had given at that time the provisional name of *Europe in Throes*.

From his diaries of this date one may quote an entry made on October 2nd, when he says: " Walked along from the English line along the Charleroi Road to La Belle Alliance. Struck with the nearness of the French and English lines to each other. Shepherds with their flocks and dogs, men ploughing, two cats and myself the only living creatures on the field."

It was in March of the following year that an American produced a dramatized version of *Tess of the D'Urbervilles*, which met with considerable success, and it was in the middle of this month that another event happened of importance, the publication in volume form of *The Well-Beloved*, which had appeared serially five years previously in the *Illustrated London News* under the title of *The Pursuit of the Well-Beloved ; a Sketch of a Temperament*. Hardy fully explains the theory which forms the basis of the story in the preface to the first edition of the novel, which was that of the reincarnation of the ideal woman, existing only in the mind of the lover, in a succession of women. Again Hardy was subject to, paraphrasing Shakespeare, " the slings and arrows of outrageous criticism," for some of his critics seemed to be able to discover immorality in the story.

From the fact that this novel was published in volume form so long after its appearance as a serial, many people have come to look upon the book as Hardy's last prose work.

Hardy, in replying to some of his critics in a letter to one of the literary weeklies of the day, explained that the story was sketched out many years before it was published even in serial form, and was the working out of an idea that had come to him as quite a young man " which," he added, " considering its charm and its poetry one could well wish to be interested in always."   He went on to say that under-lying the fantasy, upon which the book was based, there was the truth that " all men are pursuing a shadow, the unattainable."

Again certain reviewers were guilty of attacking Hardy personally, and one in particular was obviously actuated by personal malice.

Although Hardy had, of course, written this story, and it had been published some years before, as we have noted, it may be said to have closed his career as a writer of fiction and even of prose ; because with the exception of a few articles and short sketches, which he had contracted to supply, he wrote prose no more.

It was while on a cycling expedition with Hardy to " Cross-in-Hand," which stands on a lonely tableland above the Blackmoor Vale, between High Stoy and Bubb Down, on the left-hand side of the road which leads from Ever-shot station over Batcombe Down to Dogbury Gate and Minterne Magna about a hundred yards eastward of the turning to Up-Cerne and Cerne Abbas, and while resting by the roadside of the steep ascent, that he told us the legend of the stone.

"Cross-in-Hand," which is a pillar of stone resembling marble or granite, figures, of course, in Hardy's poem " The Lost Pyx," included in *Poems of the Past and Present*. In referring to the stone in *Tess of the D'Urbervilles* Hardy stated that it took its name of Cross-in-Hand from the spot which was " the scene of a miracle or murder, or both." And he describes it there as " a strange rude mono-lith, from a stratum unknown in any local quarry, on which was roughly carved a human hand." And later in the story he makes a rustic, who was questioned by Tess as to whether it was a cross, say : "Cross—no ; t'wer not a cross ! 'Tis a thing of ill-omen, Miss. It was put up in wuld times by the relations of a malefactor who was tortured there by nailing his hand to a post, and after-wards hung. The bones lie underneath. They say he sold his soul to the Devil, and that he walks at times."

Readers will remember that the poem tells how a priest going to administer extreme unction to a man who was dying, plodding up the side of the hill, with the sacramental vessels slung on his arm, lost the Pyx of the blessed sacra-ment, and the poem goes on to tell that while he was bemoaning his lost Pyx he groped with his hands along the way he had travelled.

" Till here on the hill, betwixt vill and vill,
    He noted a clear straight ray,
    Stretching down from the sky to a spot hard by,
    Which shone with a light of day.

And gathered around the illumined ground
    Were common beasts and rare,
And kneeling at gaze, and in pause profound
    Attent on an object there.

'Twas the Pyx unharmed 'mid the circling rows
Of Blackmore's hairy throng,
    Whereof were oxen, sheep and does
And hares from the brakes among.

.   .   .   .   .

Then the priest bent likewise to the sod
And thanked the Lord of Love,
And Blessed Mary, Mother of God,
And all the Saints above.

And turning straight with his priceless freight,
He reached the dying one,
Whose passing sprite had been stayed for the rite,
Without which bliss hath none.

And when by grace the priest won place,
And served the Abbey well,
He reared *this stone* to mark where shone
That midnight miracle."

It was well known among his friends, for a number of
years, that Hardy would probably eventually concentrate
his genius upon verse alone, and certainly his decision
caused no great stir among his intimates.

CHAPTER VII

HE had, indeed, always looked upon prose as a means of earning a living, and when the monetary rewards from his work became not only substantial but even handsome, the need for financial considerations of course no longer existed. Moreover, he more than once expressed an opinion that the tendency of novelists, of the period to which we are referring, who had enjoyed any vogue, was to lose sight of the high standard at which the novel, as a complete work of art, should always aim. He had, in the *New Review* in January, 1890, an essay on "Candour in English Fiction," also published in the *Eclectic Magazine* (New York) in March, 1890, given expression to the difficulties under which a novelist of that period worked. The chief of which he stated were the trammelling of his thought, through the Puritanism of his readers, difficulties which he described as being brought about through the censorship of prudery ! Hardy said that it was this that led to so many English novels composing a literature of quackery, alike false to and afraid of truth. He also expressed it as his opinion that the crash of broken commandments is as necessary an accompaniment to the catastrophe of a tragedy as the noise of a drum and cymbals to a triumphal march ! This was at least in some measure the gospel of Hardy's belief as a novelist.

It was, therefore, one may well believe, with genuine relief that Hardy turned into the paths of poetry and pursued the course that he had always desired to follow.

The scenes of natural beauty in his novels which he described so well were fundamentally poems written in prose, and he always undoubtedly aimed at an idealism which many people entirely misunderstood.

From all we have been able to gather from those who knew him best the decision he had arrived at brought him a content, peace and relief which his advancing years made doubly agreeable to him.   He now set about the collection and revision of early published and unpublished verses, some of which dated back from the time he was working under Sir Arthur Blomfield in London.

Though the Hardys visited London in 1897, as was their usual yearly practice, they lived in Town only a few weeks, and then went to stay at Basingstoke, coming up to Town occasionally.   They left in the middle of June for Switzerland, and Hardy was very much impressed with the absence of people travelling upon the Continent which was accounted for by the fact that it was the year of the Diamond Jubilee, and that people from all parts of the Continent, and indeed of the world, were flocking to London to witness the amazing pageantry of that event.

They stayed at Neuchâtel first, and then went on to Berne, where on June 20th they attended a Jubilee concert given in the cathedral in honour of Queen Victoria's sixty years' reign.   Interlaken was also visited, and Grindel-wald.

Hardy was busy writing poetry while on this holiday, and one poem which he called "The Schreckhorn" was inspired by the sight of that mountain from the train as it approached Interlaken.   They went on to Lauter-brunnen and other places, including Lausanne, where they stayed at the Hotel Gibbon, so named in honour of the author of *The Decline and Fall* who had stayed there and finished that monumental work during that period.

In *Poems of the Past and Present*, published by Harper Brothers in 1901, though dated 1902, there is a poem entitled "Lausanne" with a note that it was written in

Gibbon's garden between 11 and 12 p.m., on the evening of June 27th, 1897, which was exactly a hundred and ten years after Gibbon himself records that at the same hour he had written the last lines of the last page of *The Decline and Fall* in the summer-house of the garden.

The Hardys afterwards went on to Zermatt, proceeding along the Rhone Valley in great heat, and the result of the visit was the verses entitled " To the Matterhorn." It was while at Zermatt that Hardy was taken ill from over-exertion in the extreme heat while searching for an Englishman who had been reported missing.

They went on to Geneva where he was seriously ill, and had to stay in bed.

It is interesting to note that Hardy, while lying in bed, heard the sound of the fountain just outside his bedroom window, near which the Austrian Empress was murdered on September 10th of the same year by an Italian anarchist, Luigi Lucheni. Hardy had always possessed a great admiration for the beautiful and tragic Empress, and may indeed have seen her on her several visits to near-by Bournemouth, and had written verses to her in his early years. Indeed, it is believed that he once drafted the outline of a novel with her for a heroine, which, however, was never written.

Owing to Hardy's illness, they were unable to make as many excursions as was their custom, but on their return to London in April Hardy was invited by the editor of the *Saturday Review* to take part in a symposium which the paper was then about to publish concerning the best scenery that famous people had seen. In replying to the editor's letter, Hardy, in one dated July 9th, published in the paper August 7th, 1897, expressed his difficulty in giving a definite answer to the query, and made a very significant suggestion that " at a given moment we like best what meets the mood of that moment."

Hardy, though referring to the beauties and grandeur of the Jungfrau and the Matterhorn and the lovelier scenery of Lake Geneva, which he had just delighted in,

DOUGLAS SNOWDON

Puddletown

"Weatherbury".

finally confined his answer to scenery in his own beloved
"Wessex," the places chosen being :

(1) View from Castle Hill, Shaftesbury.
(2) View from Pilsdon Pen.
(3) New Forest vistas near Brockenhurst.
(4) The River Dart.
(5) The coast from Trebarwith Strand to Beeny Cliff,
Cornwall.

Hardy returned from London to Dorchester at the end
of July, and spent some time in rambling about in the
neighbourhood of Salisbury—which figures as "Melchester" in *Jude the Obscure*—and Frome, visiting also
Wells Cathedral.

It was in September that Rudyard Kipling came down
to Dorchester with a view to purchasing a house at Weymouth, or in the neighbourhood, and spent some considerable time with Hardy cycling about that portion of Wessex,
a companionship Hardy referred to with pleasure. Although the Kiplings eventually found a house at Rodwell,
near Wyke Regis, it was never taken owing to some
difficulty regarding the lease. They eventually settled
on a house, "The Elms," at Rottingdean, Sussex, where
they lived for a time.

Nothing of any note appears to have happened in the
autumn of this year, after the visit of Rudyard Kipling,
nor in the early portion of the following year.

In the middle of the summer Hardy was approached by
a firm of publishers who were anxious for him to write
an introductory essay to the library edition of Fielding's
works, then contemplated. Hardy declined this proposal,
not because he was not interested in Fielding ; indeed,
as a writer he had always been interested in his works ;
but because he first of all thought that Fielding's attitude
towards the peasants and the lower orders among his
characters was unsympathetic and in a measure untrue.
Moreover, he held the view—a very usual one then—that
for one writer, who was a novelist, to write in frank
criticism about another was unwise and not advisable, and
were the other author alive, impossible to do so honestly.

As further evidence of Hardy's attitude towards reviewing other people's books or expressing an opinion upon them the following letter, addressed to Mr. Stanley I. Galpin, the editor of the Year Book of the Society of Dorset Men in London, is interesting :

Max Gate,
Dorchester.
25th September, 1922.

DEAR MR. GALPIN,

I should much like to oblige you by agreeing to your request to express my opinion of Charles Dickens's writings. But apart from the fact that I am a bad estimator of novels, it is almost impossible for me to criticize Dickens without, on the one hand, being considered invidious if I am as frank on his faults as on his genius : and, on the other hand, being considered to express eulogistic commonplace if I am discriminating, so I will ask you to excuse me from saying anything, and leave it to those of your friends who stand in a more independent position, and are much better able to estimate him, or to yourself.

Yours very truly,
(Sgd.) THOMAS HARDY.

Hardy did not live to see the swing of the pendulum which has taken place, when a practice has arisen in the Press of novelists criticizing and lauding each other's works.

Hardy about this time, although approaching the age of sixty, was an untiring cyclist, and in the autumn of this year the Hardys, for Mrs. Hardy also cycled, visited places as far afield as Bristol, Gloucester and Cheltenham.

In the middle of December of this year (1898) Hardy's first collection of verse, entitled *Wessex Poems*, was published, and met with a very considerable success. The many reviews which appeared may on the whole be divided into two classes : those distinctly of a favourable kind ; and those in which respect for the writer perhaps predominated over a genuine appreciation of the merits or demerits of the

L

verses. A few critics frankly expressed their regret that Hardy should have abandoned prose fiction and taken up so entirely different a form of literary expression.

Hardy does not appear to have been altogether surprised at the attitude taken up by the last-named type of critics, for he undoubtedly anticipated that there would be some such disagreement with his attempting to create a new reputation for himself in a fresh field.

What was not generally known, of course, to the public, was that Hardy had always at heart been a poet, and, indeed, had written almost reams of verse at one time or another, before the publication of the *Wessex Poems*, much of which he had mislaid or destroyed, and that at the back of his mind throughout his life there lay the intention and hope of abandoning fiction and writing poetry, of the possibility of his making a reputation as a poet, and indeed of being remembered as such.

Hardy himself made no pretension that his poetry was new, but that, strongly intellectual and human, he might at least present age-old themes and experiences in a new way. Of course, a good deal of the criticism levelled at Hardy's verse in the early days was rather in regard to its form than its inspiration.

Just as was the case with his prose, Hardy undoubtedly constructed—and we use the word constructed advisedly— much of his verse upon architectural lines. He fully appreciated the value of somewhat irregular metre as a means not only of arresting attention, but of expressing more accurately the varying emotions and " values " of the subject of the poem. Naturally he experienced a good deal of hostile, or at all events unsympathetic, criticism in regard to his methods. Probably had some of these critics been aware that Hardy had devoted a great amount of study, both theoretical and experimental, during a long period of years to all forms of verse, they would scarcely have assumed that this was a new depar- ture on his part, or, as a considerable number of critics did, that he was now experimenting in a comparatively new medium.

An examination of the files of various newspapers in which reviews of Hardy's collections of poems appear, leads óne to the impression that on many occasions the book must have been handed either to inexperienced and unsympathetic critics, or to those who, while being competent in a general way to criticize poetry, were not able to appreciate Hardy's humour, which was often of a very dry and caustic kind.

It would appear that he met with some sort of doubt on the part of the publishers as to the possible success of his volume of *Wessex Poems* when he had sent them the manuscript, for he is known to have made an offer to the firm to bear all costs of the volume, an offer which, however, was not accepted, and the doubt as to the financial success of the volume was proved to have been uncalled for.

As undoubtedly Hardy wrote at this time, and was able to publish his poetry, without any necessity for considering financial reasons—but because he enjoyed writing it and had a very definite goal at the back of his mind—he paid very little attention to any adverse criticism which was written either ignorantly or otherwise.

A rather interesting thing happened in the early part of 1899. W. T. Stead, who founded and was the first editor of the *Review of Reviews*, wrote to Hardy, asking him to give his opinion upon a Crusade of Peace, which symposium was going to appear under the name of " War against War." A phrase, in later years, to be used so inaccurately and unjustifiably. Stead had undoubtedly at the back of his mind evidently an ideal somewhat of the kind underlying that of the League of Nations. Hardy replied to this request, but does not appear to have dealt with the subject more than to suggest that horses should only be employed in war for transport purposes, arising doubtless from his inherent hatred of all forms of cruelty, and love of dumb animals.

In April the Hardys were again in London, and had a flat at Wynnstay Gardens, Kensington, and as usual visited their friends and went out a good deal into society, attending theatres and some public functions.

Among a large circle of friends, some of whom must naturally have been those who thrust their acquaintance upon Hardy because of his eminence, there were doubtless bores, and those who might have been described as " sounding brass and tinkling cymbal." But Hardy left on record a view that when one of these callers had gone, although the visit had not been desired, there was a feeling of regret at his departure, and, as Hardy phrased it, " of the withdrawal of the grain of value in him," because he in his charity was able to overlook in the visitor what he called " the mass of chaff that spoilt it."

In the early summer Hardy was staying at a country house close to London, and visited Stoke Poges to see the grave of the poet Gray, which he did at the request of one of the guests, who was a young lady of title and of great beauty. As they stood together by the grave, Hardy records that his companion recited the whole of the " Elegy " from the first verse to the last without a single mistake, a no mean feat.

In June Hardy indulged in a rather weird excursion, and visited Westminster Abbey at midnight, by the light of a lantern, in company with some friends, having gained admission to the sanctuary by the kindness of Miss Bradley, whose father, the Rev. George Granville Bradley, was then Dean.

It was in this summer that Hardy suffered from a bad attack of influenza which left a weakness of the eye which affected his sight somewhat more or less for the rest of his life.

In July he received a letter from the Rationalist Press Association, possibly by reason of the fact that his friend Leslie Stephen was an honorary member of that body, apparently asking him also to become a member. Hardy, however, excused himself—although he admitted that he was interested—giving as a reason that he thought an imaginative writer would be out of place in such a body, which would be more suitable for philosophic, scientific and historical writers.

Hardy was cycling a good deal during the summer of

this year, and on one occasion cycled with the present writer for a distance of between thirty and forty miles, visiting among other places (at the end of a very hot afternoon) Milborne St. Andrews, figuring in *Far From the Madding Crowd* and *Tess of the D'Urbervilles* as Millpond St. Jude's.

As the village was approached, Hardy said : " We will call in at a cottage and get a cup of tea. An old lady who lives there always makes me one when I am in this neighbourhood. The cottage proved a charming, thatched one, set back from the road a matter of some twenty yards, which space was occupied by a real cottager's flower garden with a path up the centre leading one to the door and porch, and on either side of the path rows of hollyhocks, sunflowers and of less striking flowers including Canterbury Bells, Sweet Williams, candytuft and climbing and dwarf nasturtiums, while in the background were several rows of sweet peas in full bloom, a large bunch of which the old lady gathered ere we left and presented to Hardy.

He met with a warm welcome when the old lady came to the door and discovered who it was, greeting him with " Come in, Mr. Hardy, I am glad to see you again this way," adding : " Of course you will want a cup of tea." Hardy nodded his head, and afterwards introducing us, sat down in a large windsor chair not far away from the open hearth.

On the opposite side of the room near a diamond-paned window, in which there were some pieces of old bottle glass, a young girl was busily making a dress with a sewing-machine. Hardy went over and spoke to her kindly, and she smiled up at him and laughed. He then came back and told us that he had discovered that she was to be married in about ten days' time, and told us that he had known her from a child and had promised her to go to the wedding.

We suggested that the dress she was engaged in making, which was pale blue, was the actual wedding-dress, and Hardy recrossed the floor and bent down and spoke to the girl, who nodded her head and blushed rosily.

The old lady by this time had made the tea and placed it on the table at Hardy's side, and he on returning to us smilingly said : "You are quite right about the dress, but how on earth did you know it? You must be a perfect Sherlock Holmes," a reference to the stories which had made the author (afterwards Sir) Arthur Conan Doyle so famous.

We afterwards heard that Hardy had performed his promise to be present at the village wedding—probably he cycled over. How many of the society girls he had met would have felt honoured by such an act on his part?

In the autumn of that year he was deeply stirred by the Boer War, which had broken out in the second week in October, and the departure of the troops for South Africa which he had witnessed at Southampton. He wrote a number of poems and verses more or less connected with the war and what he had seen of war preparations, some of which appeared in the *Graphic*, others in a review called *Literature*, and a Christmas ghost story was published in the *Westminster Gazette*.

It was about this period, although he was only sixty years of age, that Hardy's grip of life seemed to be relaxing. We are told that he made far fewer notes such as had been his practice to do rather prolifically in former times, and it followed, perhaps naturally, that his renunciation of writing fiction had to a large extent damped down public interest in him as an active writer. He was never a personally ambitious man, taking things very much as they came and never seeking the publicity and limelight which seems the bane of many modern writers. He continued his experiments in all directions in verse writing, and a very striking poem, called "The Souls of the Slain" appeared in 1900 in the April number of the *Cornhill*.

The Hardys paid their accustomed visit to London in this year, but apparently with a view to economy stayed at the West Central Hotel in Southampton Row. There could scarcely, however, have been the necessity, if it was economy, as he must have been then comfortably off for a considerable number of years.

"Cross in-Hand"
Barcombe Hill

Douglas Snowdon

They left London rather earlier than usual, and we remember that he was back in Dorchester some time in the early part of July, and during the next month he was visited by A. E. Housman, the poet, the author of *The Shropshire Lad*, his old friend Edward Clodd, and Sir Frederick Pollock.

He went cycling a great deal during the autumn, which shows that he was in good health, covering considerable distances in Somerset, Devon and Hampshire. If Hardy may be thought in a measure to have retired, in that the cessation of writing fiction tended to decentralize interest in him, he was still asked by many people to express his opinion on various subjects, some of which must have amused him not a little. For example, a correspondent seems to have taken exception to what he had written regarding infant baptism in *Tess of the D'Urbervilles*, and got into correspondence with him on the topic.

It was about this time that he met Madame Sarah Bernhardt at the house of Maurice Hewlett, the novelist, and the great French tragedienne appears to have spoken to him of her consciousness of getting old, but most who saw her years after—as we did in such pieces as *La Dame aux Camelias*—would have been prepared to say she still then possessed a good share of the elixir of eternal youth.

At the end of July the then famous literary organization, "The Whitefriars Club," which had a custom of paying a visit at least once a year to some spot having associations with English literature, or to some distinguished writer, decided to make the Hardy country the locale of their visit, and, if it could be arranged, to pay a call on the famous novelist himself at Max Gate.

Living at that time, as he had, indeed, from birth, on the borders of Dorset, and possessing a knowledge of Hardy's "Wessex," acquired during many years of study and of exploration, the present writer was asked by the club, of which he was a member, to undertake the organization of the visit. A tour was planned which included a considerable portion of the district in which were laid some of the principal scenes of at least four of Hardy's best-known novels—namely, *Tess of the D'Urbervilles*, *The Return of the Native*, *Far from the Madding Crowd*, and *The Mayor of Casterbridge*.

The party arrived by special train from London at Wool station at about midday, and were met by coaches, in those days drawn by horses, which took them to the ancient Manor House known to readers of *Tess* as Wellbridge Manor House, once the seat of a junior branch of the D'Urberville family, less than half a mile from the station.

After an inspection of the building, including the frescoes of the sinister women referred to in the story, the party visited Bindon Abbey, the mill at which Angel Clare studied milling, and saw the empty coffin in which Tess was laid by her husband.

Then the way lay across Bere Heath, the " Egdon " Heath of Hardy, a magnificent description of which appears in the first chapter of Hardy's *Return of the Native*. Hardy wrote as follows : " The face of the heath, by its mere complexion, added half an hour to eve ; it could, in like manner, retard the dawn ; sudden noon, anticipate the frowning of storms scarcely generated, and intensify the opacity of a moonless midnight to a cause of shaking and dread."

Even on that sunny summer's day the heath wore a sombre look, but perhaps, as Hardy wrote : " Men have oftener suffered from the mockery of a place too smiling for their reason than for the oppression of surroundings over-sadly tinged."

Bere Regis, or as Hardy calls it " King's Bere," was soon reached—" the half-dead townlet " mentioned in *Tess* and *Far from the Madding Crowd*, where John Durbeyfield with his shiftless family migrated, and in the church of which are the ancient memorials of the D'Urbervilles.

Still in certain parts of Dorset the villages lie away off the high road and are approached by little-frequented lanes, and thus have managed to escape the attention of those for whom the highways have attraction, and to our mind Hardy never did finer work nor was more absolutely at home than when he dealt with the life of a village of this type. In these all the people know one another, but even to-day in some they know very few " outsiders," or " Kimberlins," as the people of " the Isle of Slingers " (Portland) call strangers, and not much of the great world outside. Their emotional resources are drawn upon for each other, and if only they were left alone the most tragic incidents of their lives might be avoided.

Hardy, however, in most of his books delighted to introduce persons from the outside world into these regions of tranquillity, and these often proved human " apples of discord." So long as peasants deal with peasants there is comedy in the community, and, indeed, the peasants seem almost to play the part of a Greek chorus.

Certainly some of those who drove with us along the enchanted ground, which Hardy had discovered and created for the outside world by his books, must have been haunted by his immortals, and when village folk came out to gaze upon us and wonder whence we could have come and why, surely there were among them Marty Souths, Giles Winterbornes, Diggory Benns, Grandfer Cantles, and Joseph Poorgrasses and a score of others.

At all events some of us remembered that it was in the church at King's Bere that Alec D'Urberville, the evil genius of Tess, repaired, to find her meditating upon the monuments of her ancestors' fallen greatness.

High above the straggling street with its tumbledown-looking and ancient dwellings rose the green slopes of Woodbury Hill, which figures so prominently as Green Hill in *Far from the Madding Crowd*. One passed onwards through the meads where shepherd Gabriel Oak tended his lambs and almost silently courted Bathsheba ; where Jan Coggan and other farm-hands, Boldwood and Bathsheba herself had assembled for the famous sheep-washing, along the road leading to Casterbridge down which Laban came at midnight at the end of the story, bringing the news of Boldwood's reprieve to waiting Gabriel Oak, Jan Coggan and the villagers, till the stretch downhill, shut in on either side by trees, is reached where poor Fanny Robin met Sergeant Troy and Bathsheba, and this way came to Dorchester, so well known to Hardy's readers as Casterbridge. With just a glance at a few of the " lions " of Casterbridge —and nothing more than a glance—which included the bay window of the King's Arms, associated with Henchard in *The Mayor of Casterbridge*, we came to Max Gate, where the whole party was cordially welcomed by Mr. and Mrs. Hardy.

Among the most notable guests, many of whom have since passed away, may be mentioned Clement Shorter, then editor of the *Sphere*, who was Prior for the day ; Robert Leighton, the well-known writer and collaborator, with his wife ; William Senior ; W. H. Rideing, the editor of the famous American journal, the *Youth's Companion* ; G. W. Sheldon, then London representative of Appletons, New York ; I. N. Ford of the *New York Tribune* ; J. Foster-Fraser, the well-known writer (now Sir John Foster-Fraser); W. H. Boucher, the artist ; Mackenzie Bell, the poet ; the well-known book collector, W. G. Lacey ; J. Farlow-Wilson, then Director of Cassells ; the late Sir William Treloar ; Judge Bingham and Judge Curler, distinguished American judges ; Miss May Rockman, actress and friend of Sarah Bernhardt; and the secretary of the club, Arthur (now Sir Arthur) Spurgeon.

After tea on the lawn, Richard Whiteing, the author of *No. 5 John Street*, in a very graceful speech claimed that our host had always been a true and conscientious artist, and added : " Whatever else may be said of him, whatever judgment one may form as to his view of life, no one can deny that he has spent the whole force of his genius in giving life to the scenes and the people among whom he was born and grew up ; and to whom he returned as soon as he could from all-devouring London and where he still remains." The speaker added, and many of us shared the feeling, " that the interest in Dorsetshire scenery did not arise so much from its own intrinsic beauty, which is, indeed, easily and often equalled and surpassed, but from the interpretation that had been given to it by a great genius."

In brief acknowledgment, Hardy said that he and Mrs.

Hardy were delighted to see so many guests. He likened the "Pilgrimage" to that of which Chaucer wrote, only that here to-day there was surely no "poor man," a statement which caused considerable laughter. It was a surprise to him that the club had managed to see so much. Should they ever visit Dorset again, he would suggest that they should start their drive at Bulbarrow, towards the north of the county, and proceed along the edge of the valley to Wynyard's Gap. This way would show them that Dorset had views which would compare with that from the famous Richmond Hill, of which just then so much had been written.

He did not know why Dorset had been so little thought of. Perhaps it was the result of the report given by certain commissioners, who were sent thither during the agitation against the Factory Acts. So depressing was their report of the industrial and social conditions of the county that it had seemed unjustly to cut it, Dorset, quite off from England ever since.

After Mr. Hardy had spoken, Mrs. Clive Holland presented Mrs. Hardy, on behalf of the club, with a beautiful album of Wessex pictures, bound in art linen and tied with orange ribbon.

The photographs had been taken by her husband during his many visits to the scenes of their host's novels. The gift was suitably acknowledged by Mrs. Hardy, who expressed her pleasure at receiving the collection of Wessex pictures, many of them so closely connected with the scenes her husband had described in his novels and poems.

Dr. Robertson Nicoll, the then editor of the *Bookman*, who was one of the party, said in conversation afterwards : "I felt more strongly than ever that Mr. Hardy is almost the only novelist who can weave together the life of a man and woman, and the life of Nature. The landscape is always playing an important part in his books, and a truer, more fortunate, more proven reader of landscape than Mr. Hardy might not easily be found, but the special characteristic of his work is that the landscape scenes form an essential part of the story. In many novels we have bits about Nature which may be good or may be bad, but which in either case might be removed without interfering with the narrative.

"Mr. Hardy, on the other hand, sees and understands the link that binds in indissoluble union humanity and Nature. It is no doubt by living in his own land so long, loving it so well, brooding over it so patiently, that he is able to make his books appealingly fresh and interesting. We should never wish him to go outside his kingdom, that kingdom in which he has room and energy enough."

A very true estimate of the great writer to whom the speaker was referring.

Hardy himself took considerable interest in showing, those of his guests who were interested, the Druidical and supposedly sacrificial stone which he had erected in the garden, and also the "curiosities," consisting of the Roman-British remains, fragments of glass, jewellery, etc., which had from time to time been dug up in his garden, to be seen in the attractive drawing-room where also many sketches of the illustrations to his books, and water-colour drawings of "Wessex" scenery were on the walls.

It was not until afterwards that the "Whitefriars" learned, to their deep regret, because they had been unable to greet her, that Hardy's old mother, then in her eighty-eighth year, accompanied by her daughters, Mary and Katherine, had been wheeled to a point, which the coaches would pass on their way to Dorchester, at the end of the lane from Upper Bockhampton to the foot of Yellowham Hill.

For a considerable period after this visit Hardy was engaged in collecting together and preparing for publication a number of miscellaneous verses which he had written since the *Wessex Poems* had been published, and had found among his papers, and had either recopied or entirely re-written. The volume appeared in the middle of November and was entitled *Poems of the Past and Present*.

An interesting sidelight on Hardy's character, and an explanation in a measure to what to a certain extent might have been held to have inspired his reputed pessimism, is given by a note he made for January 1st, 1902, where he says that " pessimism is in brief playing a sure game ; you cannot lose at it, you may gain.   It is the only view of life in which you can never be disappointed.   Having reckoned what to do in the worst possible circumstances, when better arise, as they may, life becomes a child's play."

Life onward at Max Gate during the next few months was very uneventful, but in April Hardy wrote what he considered upon the whole his best poem called "A Trampwoman's Tragedy," which was based on a local story of an incident that took place in the early part of the 19th century, which Hardy more or less embodied in his verses.

Many people have expressed curiosity from time to time regarding Hardy's attitude towards what is generally known as agriculture during the later years of his life. Hardy paints two pictures which are very informative as regards the past and the present in a letter which he addressed to H. Rider Haggard, the well-known writer of *King Solomon's Mines* and many other novels, who was afterwards knighted.   Of the past he speaks of a labourer whose wages were but six shillings a week, with about two pounds earned by overtime during the harvest ; a cottage rent free, and an allowance of firewood.   He also speaks in that letter of the average wages ranging from seven shillings to nine shillings a week with allowance better in proportion.   At the time he wrote (1902), he contrasted the old hiring fairs of his boyhood, dating from ancient times, which took place yearly in Dorchester, where he states : " The old positions are absolutely reversed.   The farmers walking about and importuning the labourers to come and be hired, instead of, as formerly, the labourers insistently entreating the stolid farmers to take them on at any pittance."

He says that the agricultural labourers' life at the time at which he wrote was one of comfort if only they observed ordinary thrift, and that he could take his correspondent " to the cottage of a shepherd not many miles from here that has a carpet, and brass rods to the staircase, and from

Douglas Snowpon

West Bay. Bridport.

"Port. Bredy".

the open door of which you can hear a piano strumming. Of course, bicycles stand by the doorway, while at night a large paraffin lamp throws out a perfect blaze of light upon the passer-by."

Hardy's view expressed in this letter was that the migration to the towns—concerning which probably Rider Haggard had written to him—was caused not so much from sheer choice except as regarded " that percentage of young, adventurous, and ambitious spirits among them, which is found in all societies—the prime cause is unquestionably uncertainty of tenure. If they do not escape this in the towns it is not fraught with such trying consequences there as in a village, whence they have to travel ten or twenty miles to find another house and other work."

Some interesting letters are to be found in the files of the *Dorset County Chronicle* from Hardy, relative to Edmund Kean's connection with Dorchester. The great actor visited the town before he became famous, and stayed with his wife and child at an inn called The Little Jockey, which was still standing in Hardy's time on Glyde Path. While staying here Kean lost his little son who was buried in Trinity Churchyard.

It would seem that at the time of this visit, the company of which Kean was a member had the misfortune of a very wet night. The play was *Coriolanus*, and apparently Kean did not act at all well. In one way, however, he was in luck, for Arnold, the stage-manager of Drury Lane Theatre, was present at the performance, and came to the conclusion that, notwithstanding his bad acting on that occasion, Edmund Kean was worth bringing to London.

The cause of Hardy's correspondence was his desire to defend the actor, and he wrote under the pen-name of " History."   A correspondent, signing himself " Dorset," had written stating that because Kean had been guilty of immoral conduct he was not worthy to be highly thought of. And this, notwithstanding the fact that he was one of the greatest actors that the English stage has known. Hardy went on to point out how many of the greatest men of the past, now acclaimed as geniuses, were guilty to a far greater degree of moral offence than was the actor who was attacked. He went on to show how Kean, from his birth, was handicapped by his illegitimacy, and how the hardships he underwent in his youth and young manhood had probably had the effect of leaving him without moral ballast when he had won success and was assailed by flattery and temptation.

On Saturday, March 21st, 1903, Madame Sarah Grand, who had been lecturing in Bournemouth at the Winter Gardens, and was staying with the present writer and his wife, having expressed a wish to pay a visit to Thomas Hardy, one was arranged.

The authoress of several notable novels, she had strangely enough undergone a few years previously, on the publication of *The Heavenly Twins*, her most famous book, a storm of criticism and abuse such as had greeted the appearance of Hardy's *Tess of the D'Urbervilles* two years previously.

Hardy readily agreed to a visit, and invited us to lunch, and so shortly before midday we arrived at Max Gate, then much less secluded than it is now, owing to the fact that the trees had not to the same extent grown up and thereby shut it in. Hardy greeted his distinguished guest cordially, and Mrs. Hardy was particularly charming, and expressed her admiration of the novel which had made her visitor one of the most talked-of authoresses of the period when it was published. Indeed, she in conversation in the drawing-room before lunch, expressed her general approval of the tendency of the book, and its subject, Hardy, we remember, looking on with a somewhat sardonic smile, until Madame Sarah Grand directly challenged his opinion.

" Of course," he said, " I hold that a writer should be free to state frankly his views of life, and to depict his characters as undergoing experiences of life that would naturally follow certain conditions and happenings. I can sympathize with you in what you went through," adding with a smile : " I know it all ; I have been through the mill myself with *Tess*."

At lunch, Hardy's conversation ranged over a variety of

M

subjects, and the brilliant woman who took part in it contributed not a little to the gaiety and alternating serious-ness of the conversation.

We remember that Hardy expressed very decided views upon the " spinelessness " of the drama of the day, as presented by the usual type of actor-manager, and de-plored that in (then) recent times the stage, in his opinion, had declined both in artistry and importance.

He stated, if our memory serves, that he had tired of fiction as a means of literary expression, and had definitely decided that he would write no more novels. This in reply to Madame Sarah Grand's suggestion regarding the possibility of another novel from his pen.

Gradually the conversation drifted on to the more philo-sophical aspects of life generally. Then a remark of Mrs. Hardy's caused her husband to give expression to some very unorthodox views upon conventional Christianity and his abhorrence of religious pretensions which had no counter-part in the actual lives of the persons making them.

We could see that Mrs. Hardy, who was in many ways a delightful and interesting personality, was being shocked, no doubt owing to her early clerical upbringing and association with regularized religion, while an inmate of her brother-in-law's rectory at St. Juliot, Cornwall, and the fact that she was an archdeacon's niece. Madame Sarah Grand was, we think, amused by Mrs. Hardy's efforts to neutralize any unfavourable impression that might have been created by her husband's expression of unorthodox opinions.

In the end Hardy himself appeared bored by the trend of the conversation into the " safer " channels that Mrs. Hardy had steered it, and we all adjourned to the garden with the especial view of inspecting the Druidical stone and seeing the famous cats.

Hardy in conversation told us that just then he was interested most in going through some old manuscripts, seeing, as he put it, if there was anything worth saving. He told Madame Sarah Grand, too, that although he had a horror of making photographic portraits in print, and often blended the characteristics of several people he had met to make a composite whole, he had a great belief in the value of notes made of striking incidents or characteristics of people at the time or as soon after as possible that these things were observed.

We left soon after an early cup of tea, and returned to Bournemouth.

Next morning the present writer received—as he did on several other occasions—a note from Mrs. Hardy, stating that she hoped that neither he nor her visitor would regard what her husband said on religious matters as serious, adding the information that he regularly read his Greek Testament. She also gave several facts about Hardy " in case you might want to write something about him," which were, however, of no real or public interest.

Needless to say they were never used.

During the later half of the same year Hardy was more or less at work definitely shaping the first portion of *The Dynasts*, although he was away from Dorchester, at Bath and other places from time to time.

It is interesting to note Hardy's opinion on such a subject as capital punishment, which has always been more or less a burning question at all events since the days when certain humanitarians first opened up the question of the need for its abolition.

A correspondent in America, who was engaged in preparing a report on the subject for the Department of Economics of a Californian university, drew from Hardy the following opinion on the advisability of abolishing the death penalty : " As an acting magistrate, I think that capital punishment operates as a deterrent from deliberate crimes against life to an extent that no other form of punishment can rival. But the question of a moral right of community to inflict that punishment is one that I cannot enter into in this necessarily brief communication."

With reference to this subject one may record an experience of Hardy's when a boy. A woman was tried at Dorchester Assizes for the murder of her husband, who, it would appear from the evidence, was a dissipated rascal.

She knew him also to be unfaithful, and finding him with her rival fatally stabbed him.

She was convicted and sentenced to death. Young Hardy and a companion, having heard of this public event, walked into Dorchester, climbed up into a tree near the gaol, and saw the execution.

The two boys seem to scarcely have realized the tragic incident of which they were witnesses, and it was not, the story goes, until the drop fell with a thud, and his companion on another branch of the tree fell fainting to the ground, that young Hardy was at last brought to a complete realization of the horror of the scene that he had witnessed.

The event probably haunted the imagination of the future novelist for many a long day, and it may have proved the germ of much of the tragedy of the latter part of *Tess of the D'Urbervilles*. It will be remembered that she too murdered her victim by stabbing.

Although Hardy was a Justice of the Peace, it does not appear that he made very regular attendances on the bench ; but he was, one gathers from newspaper reports, not infrequently summoned at Grand Juries at the Assizes where he doubtless met occasionally with cases involving the death penalty.

One can imagine the interest of the Judges when his name was called, and the " dapper " figure of the famous novelist stepped into the jury box.

In the middle of the year he was able to complete the first portion of *The Dynasts*, and sent the manuscript off to Messrs. Macmillan towards the end of September.

Once more, it appears, Hardy had met with a rebuff when offering a masterpiece (his poem) "A Trampwoman's Tragedy" to an English publication, for it is recorded that before offering it to the editor of the *North American Review*, in which it appeared in November, it was offered to the *Cornhill* magazine, whose editor declined it on the grounds that it was not fit for a publication going into the family.

The close of this year was memorable for the publication of the first portion of *The Dynasts*.

Another notable event was the erection in Stinsford Church, the locale of *The Mellstock Quire*, of a brass tablet, with an inscription in Latin, to the memory of his grandfather, father and uncle, commemorating their connection in the early part of the 19th century with the musical portion of the services of that church. The gallery in which the two generations of Hardys had been wont to perform on various instruments had been long ago removed.

Amazing, indeed, to those who knew him was the diligence with which Hardy sought for information likely to be of service in the writing of his great drama and the skill and perseverance with which he tracked down all references and incidents likely to add either to the importance or accuracy of his work.

Unfortunately the first part of *The Dynasts* met with an unfavourable reception at the hands of the critics, many of whom were quite incapable of adequate or intelligent criticism of such an unusual work. Indeed, to some critics, as well as to many other people, it presented considerable difficulties, arising from its philosophic basis, and as a consequence there was not a great demand for the book. Those, however, who were fortunate enough to obtain copies of the first edition, and have retained them, are probably congratulating themselves on their greatly enhanced value.

Hardy seems to have had at the back of his mind, and, indeed, he once mentioned it to the present writer, long prior to its publication, a doubt as to whether the great work upon which he was then engaged would be understood or accepted ; a doubt as to whether it would not be held to run counter to established philosophies and notions, and he even feared that *The Dynasts*, when published, might prove a stumbling-block to his acceptance as a poet.

There were, however, not a few of his literary friends who recognized the merit of his book, and no doubt the pleasure that they expressed did much to soften the attack made upon it by the critics. It was not Hardy's original intention to publish the book until it was completed, but he appears to have sent off Part I to the publishers after turning over the whole matter in his mind.

Strangely enough the criticism that it created seems only to have determined him the more strongly to complete a work which, when he had finished the first part, he had almost decided he would never be able to finish.

Hardy suffered a great blow in the loss of his mother, who died after only a few days' illness on Easter Sunday, April 3rd, 1904. She lies buried at Stinsford in the family grave. Those who met her recognized in her not only a woman of great charm and of very considerable knowledge, but one having an extraordinary memory for the things that had happened not only in Hardy's youth, but going back to her own. She possessed, moreover, an excellent taste in literature, which may have been gathered from what has already been said regarding the books that she influenced Hardy to read in his childhood and boyhood.

We have more than once drawn attention to the love of animals that Hardy undoubtedly possessed and his hatred of any suffering being unnecessarily inflicted upon them. A correspondent about this time wrote to him regarding his views upon sport—probably we think what have become known as " blood " sports. In his reply Hardy made it quite clear that he did not approve of any kind of hunting or sport which, in pursuit of it, inflicted suffering or death upon dumb creatures, and he also said that he thought that the then devotion to sports of this kind was convincing evidence that as a nation we had not yet emerged from barbarism. He even suggested, and this is truly a Hardyesque touch, that he saw no logical reason " why the smaller children, say of overcrowded families, should not be used for sporting purposes," and added that Darwin himself had shown that to do so would involve no difference in principle, and that probably the children would by this means often escape lives which would have proved to be less happy than those of wild birds and other animals !

He was in London during the spring for a time, returning to Dorchester after the close of the Season. One cannot, however, trace that he published very much during this year.

In the early part of 1905 Hardy sent a poem called " A Noble Lady's Tale" to the Editor of the *Cornhill* magazine, which was printed, occupying a page, in the number for March.

In April of this year a well-deserved honour was offered to Hardy by the University of Aberdeen, which seat of learning wished to confer upon him its honorary LL.D. degree. Hardy in accepting this remarked that he had never visited that part of Scotland, but had always possessed an admiration for the excellent work and services rendered by that northern University. In April Hardy set out from Dorchester to travel via London to Aberdeen, which lay some six hundred and fifty miles distant from Dorchester. Part of the journey was, we are told, very wintry, with snow, but Hardy reached the " Granite City " comfortably, and found a good many visitors from London who were present in Aberdeen in connection with the opening of the then new Gallery for Sculpture.

He was the guest of Principal and Mrs. Marshall Lang at the Chanonry Lodge. Several distinguished men of science received degrees at the same time, and Hardy next day, after being present at the opening of the Gallery, dined with the Corporation at the Town Hall.

The following day (Sunday) Hardy paid visits to several places in and in the neighbourhood of Aberdeen which had literary associations, and during his visit to the northern city made several friendships which endured as long as he lived.

CHAPTER VIII

I T WAS in this year that the Hardys again visited London, and he not only went out a good deal, visiting and meeting old friends at people's houses and at the Athenæum Club, but it is recorded that he met Sir Henry Irving at the Garrick Club, and that not unnaturally, perhaps, his conversation with the famous actor was concerned with Shakespeare. Hardy afterwards expressed an opinion that actors were incapable of seeing the play in which they were appearing, as a whole, but only so far as concerned the particular character they themselves were portraying.

In June of this year he went to see an exhibition of " Wessex " water-colours at the Leicester Galleries by the well-known artist, Walter Tyndale, which pictures had been commissioned by Messrs. A. & C. Black to illustrate the book upon " Wessex " of the present writer, in which Hardy had been much interested, and upon the writing of which he had made valuable suggestions. Hardy, too, had been of assistance to the artist in suggesting subjects for the pictures, which were many of them definitely connected with scenes in his various novels and poems.

In July when Hardy was back again in Dorset there was a most interesting exhibition in Dorchester comprising relics connected with Nelson's Hardy, who had been born and lived near the town and indeed belonged to a branch of the Dorset Hardys.

Early in September a large number of members of the Institute of Journalists visited Hardy at Max Gate after a driving tour similar in character to that which had been made by members of "The Whitefriars Club" four years previously. The members of the party were entertained on the lawn to tea in a large marquee, which had been erected for the purpose in case the weather should prove unkind. Whereas the "Whitefriars" had journeyed from Wool to Dorchester, the Institute of Journalists party had reversed the process and returned to London from Wool by way of Bockhampton, Puddletown, Bere Regis and across "Egdon" Heath.

It is recorded that notwithstanding his visitors on this occasion were journalists, Hardy made it a condition, before agreeing to receive the party at Max Gate, that no interviews or detailed report of the visit should be printed, and this restriction was observed to the letter.

It was Hardy's distaste for interviewing—and one might almost say horror of interviewers—that served to make him so remote a figure of the literary world in which he lived. Even in the days when interviewing, almost unknown in his early life, had become so popular, Hardy was very seldom interviewed, and on the one or two occasions on which his kindness of heart induced him to chat with callers about whom he knew very little, the interviews or articles which appeared were often not only inaccurate but very distasteful to him.

Hardy paid a visit in the middle of September to his friend Edward Clodd, at Aldeburgh, Suffolk, to attend the one hundred and fiftieth anniversary of the birth of George Crabbe, which was celebrated on the 16th, a poet who, perhaps, more than any other in his love for the poor and genius for describing Nature, possessed characteristics common to Hardy himself. On returning to Dorchester he set to work to finish the second part of *The Dynasts*, and sent off the manuscript to his publishers towards the end of October.

In the autumn of this year Hardy was approached by a correspondent as to his connection with the branch of the Hardys to which Nelson's Admiral, Sir Thomas Masterman Hardy, had belonged. He said in a letter dated November 5th, 1905 : "All I know about my family history is that it is indubitably one of the several branches of the Dorset Hardys—having been hereabouts for centuries. But when or how it was connected with the branch to which Nelson's Hardy's people belonged—who have also been hereabouts for centuries—I cannot positively say."

Hardy goes on in this letter to mention that locally the branches were traditionally connected; also made a note of the interesting fact that members of them bore a strong family likeness.

In connection with Hardy's declining—we believe on several occasions—the honour of a knighthood or baronetcy which succeeding Governments wished to bestow upon him in acknowledgment of his services to English literature, it is interesting to note what he himself says about such honours and the reason that no doubt actuated him in his refusals. "I have always thought that any writer who has expressed unpalatable or possibly subversive views on society, religious dogma, current morals, and any other features of the existing order of things, and who wishes to be free to express more if they occur to him, must feel hampered by accepting honours from any government."

At the end of the year he received a letter from a correspondent as far afield as the Philippine Islands, in the China Sea, who, among other things, told him that he was like some terrible old prophet crying in the wilderness, an opinion of Hardy which had doubtless arisen from a reading of *The Dynasts*, and possibly by an intellectual appreciation of the real lessons to be learned from the two novels *Tess of the D'Urbervilles* and *Jude the Obscure*, which had aroused most hostility in conventionally-minded people.

The second part of *The Dynasts* was published in the first week of February, 1906, and met with a much more favourable reception from the reviewers and from the public than its preceding instalment.

The Hardys visited London as usual this year, and were again at a flat in Hyde Park Mansions, where they had been a year before. Their life seems to have consisted of the usual routine of visits to various entertainments, receptions,

Marnhull
(The Crown)

Hough Snowdon

"Marlott"

the Academy, to friends and the receiving of visits from the latter.

From a letter of Hardy's published in *The Times* on May 21st, 1906, dated from Hyde Park Mansions on the anniversary of the birth of John Stuart Mill, we quote the following as describing an interesting incident of Hardy's own life in London when a young man. He wrote : " It was a day in (early in January) 1865, about three in the afternoon during Mill's candidature for Westminster. The hustings had been erected in Covent Garden near the front of St. Paul's Church, and when I—a young man living in London—drew near to the spot, Mill was speaking. The appearance of the author of a treatise 'On Liberty' (which we students of that date knew almost by heart) was so different from the look of persons who usually addressed crowds in the open air that it held the attention of people for whom such a gathering in itself had little interest. Yet it was, primarily, that of a man out of place. The religious sincerity of his speech was jarred on by his environment— a group on the hustings who, with few exceptions, did not care to understand him fully, and a crowd below who could not. He stood bareheaded, and his vast pale brow, so thin-skinned as to show the blue veins, sloped back like a stretching upland, and conveyed to the observer a curious sense of perilous exposure." Then follows a really Hardyesque thumb-nail sketch of the speaker : " The picture of him as personified earnestness surrounded for the most part by careless curiosity derived an added piquancy —if it can be called such—from the fact that the cameo clearness of his face chanced to be in relief against the blue shadow of a church which, on its transcendental side, his doctrines antagonized."

It was during the summer that Hardy gave several sittings to a well-known French portrait painter, Monsieur Jacques Blanche, then resident in London, for his portrait in oils.

About this time the annual meeting of the Society for the Protection of Ancient Buildings, which had always enjoyed Hardy's support and interest, took place, and a paper

which he had written was read in his absence by Colonel
Eustace Balfour.   Not only was it a valuable paper in many
respects for its advocacy of the careful preservation of
ancient buildings and monuments, but Hardy had in it laid
special stress on the value he attached to the human associations of these things, and this point of view was warmly
supported by several of the speakers.

Hardy was now busily engaged in collating his materials
already gathered and obtaining other details for the concluding part of *The Dynasts*, and worked a good deal, as
was his custom, in the British Museum library.

It was in July that he received from Mr. Carnegie, the
American millionaire philanthropist, and the Trustees of
the Pittsburg Institute an invitation, which included Mrs.
Hardy, for him to attend the dedication of the Institute.
He, however, felt unable to undertake the long journey to
the United States.

In the January number of the *Fortnightly Review*, 1907,
there appeared a poem, which was afterwards reprinted
in *Time's Laughing Stocks and Other Verses*, and about this
time Hardy seems to have contemplated an article em-
bodying his views upon the religious situation and ten-
dencies of the times.   Some notes that he made for this
article are interesting.   Here are one or two quotations.
He says: " When we enter church and have to say ' We
have erred and strayed from Thy ways like lost sheep '
what we really wish to say is : ' Why are we made to err and
stray like lost sheep ? '   Then we have to sing ' My soul
doth magnify the Lord,' when what we want to sing is :
' Oh ! that my soul could find some Lord that it could
magnify.' "   He goes on to say in these notes : " Till it
can, let us magnify good works and develop all means of
easing mortals' progress through a world not worthy of
them."

Hardy also expresses the view that religious religion
should consist of inspired feelings towards humanity and
emotional goodness and greatness, and that the days of
creeds are dead and done with, and that the old meaning
of the word ritual is either nearly or actually abolished.

Mrs. Hardy, it is interesting to note, was connected locally and nationally with the Suffragist Movement, though we were always astonished that this should have been so. It may, indeed, have been a gesture of self-expression against her being overshadowed by her distinguished husband. On February 8th she went to London to walk in a procession, of which there is a note in *The Times* of the day following. (Although those who knew her would scarcely have credited her with militancy.)

The eve of Good Friday of this year, almost approaching midnight, saw Hardy finishing his draft of Part III of *The Dynasts*. It is not likely, seeing the hostility with which the first portion of this monumental work had been greeted, and the coldness, generally speaking, of the reception of Part II, that Hardy had any great hopes of appreciation from the critics for the conclusion of the work, and he makes a note on critics in which he accuses them of being unable to understand that sometimes failure may actually be greater than success.

What he evidently means, and the idea he expressed more than once to us, was that a splendid failure, when the aim has been a high one, is infinitely more satisfactory to the real artist than a success won when he has aimed less high.

During this visit to London, where they were at Hyde Park Mansions again, they had the usual round of calls to pay and receive, and among those who came to see them were Mr. and Mrs. Bernard Shaw ; the Russian novelist Maxim Gorky, the author of *The Outcasts* and *The Orloff Couple*, novels which had attracted much attention, and his wife ; H. G. Wells ; and Richard Whiteing.

Towards the end of September they were back in Dorset following their usual occupations, and he finished off the final copy of the third part of *The Dynasts* and sent the manuscript to the publishers. The publication of the third and concluding part of *The Dynasts* took place at the end of the year, and rather to Hardy's surprise, one imagines, he received a number of congratulatory and enthusiastic letters from friends and strangers, and later was cheered by the more favourable reception accorded the book by the Press.

At the annual general meeting of the Society of Dorset Men in London held at the Holborn Restaurant on November 15th, on the proposition of the Chairman of the Society, Mr. J. C. Swinburne-Hanham, J.P., the great novelist-poet was elected as president in succession to Sir Frederick Treves, Bart., G.C.V.O., C.B., LL.D., who had been elected the first president and had served in that capacity from 1904, when the Society was founded, until 1907.

Hardy wrote an address to be read by a deputy as he was unable, owing to ill health, to be present at the meeting. This was published in the 1908-9 Year Book of the Society, and the original manuscript is a treasured possession in the archives.

A very interesting note of Hardy's in this presidential address is that relating to the changes in the social life of the metropolis since he had lived there as a young man. He said : " No more curious change has come over London social life of late years than the rise of that almost total disregard of provincialism among its constituents and casual sharers which nowadays pervades the City. Incomers are allowed to preserve personal peculiarities that they formerly were compelled to stifle, if they wished to be accepted. A hundred or even fifty years ago the object of every sojourner in the metropolis from the west —as from east, south and north—was to obliterate his local colour, and merge himself in the type Londoner as quickly as possible. But now Town society has become a huge menagerie, and at what are called the best houses visitors hear with no surprise twangs and burrs and idioms from every point of the compass. . . . In former times an unfamiliar accent was immediately noted as quaint and odd, even a feature of ridicule in novels, memoirs, and conversations of the date. So that while it was the aim of every provincial, from the squire to the rustic, to get rid of his local articulation at the earliest possible moment, he now seems rather to pride himself on retaining it, being, in fact, virtually encouraged to do so.

"Even dialect words are respected. Within my own recollection it was, for instance, thought comical in London to hear a West of England man speak of the autumn as ' the fall.' But now that the American multi-millionaire also speaks of the autumn as ' the fall,' the expression is voted poetical—which, indeed, it is."

The address dealt with a number of topics, not the least interesting of these being the fact that Dorset men in London would find many familiar names confronting them at street corners, in squares and other places in the names given to these. For examples: "Dorset" Square, "Bryanston" Square, "Portland" Place, "Bindon" Road, and "Cranbourne" Street.

It is interesting to know that although the motto of the Society in its present form "Who's A-Fear'd?" was proposed by the editor of the Society's Year Book, Mr. Stanley I. Galpin, it originated in a letter from Hardy himself in which he wrote: "It is a sign of the times that modest little Dorset should at last have the courage to stand up to great London and say: ' Who's afraid?'"

It was in the following year that he seriously set to work on a book which he had been asked to prepare for the Clarendon Press, Oxford, comprising selections from the poems in the Dorset dialect of his friend the Rev. William Barnes, who had been vicar of Winterborne Came. He wrote a critical preface, and also provided a glossary for the enlightenment of those, other than Dorset folk, who might read the poems.

In April of this year the local Dramatic Society, which was in after years identified with the production of several dramatized versions of Hardy's novels, and attained considerable fame on account of the ability of its members, presented some scenes from *The Dynasts*, which was not, of course, a drama ever intended to be presented as a stage play.

For the first time for many years the Hardys did not take up any definite quarters in London for their usual annual visit, and indeed only paid short visits this year to Town, staying in hotels.

In July the first Lord Curzon of Kedleston unveiled a memorial to Mrs. Pearl Mary Teresa Craigie, the writer best known under the pseudonym of "John Oliver Hobbes," at University College. Hardy was present, and an amusing incident was afforded when one of the speakers attacked his, Hardy's, writings in comparison with those of Mrs. Craigie, not knowing that he was there. One can well imagine his sardonic amusement.

During this short visit to London the portrait Sir Hubert Herkomer painted of Hardy and presented to him, which was considered to be an excellent likeness, was finished.

He went on to Cambridge to the tercentenary celebrations of Milton's birth, and met among others, Sir James Murray, the great lexicographer and editor of the great English Dictionary, with which, as a boy at school, the present writer used to assist by collecting the slips of quotations prepared by some of the army of assistants who acted as readers for Murray in the village.

The autumn of this year was filled in by visits to cathedrals and to Swanage, where his sister had gone on account of her health. From now onwards Hardy's life—he was approaching sixty-nine years of age—was a very quiet and comparatively uneventful one, although it is true that one or two happenings of great importance to him took place in the succeeding years.

Early in 1909 Hardy had the honour paid him of being appointed a Representative Governor of the Dorchester Grammar School, which had been founded by a namesake, who died in 1599, and who is thought to have been of the same branch of the family as the great novelist himself. He remained a Governor till within a year or two of his death.

In the following months Hardy was destined to lose two friends whom he valued, outstanding figures in the poetry and fiction of the Victorian era: Swinburne, who died on April 10th; and a month later while in London, walking

N

down Dover Street on May 18th to visit the Academy, Hardy saw the announcement of the death of George Meredith on a newspaper placard.

He was very much grieved, and went into his club, the Athenæum, in Waterloo Place, and wrote some memorial verses. He attended the service on the 22nd held in Westminster Abbey. There were also present several of Hardy's friends and acquaintances, including the novelists Maurice Hewlett and Henry James, Alfred Austin, who at that time was Poet Laureate, and Max Beerbohm, the artist and essayist. On this day the poem that he had written on his friend was published in the columns of *The Times*, under the title of " G.M. 1828–1909," and was afterwards reprinted.

Meredith at the time of his death was the President of the Society of Authors, and Hardy received early in June a letter from Maurice Hewlett, asking him to permit his nomination as Meredith's successor. In declining this honour, Hardy's reply set forth the chief reasons for that decision, though he expressed himself as highly honoured and touched by the wish of the Council that he should become President. The principal reason was a very unselfish one, namely, that Hardy thought it was essential that the Society should have a President capable of taking an active part in its meetings and work, and also one who, by living in or near London, would be available for these duties and other purposes. His decision was ultimately overcome by great pressure exercised by the Council, and his refusal was withdrawn and he became President.

An event of great importance to Hardy and one in which he was very interested was the preparation by Baron F. D'Erlanger of an opera founded upon *Tess*. This was produced at Covent Garden on July 14th, and naturally Hardy and Mrs. Hardy were present. Among the distinguished audience, in a crowded house, was Queen Alexandra, and the opera was received with great enthusiasm. It was somewhat difficult, however—indeed Hardy himself found it so—for anyone who saw Baron

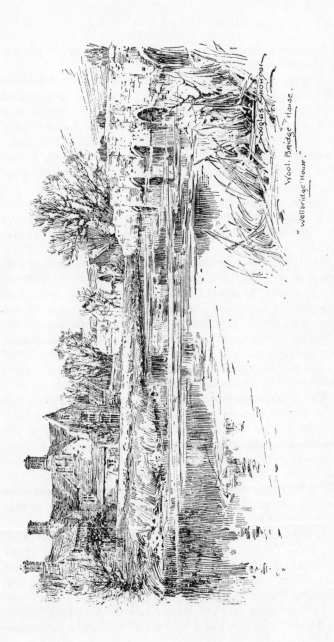

"Wellbridge House."

Wool Bridge House.

Douglas Snowdon.

d'Erlanger's version of *Tess* to recognize its origin as that of Hardy's novel.

It was at the end of autumn of this year that he had succeeded in gathering together from various sources and from boxes of manuscripts sufficient poems written, and some of them already published in periodicals, from 1865 onwards for issue in the volume he called *Time's Laughing Stocks and Other Verses*, which consisted of fifteen poems that had already seen the light of print, and seventy-nine other pieces.

In the autumn he paid visits to places as far apart as Chichester, York and Durham to see the cathedrals, and went on to Edinburgh, a city which he much admired and liked.

The Dorchester Debating and Dramatic Society, which was a strong one, and contained a considerable number of members of real talent, had meanwhile put into rehearsal a dramatic version, prepared by one of the members, Mr. A. H. Evans, of *Far from the Madding Crowd*. The play was performed as usual in the Corn Exchange, and the success was such that the whole company journeyed to Town a few days later, and gave a performance before the Society of Dorset Men in London.

The local performances always afforded both Hardy and Mrs. Hardy pleasure, and on occasion Mrs. Hardy was present at the tea, or other refreshments, served to the players after the performances.

It will be remembered that as long ago as 1882 a version had been prepared by an author and journalist, J. W. Comyns Carr, and Hardy's own opinion was that the version prepared by the local author was superior to that we have just mentioned.

It was a custom of Hardy's, he once told us, always to see the New Year in, and on this occasion he did so under unfortunate circumstances, as he had returned from a visit to London suffering from a cold and sore throat, and was for some time obliged to remain in bed.

In the spring of 1910 Hardy was in the Isle of Wight, and went to Ventnor and paid a visit to Swinburne's grave in the picturesque little churchyard at Bonchurch. Hardy's friendship with Swinburne was not merely one of a conventional kind because they happened both to be poets, but arose from a real admiration for his brother poet's gifts, and as a result of the visit he wrote a tender poem : " The Singer Asleep."

For some time, indeed, from when Hardy was sixty years onwards, many friends and people, including several well-known publishing firms, had urged him to set to work and write his memoirs or reminiscences. Hardy, however, had always declined any suggestion of the kind ; indeed, had written to several correspondents saying not only was he unwilling to undertake the work, but that it was unlikely that he would ever change his decision not to write anything of this nature.

However, in the early part of 1910 Hardy was again approached, this time by the editor of *Harper's Magazine*, with a view to the publication of his memoirs in his pages. Hardy again wrote saying that what was suggested was impossible, although there was no magazine that he would consider more suitable in which such a work could appear.

In May the Hardys were again in Town and located at Blomfield Court, Maida Vale. One wonders whether the building was named after Hardy's former employer, Sir Arthur Blomfield.

It was on the third night of their arrival in Town that King Edward passed away, an event which Hardy recorded in his verses "A King's Soliloquy on the Night of His Funeral."

The next month Hardy was given the Order of Merit by King George, and the announcement appeared in the Birthday Honours List of June. It is possible, of course, that this distinction had been decided upon by King Edward, who is believed to have had an admiration for his distinguished subject.

Hundreds of letters and telegrams of congratulation upon this honour arrived at the flat and even more at Max Gate, not only from friends and persons connected with public bodies, but from entire strangers and from many quarters of the globe.

Unfortunately in June Hardy was taken ill, but the illness was not serious, and on July 19th he was able to go to Marlborough House to be invested with the Order of Merit.

Although approaching seventy years of age, he was still able to ride his bicycle, and during the summer of this year went to various places a-wheel.

It was in September that he sat to William Strang, R.A., for a sketch portrait, as it was the custom to hang those of all recipients of the Order of Merit in a gallery at Windsor Castle.

On November 16th of the same year the Corporation of Dorchester presented Hardy with the Freedom of his native town, and it is well known that this honour was one that he most deeply appreciated, not only because of the recognition of his work and distinction, which the authorities marked by this means, but from purely sentimental feelings.

The presentation took place in the Town Hall, and the Mayor, Mr. C. Francis Symes, in his speech referred to Hardy's lifelong association with Dorchester, his boyhood, his family, and the pride that the town and the municipal authorities felt in him, the fame that he had achieved, and in the great and, he believed, lasting place his works would occupy in English literature. After a speech in support by one of the Aldermen, Mr. E. W. Kerr, the Town Clerk, Mr. A. G. Symonds, read the Presentation Address, and the casket containing the scroll was handed to Mr. Hardy. In addition to members of the Corporation, among those present were Mrs. Hardy, Mr. Henry Hardy, and Miss Hardy.

After the conclusion of the Town Clerk's reading of the Address, Thomas Hardy, who made few public appearances during his life, and still fewer public utterances, addressed the assembly in the following interesting and happy speech :

He said : " Mr. Mayor and Gentlemen of the Corporation—This is an occasion that speaks for itself, and so, happily, does not demand many remarks from me. In simply expressing my sincere thanks for the high compliment paid me by having my name enrolled with those of the Honorary Freemen of this historic town, I may be allowed to confess that the Freedom of the Borough of Dorchester did seem to me at first something that I had possessed a long while, and had helped myself to (to speak plainly), for when I consider the liberties I have taken with its ancient walls, streets and precincts through the medium of the printing press, I feel that I have treated its external features with the hand of freedom indeed.   True, it might be urged that my Casterbridge (if I may mention seriously a name coined off-hand in a moment with no thought of its becoming established and localized) is not Dorchester— not even the Dorchester as it existed sixty years ago, but a dream-place that never was outside an irresponsible book.

" Nevertheless, when somebody said to me that ' Casterbridge ' is a sort of essence of the town as it used to be, ' a place more Dorchester than Dorchester itself,' I could not absolutely contradict him, though I could not quite perceive it.   At any rate, it is not a photograph in words, that inartistic species of literary produce, particularly in respect of personages.   But let me say no more about my own doings.   The chronicle of the town has vivid marks upon it.   Not to go back to events of national importance, lurid scenes have been enacted here within living memory, or not so many years beyond it, whippings in front of the town pump, hangings on the gaol roof.   I myself saw a woman hanged not 100 yards from where we now stand, and I saw, too, a man in the stocks in the back part of this very building.   Then, if one were to recount the election excitements, Free Trade riots, scenes of soldiers marching down the town to war, the proclamation of Sovereigns now crumbled to dust, it would be an interesting local story.

" Miss Burney, in her diary, speaks of its aspect when she drove through with the rest of King George's Court on her

way to Weymouth.   She says : ' The houses have the most
ancient appearance of any that are inhabited that I have
happened to see.'   This is not quite the case now, and
though we may regret the disappearance of these old
buildings, I cannot be blind to the difficulty of keeping a
town in what may be called working order while retaining
all its ancient features.   Yet it must not be forgotten that
these are the chief attractions for visitors, particularly
American visitors.   Old houses, in short, have a far larger
commercial value than their owners always remember, and
it is only when they have been destroyed, and tourists
who have come to see them vow in their disappointment that they will never visit the spot again, that this is
realized.

   " An American gentleman came to me the other day in
quite a bad temper, saying that he had diverged from his
direct route from London to Liverpool to see ancient
Dorchester, only to discover that he knew a hundred towns
in the United States more ancient looking than this !
Well," the speaker added with a smile, " we may be
older than we look, like some ladies—(laughter)—but if
for instance, the original All Saints and Trinity Churches
with their square towers, the castle, the fine mansion of
the Trenchards at the corner of Shirehall Lane, the old
Three Mariners' Inn, the old Greyhound, the old Antelope,
Lady Abingdon's house at the corner of Durngate Street,
and other medieval buildings were still standing, more
visitors of antiquarian tastes would probably haunt the
town than haunt it now.   Old All Saints was, I believe,
demolished because its buttresses projected too far into the
pavement.   What a reason for destroying a record of
500 years in stone !   I knew the architect who did it ; a
milder-mannered man never scuttled a sacred edifice.
Milton's well-known observation in his *Areopagitica*—' As
good almost to kill a man as kill a good book,' applies not a
little to a good old building ; which is not only a book but
a unique manuscript that has no fellow.   But Corporations,
as such, cannot help these removals ; they can only be
prevented by the education of their owners or temporary

trustees, or, in cases of churches, by Government guardianship."

Hardy then went on to refer to the days of his boyhood. He said : " Where is the Dorchester of my early recollections —I mean the human Dorchester—the kernel of which the houses were but the shell ?   Of the shops as I first recall them, not a single owner remains : only in two or three instances does even the name remain. . . . Here in Dorchester, as elsewhere, I see the streets and the turnings not far different from those of my schoolboy time ; but the faces that used to be seen at the doors, the inhabitants, where are they ?   I turn up the Weymouth Road, cross the railway bridge, enter an iron gate to a ' slope of green access,' and there they are ! There is the Dorchester that I knew best : there are the names on white stones, one after the other, names that recall the voices, cheerful and sad, anxious and indifferent, that are missing from the dwellings and pavements. Those who are old enough to have had that experience may feel that after all the permanence or otherwise of inanimate Dorchester concerns but the permanence of what is minor and accessory."

On the same evening a performance was given for the first time by the Dorchester Dramatic Society of an adaptation by their own dramatist of Hardy's novel *Under the Greenwood Tree*, to which had been given the title *The Mellstock Quire*, the sub-title of the novel. Hardy himself took some part in the preparation of this dramatic version in that he supplied the original carols, which had been sung in former days by the choir in Stinsford Church, which village appears, of course, in the novel as " Mellstock." Among those present at the performance was Henry J. Newbolt, the poet-author, who was knighted in 1915.

At the beginning of the next year Hardy was again contributing poems to the Press, and in April a group of verses, divided into twelve sections, called *Satires of Circumstance* appeared in the *Fortnightly Review*.

Hardy, during this year, went on several holidays with

his brother Henry, visiting some of the cathedrals, and in June was in the Lake District, where he spent Coronation Day at Windermere instead of at Westminster Abbey, to which he had been invited. While in the north Hardy wrote some verses, and with his indomitable love of acquiring knowledge, on his way back to Dorchester saw several cathedrals and visited and went over Rugby School.

In view of the present disquietude regarding the future of aerial warfare, it is interesting to note that as long ago as 1911, Hardy, in company with many other distinguished people, signed a protest against the use of airships and aeroplanes in war, and appealed to all governments " to foster by any means in their power an international understanding which shall preserve the world from warfare in the air." It will be remembered that two years previously Louis Blériot, the French pioneer airman, had flown the Channel for the first time in a monoplane, and that this, in those days, startling event had at least concentrated public attention upon the future possibilities of the aeroplane in warfare.

After Hardy returned to Dorchester, during the summer he was engaged in searching for his old manuscripts in consequence of a visit from Mr. Sydney C. Cockerell, M.A., director of the Fitzwilliam Museum, Cambridge, who came to Max Gate to enquire about them, hinting that they would be historically valuable, and accordingly that Hardy should, if possible, ascertain their whereabouts, and collect them together.

Ultimately, after considerable search, he found a number of them, which were handed over to Mr. Cockerell to distribute, as Hardy himself thought it would be invidious for him to undertake that work. Mr. Cockerell, having accepted the responsibility, in the autumn sent to the British Museum perhaps the two most important, *The Dynasts* (as representing Hardy's high-water mark in verse) and *Tess of the D'Urbervilles* (as representing his greatest work of fiction, or at least that assumed to be so by public popular consent). To the Fitzwilliam Museum at

Cambridge was given the manuscript of *Time's Laughing Stocks and Other Verses*, and *Jude the Obscure* ; and the most interesting volume of verse, *Wessex Poems*, which was the only volume he ever to any extent illustrated, went to Birmingham. Other manuscripts were given to various public libraries from that time onward, till all the manuscripts that Hardy had then been able to recover or find were distributed.

In October of this year the Debating and Dramatic Society in Dorchester gave another of their performances of plays having their origin in Hardy's works. Among those performed was the one-act play he had himself dramatized eighteen years before, which had been produced at Terry's Theatre, from the story called *The Three Strangers*, which as a play, it will be remembered, was called *The Three Wayfarers*, and a dramatic version, prepared by Mr. A. H. Evans, of the tale *The Distracted Preacher*.

Not unnaturally there was a desire that Dorchester should possess at least some of the manuscripts of its famous townsman, and towards the end of 1911 Hardy sent the original manuscript of *The Mayor of Casterbridge* to the curator of the Dorset County Museum.

Though over seventy years of age, Hardy was still keenly interested in architecture, especially that branch of the Gothic represented by the Perpendicular of the 15th century, and most purely English, and to enable him to study it he went to Gloucester. The result of this visit is chiefly interesting from the fact that Hardy's discoveries regarding this particular type of architecture in Gloucester suggested to his mind a poem called "The Abbey Mason," and records the fact that the originator remains unknown. This poem appeared later in *Harper's Magazine*.

One of the greatest shipping disasters the world has ever known occurred with the loss of the *Titanic* on April 15th, 1912, on her maiden voyage to New York, after collision with a sunken iceberg, and Hardy, to assist a fund which had been opened for the relief of the sufferers, wrote a poem called "The Convergence of the Twain." Several of the novelist's friends, including W. T. Stead, formerly editor of the *Pall Mall Gazette*, and founder of the *Review of Reviews*, were lost with the vessel.

A little later in the year Hardy was busily engaged in correcting proofs for the fine, large-type "Wessex" edition of his works, in many cases making alterations and revisions. It is interesting to his admirers to note that in a letter to a correspondent, he says : " I got to like the character of Clym (Yeobright in *The Return of the Native*) before I had done with him. I think he is the nicest of my heroes, and *not a bit* like me. On taking up *The Woodlanders*, and reading it after many years, I think I like it as a story the best of all. Perhaps that is owing to the locality and scenery of the action, a part I am fond of. It seems a more quaint and fresh story than *The Native*, and the characters are very distinctly drawn."

The Hardys were again in London this season, staying at the West Central Hotel in Southampton Row, which they had on several occasions patronized. On June 1st, Hardy's seventy-second birthday, the two poets, Henry Newbolt and W. B. Yeats, as representatives of the Royal Society of Literature, came down to Max Gate to present Hardy with the Society's gold medal. He, in a note, pays a tribute to Newbolt's well-known facility for speech-making by saying he " wasted on a nearly empty room the best speech he ever made in his life, and Yeats wasted a very good one," adding modestly : " Mine in returning thanks was as usual a bad one."

It is very interesting, because of what happened more than twenty years later in regard to Hardy himself, to know in the autumn of this year a letter was addressed to him, protesting against the publication (not by him, of course) of details of a lately deceased person's life in the pages of a novel.

Hardy replied that the thing that should certainly be protested against was " the mixing of fact and fiction in unknown proportions," because, he added, " unbounded mischief would lie in that. If any statements in the dress of fiction are covertly hinted to be fact all must be fact and nothing less but fact for obvious reasons. The power of

getting lies believed about people through that channel "
(the publication of details of their lives in a work of fiction)
" after they are dead by stirring in a few truths, is a horror
to contemplate."

Only a year or two ago a work of fiction was published
by a popular author which was stated—and by some supposed—to be founded on Hardy's life, or at least upon some
incidents connected with it, and the supposition that fact
had been blended with fiction in this particular story was
blazoned in the newspapers, and at least directed a great
deal of attention to the novel in question.

Readers who had any acquaintance with Hardy or
Hardy's life, of course, knew that the claim that had been
advanced was entirely apocryphal, and his friends were
naturally indignant at the suggestion. But there is little
doubt that two things resulted from the ridiculous story
which had been set about, namely an increased sale for
the book—which may even have been the object of the
rumour—and pain caused not only to Hardy's surviving
relatives, and friends who knew him, but also to literary
people generally.

It was in autumn of this year that Mrs. Hardy, who
had not been in good health for some time from heart
trouble, fell ill ; and on November 25th, when two callers
visited Max Gate, though advised not to go downstairs to
see them, she did so, and was obliged to go to bed immediately they had left. It proved to be the last occasion
on which she was downstairs. The next day she saw a
doctor, who apparently did not think very seriously of his
patient's condition, but on the following day early in the
morning, although her maid reported to Hardy her mistress had expressed herself as feeling better and would get
up later, he found on going to her room that she was
unconscious, and before the doctor, who was immediately summoned, could reach the house she had
passed away.

On the previous afternoon, not for a moment thinking
that Mrs. Hardy was seriously ill, Hardy had, at her desire,
attended a rehearsal of a version of *The Trumpet Major*,

prepared for performance by the local Debating and Dramatic Society.

Naturally the death of Mrs. Hardy caused a great stir in the town and, indeed, a widespread regret.

She was buried in Stinsford Churchyard, a mile or so distant, where the Hardys had a family grave. Possibly, but for the distance, she might have reposed in the grave-yard of the church of St. Juliot, Cornwall, of which her brother-in-law was for many years the incumbent.

Her death was a heavy blow to her husband, who at that time had passed the age of seventy ; but at the end of the year he wrote quite a number of verses, and, in fact, seemed to find consolation and distraction in what might almost be called strenuous literary work.

CHAPTER IX

EARLY IN March, almost on the very anniversary of the day on which, forty years earlier, he had visited St. Juliot for the first time to superintend the restoration of the church, he set out for Cornwall, making his headquarters at Boscastle, and visiting several places which had become familiar to him during the time he was engaged on his architectural work, and afterwards in visiting at the rectory to see his future wife. It was during his stay that he arranged for the erection of a memorial tablet to Mrs. Hardy in the church where, when he first knew her, she was acting as organist, and was also engaged in much parish work. He personally designed both this tablet and the tomb in Stinsford Churchyard.

The following is the inscription which was placed on the tablet at St. Juliot.

TO THE DEAR MEMORY OF EMMA LAVINIA HARDY, BORN GIFFORD, THE WIFE OF THOMAS HARDY, AUTHOR, AND SISTER-IN-LAW OF THE REV. C. HOLDER, FORMERLY INCUMBENT OF THIS PARISH : BEFORE HER MARRIAGE SHE LIVED AT THE RECTORY 1868–1873, CONDUCTED THE CHURCH MUSIC, AND LAID THE FIRST STONE OF THE RE-BUILT AISLE AND TOWER : SHE DIED AT DORCHESTER 1912, AND IS BURIED AT STINSFORD, DORSET. ERECTED BY HER HUSBAND 1913.

In the middle of the year a further distinction was conferred upon him by the University of Cambridge in the shape of the honorary degree of Litt.D. He went to Cambridge to receive the honour, and met a number of old friends and other distinguished people, spending a very interesting visit largely by reason of the fact that he had, during his long life, made many friends who were graduates or members of the university.

About this time Hardy gave permission to the authorities of the National Institute for the Blind to print some of his books in Braille type, and *The Mayor of Casterbridge, Tess of the D'Urbervilles, Far from the Madding Crowd, The Trumpet Major, Life's Little Ironies, Desperate Remedies, A Pair of Blue Eyes* and several other works, and *The Dynasts*, were ultimately issued as manuscript or stereotyped Braille volumes by the society, for the use of the blind.

In the autumn Hardy seems to have had a good deal of domestic worry, and, unfortunately, several of the late Mrs. Hardy's cats either died, or were lost, causing Hardy a great deal of regret, especially those which were lost and could not be traced, as one naturally could not know what had become of them or what suffering they might have undergone.

Hardy was again in Cambridge in November on the occasion of his being installed as an Honorary Fellow of Magdalene College, which had conferred upon him the Litt.D. degree.

From a report in the *Cambridge Review*, one learns that Hardy dined in the Hall in the evening, and his health was proposed by the Master, who charmingly referred to him as no longer a guest but one of themselves. The ceremony of admitting a Fellow takes place before the altar of the chapel, and the handing of the newly made Fellow into his stall is a ceremony not without picturesqueness and impressiveness.

It is the custom of Magdalene College to hang portraits of Fellows in its Hall, and for this purpose a sketch was commissioned by the late Master of the College, Dr. Arthur Christopher Benson, C.V.O., and made in the autumn by Mr. R. E. Fuller Maitland.

In February of the following year, 1914, at the age of

o

seventy-three, Hardy re-married, his bride being Miss
Florence Emily Dugdale, herself a contributor to various
papers and magazines, and author of books for children.
A step that he doubtless took because of his great loneliness, and the fact that with increasing years, like most
artists, he felt very keenly the need of care and sympathetic companionship.

The Hardys visited their friends in London in the spring,
and afterwards went to Cambridge, where they met
among other people the well-known Cornish writer, Sir
Arthur Quiller-Couch, who at that time had been Professor
of English Literature at the University for a couple of
years.

The Hardys did a good deal of motoring in the summer
of this year, which pleasure was, however, a few months
afterwards somewhat restricted by the outbreak of the
Great War.

Hardy, in common with most people, had very little idea
of the possibility, and, indeed, the imminence of war.   The
murder of the Archduke Francis Ferdinand of Austria and
his Archduchess at Sarajevo, on Sunday, June 28th, 1914,
shot by a Bosnian student named Prinzip after two previous
attempts with bombs had, earlier in the day, been made
upon their lives, was the signal which was to plunge Europe
into the greatest war of history.

Just a month afterwards the Hardys were visiting friends
at Ilsington, near Dorchester, when war was declared by
Austria on Serbia, and proved to be " the match in the
powder barrel of Europe." A few days later they were
lunching at Athelhampton Hall with their friends, the
Martins, whose family had owned the place for generations,
when a telegram reached the party confirming the rumour
that had been prevalent all that day that England had
declared war with Germany.

Hardy from the first appears to have had no delusions
as to the brief duration of the War, prophesied by the
optimists.   Indeed, by some prescience, he foresaw a long
struggle and universal disaster.   Curiously enough Hardy
had some time before written a poem entitled " Channel

Firing," which had appeared in the *Fortnightly Review* in May.

Doubtless a study of the wars of the Napoleonic era and those of more recent years had served to incline him to the belief that wars had, to use his own expression, " declined in popularity," and he had, from time to time, written verses which bore out this belief. One which is very well known, named "His Country," provides evidence of this.

Much as he was shocked and amazed at the rude shattering of this theory, his still active mind, although he was nearly seventy-four, cast about to see whether there was any service that he was capable of rendering his country in its emergency.

A very short time afterwards, at the end of August, he was included in a group of eminent men and women of letters, whose names were specially well known abroad, who were invited by the then Chancellor of the Duchy of Lancaster, the Rt. Hon. Charles F. G. Masterman, to a conference in London, called for the purpose of considering the best way in which to place the facts of the British case, and the principles for which the Allies were fighting, before neutral countries.

The meeting was held at Wellington House, Buckingham Gate, and there were quite a number of Hardy's friends, including Sir James Barrie, Bart., Sir Henry Newbolt, Dr. Arthur Christopher Benson, C.V.O., Monsignor Benson, John Galsworthy, Arnold Bennett, John Masefield and Robert Bridges, LL.D., then Poet Laureate, and many others. The meeting was undoubtedly productive of considerable results, for very soon neutral countries were being informed in the way that had been decided upon after considerable discussion, in many cases by very graphic descriptions and logical arguments, written in various forms by the members of the conference, and others who were induced to place their literary services at the nation's disposal.

Hardy had returned to Dorchester after the conference the same evening, evidently very tired, but immediately gave consideration as to how he could best carry out the recommendations and suggestions of the conference. Very soon he was busily at work, writing in connection with the propaganda scheme and also a number of poems dealing with aspects of war. One of his best-known War poems was published in *The Times* on September 9th. It was called " Song of the Soldiers " and proved extraordinarily popular. It was afterwards called " Men who March Away." He also contributed to the famous *King Albert's Book*, published in aid of the Belgian refugees, a sonnet " On the Belgian Expatriation." In September, too, his volume of poems *Satires of Circumstance : Lyrics and Reveries, with miscellaneous Pieces*, was published.

In November, notwithstanding the stress of war, and social disturbances, Granville Barker decided to stage at the Kingsway Theatre a portion of *The Dynasts*, and the Hardys went to London for the rehearsal. The play was produced on November 25th, but the author was unable to be present owing to illness. Although the production was an artistic success, Hardy was in direct conflict with the method that Granville Barker had adopted, which, it will be remembered, included indoor architecture for outdoor scenes. No doubt these anomalies were largely unavoidable owing to the small stage.

As was perhaps only natural, when one considers Hardy's age at the time, the War undoubtedly destroyed his preconceptions that men had made considerable progress towards a nobler outlook upon life, and that in the coming years this process would be enhanced.

In April of the next year Hardy gave a sitting to the well-known sculptor, William Hamo Thornycroft, R.A. (afterwards knighted) for his head, given some years ago to the National Portrait Gallery by his widow, Lady Thornycroft ; and in the same month had the satisfaction of knowing that two short manuscript poems " The Night of Trafalgar " and " Men who March Away," which he had contributed to the Red Cross sale, had fetched under the hammer at Christie's no less a sum than £48 for the fund.

Douglas Snowport

Stonehenge

During May and June of this year, although Hardy and Mrs. Hardy did a considerable amount of motoring, and called on Eden Phillpotts at his charming Torquay home, very little seems to have disturbed the quietude of their lives.

Mrs. Hardy, about this time, and during the autumn, was almost continually at work at the soldiers' canteen which had been established in Dorchester Corn Exchange, and not infrequently Hardy himself went down to chat with the men, and doubtless to make mental notes.

Towards the close of November, Hardy had the great sorrow of losing his elder sister Mary, who was living at the time with her brother at Talbothays. This was the sister who had a decided gift for painting, and whose portrait of her mother was recognized as an admirable likeness. She had, however, for various reasons, never been able to develop this talent, or to pursue it other than as a hobby.

Unfortunately Hardy took cold at the funeral on November 29th, and was laid up for some considerable time with bronchitis, but in December he wrote and sent off to London facsimile paragraphs taken from *The Dynasts*, which he entitled "England at Bay" and "England Resolute," for exhibition in a pro-Ally film which it was intended to exhibit throughout the world. The extracts were to be of a nature likely to appeal and impress neutral nations.

In January, 1916, was published his verses, "The Dead and the Living One," in the *Sphere* and also the *New York World*.

In February of this year he again contributed to the Red Cross sale, sending on this occasion a bundle of letters, which he had received from many well-known people, of a very interesting nature, and the fund also benefited to a handsome extent by three short manuscripts of his, which Mrs. Hardy had forwarded, consisting of a fragment of a story, "The Oxen," and "The Breaking of Nations," the latter a poem, the subject of which, strangely enough, originated in Hardy's mind so long previously as the Franco-Prussian War of 1870, but had lain germinating there for forty-four years before gaining expression.

June of the same year saw Wessex scenes from *The Dynasts*, produced by the company which had become known as " The Hardy Players."   It was quite a different arrangement to that of Granville Barker, and contained only scenes of a local, and therefore rural, character.   The producers had acted wisely, and they certainly succeeded in conveying the disturbed and unrestful nature of the times and the great events which were taking place on the Continent in Napoleonic days, by the methods adopted.   This selection was afterwards performed in the Weymouth Pier Pavilion, and was well noticed in the London Press.

The summer appears to have been filled up chiefly with motoring excursions and quiet work at Max Gate, but in September the Hardys went to Cornwall, visiting Boscastle and St. Juliot, so that they might see if Hardy's design and inscription for the tablet in the church had been carried out correctly.

An interesting sidelight is thrown upon the statements made by the German authorities to the soldiers, by Hardy's discovery when visiting the hospital, and the German prisoners' camp at Dorchester, that the men had been told that the British were fighting to destroy Germany.   This statement he combated by telling them that what we were fighting for was to save all that was best in Germany.   He was evidently greatly impressed by the knowledge that Germans and British, only separated by a few hundred yards, were lying in the hospital suffering and dying because of the actions of their rulers.

Performances of Wessex scenes from *The Dynasts* were given in aid of the Red Cross Fund at Dorchester in October, and several of Hardy's friends came down for the performance, among whom was Sir James Barrie.

About this period Hardy began, perhaps for the first time, to feel or realize his age, and sought to obtain relief and more rest by resigning from several societies with which he was connected.

In March a stirring sonnet of his was published in the newspapers entitled " Call to National Service." A sympathetic review by the well-known critic, Mr. W. L. Courtney, in the April *Fortnightly Review* of this year, dealing generally with Hardy's writings, and especially with reference to *The Dynasts*, by reason of its final conclusions aroused Hardy's dissent, for the writer of the article seemed to be advocating the belief of a God of Mercy, while Hardy, stunned and bruised by the awful years of war, slaughter and misery, appeared to be confirmed in his idea that to believe in a God of infinite goodness and mercy without any qualifying characteristics was a delusion. In a note made about this time he again reiterated his belief that the only reasonable meaning attached to the word God, of which, indeed, there were so many meanings in use, was that of " The Cause of Things," whatever that cause may be. And no modern thinker (he added) " can be an atheist in the modern sense, while all modern thinkers are atheists in the ancient and exploded sense," which we take to mean at least the adoption of a form of agnosticism.

An interesting light is thrown upon what Hardy's ideas were on this question by the preface to *Late Lyrics and Earlier, with many other Verses*, to which the reader is referred.

In June of this year, 1917, his friend Sir James Barrie had arranged to go to the front in France, and had written to Hardy inviting him to go. The latter, though no doubt the idea attracted him by its sense of adventure and opportunities for personal observation of conditions in which he was deeply interested, felt compelled on account of increasing age, and the fact that he was by no means in robust health, to decline the invitation.

Moments of Vision, and Miscellaneous Verses was published during November.

It is recorded that during the immediately succeeding period, Hardy seems to have been engaged in deep introspection, and in a note he states that he felt he had been a child till he reached sixteen, a youth till twenty-five, a young man till forty or fifty. Certainly to this entry might be added that he was, in mental grasp and indeed almost in physical qualities, a young man for a period of ten or fifteen years beyond that he mentioned.

In the following year, in January, he saw a performance by the women landworkers of the neighbourhood in the Corn Exchange, Dorchester, doubtless with a view to inducing other women to take up field work. Hardy met Mrs. Alfred Lyttelton, who was very active in the movement, and also other interested society people. Hardy notes that the girls looked very picturesque in their pseudo-male garments, and that they evidently delighted in the freedom of that form of clothing.

A rather interesting event occurred on New Year's Eve of this year when a performance of *The Mellstock Quire* was given by "The Hardy Players" in aid of the hospital, for Hardy had arranged that the then Mellstock choir should be present to enable them to see what their predecessors, as represented in the play, were like.

The annual Red Cross sale took place at Christie's in April, and was additionally interesting by reason of the fact that the manuscript of Hardy's *Far from the Madding Crowd* was offered for sale, and realized a large sum. Hardy himself was entirely ignorant that this manuscript, which had been sent to the *Cornhill Magazine* for publication in 1874, was still in existence, it not having been returned to him with the proofs. After the sale it went to America, and was ultimately bought by Mr. A. E. Newton of Pennsylvania, a well-known collector of books and manuscripts, from a New York dealer who had acquired it.

In May Hardy was laid aside by a cold, but later in the month he took part in what he had described as the only War work of which he was capable, namely, sitting on the Bench, and hearing several food profiteering cases.

In the September of this year (1918) Hardy received a letter, issued to well-known people, asking him to help in making known to people facts relative to the future, with the view of impressing upon them the terrors which would undoubtedly distinguish future wars, and of finding some way out.   In which letter occurred the following : " It is agreed by all students of modern military methods, that this War, horrible as it seems and was, has mercifully no comparison to what future wars must be. Scientific ammunition-making is only in its infancy. The next world war, if there is another, will find the nations provided not with thousands, but with hundreds of thousands of submarines, and all these as far surpassing the present types in power and destructiveness as they surpass the feeble beginnings of ten years ago."   Hardy remarked in reply, if all the letter said were true, and the grounds in support of the views of its originators were set forth in detail, " I do not think a world in which such fiendishness is possible to be worthy of saving. Better let the Western civilization perish, and the black and yellow races have a chance."

Hardy always showed a sympathetic interest in the scheme for the " reconstruction of Palestine as the national home for the Jewish race," and one can imagine with what horror he would have regarded the policy of Hitler towards Jews of to-day.

He was in London in May of this year with his friend Sir James Barrie, and attended the dinner of the Royal Academy, which happened to be of additional importance as during the War the function had been suspended.

Towards the end of June, and after his seventy-ninth birthday, he received a very valuable and delightful present in the shape of a beautifully bound volume containing the originals of some forty or fifty poems by a large number of living poets.

Although of so great an age, Hardy, at considerable labour to himself, we were told, wrote a letter of thanks to each of the contributors. This volume was brought down to Dorchester by one of the poets, Siegfried Sassoon, and as a matter of fact, we believe the idea originated with him, himself the author of a number of War poems.   One may imagine the competition that would arise, especially from Americans, if this valuable volume of original poems by some of the most distinguished poets of that day came into the market.

A collected edition of Hardy's verses was published in August, 1919, in two volumes, the first containing the War poems, and the second being devoted to *The Dynasts*.

Many years before the time of which we now write Hardy had written a short story called " A Tradition of Eighteen Hundred and Four " describing an imaginary visit of Napoleon to England in that year. This perilous adventure was to enable him to ascertain a suitable spot on which to land his troops and carry out the contemplated invasion.

As a matter of fact, there was in our own boyhood, in the neighbourhood of Poole and along the coast westwards, a tradition, or at least a story, relative to such a landing. Indeed, we, ourselves, knew a very old fisherman of Poole, who, at the time of which we are speaking, was a " long-shoreman," with a white beard, at Sandbanks, at the entrance to the harbour, talking of Boney, and telling us he had heard his father say that " the little Corporal " had once landed on the sand dunes near Studland, a by no means unsuitable spot in those days for disembarking troops, and perhaps, indeed, the most suitable of all along the South Coast. In fact, when, at the end of the 18th century, a survey was made by the authorities regarding the most feasible places at which an enemy might land, the spot we have mentioned was recorded as dangerous.

Hardy's story, however, led to enquiries being made by people interested in the history and tradition of their own county, with the result that they came to the conclusion that whatever might be said for the interest of the local " yarn," it did not amount to a tradition, and that nothing was now discoverable in support of the story that Napoleon had ever so visited these shores.

Hardy was many times asked by correspondents to

furnish some biographical details, and on more than one occasion the correspondents suggested that *Jude the Obscure* might be in part autobiographical. Mrs. Hardy, replying to one of the letters, remarked that the rumour that such was the case was started some years before, and that there were no personal details in this novel, going on in her reply to say what Hardy himself years before had written to the present writer—namely, there is autobiography in his poems, but not in the novels.

On December 19th of this year the village War Memorial in Bockhampton, which had taken the form of a reading room and club, was opened by Hardy, who made a short speech, and in this gave some very interesting historical details regarding the village, which at the time of the Conquest was given to a Norman countess, and later became the property of a French priory, as was the case with a considerable number of the grants of land made by the Conqueror. An interesting fact regarding this club is that it was built on the site formerly occupied by the shoemaker's shop kept by a Robert Reason, who appears in *Under the Greenwood Tree* as Robert Penny.

It stood also close to the first village school which Hardy as a child attended. The club was not named, by the way, the Bockhampton Club, but, no doubt in compliment to Hardy's work, was given the name of the Mellstock Club, by which name the village is referred to in several of his novels, short stories and poems.

Hardy, much to the sorrow of his friends, was undoubtedly failing at this time, and as he was in his eightieth year this caused no surprise ; and, towards the end of the year, he wrote to a correspondent who had asked him for a poem worthy of the 8th of August, 1918, saying that he felt that the length of the late War had exhausted all his energy for writing impromptu verses, and he suggested that one of the younger poets should be asked to write such a poem.

In February of the next year Hardy was to go to Oxford

to be present at a performance of some of the scenes in
The Dynasts, which the Oxford University Dramatic
Society had obtained his permission to stage in the previous
November. The opportunity was taken by the University
authorities to confer the Honorary Degree of a Doctor of
Letters upon their distinguished guest at the time. Mr.
and Mrs. Hardy reached Oxford on February 9th, and
were, according to the Press, met at the station by a crowd
of enthusiastic students of the O.U.D.S. and others, and
were conducted round the city, and afterwards taken to
the house of Sir Walter and Lady Raleigh, who were acting
as their hosts.

On the next day Hardy was presented with the Degree in
the Sheldonian Theatre, and the Public Orator, Mr. A. D.
Godley, made the usual speech in Latin ; one happy
phrase of which is as follows : " His (Hardy's) work is
marked not only by the eloquence of the author, but by
the magnitude and importance of the events which he
describes." The concluding words of the orator were as
follows : " Now that you may confer distinction, not so
much on him as on our own selves, by granting a deserved
honour to one who is a friend of the Muses and Pastoral
Gods, I present to you the revered and renowned Thomas
Hardy."

In the afternoon, after the ceremony, his host invited to
meet him Robert Bridges, the Poet Laureate, John Masefield and many other friends.

The thought, we know, presented itself to Hardy on
many occasions that honours came late to most people,
for it was not till he had attained the age of eighty that
the Royal Institute of British Architects proposed to make
him an Hon. Fellow of the Association.

A very old friend wrote to him asking that he might be
nominated for that distinction and Hardy wrote back
saying that whereas he felt that he cared very little for such
honours at his age, and more especially because he could
not look forward to taking any part in the conduct of
affairs, he left the decision to his correspondent's judgment.
A Hardyesque touch is the sentence in which he says he

likes " to be reminded in such a way that he once knew what a T-square was."

Of course he was elected, and we are told that he regretted that he was unable to attend the meetings which were held in the same room in which he had received the prize medal for his essay from the hands of Sir Gilbert Scott, more than half a century earlier.

On April 21st, Hardy paid his last visit to London, staying at Sir J. M. Barrie's flat in 3, Adelphi Terrace, near to which George Bernard Shaw also had his home, so that they might attend the wedding of Mr. Harold Macmillan to Lady Dorothy Cavendish, which took place at St. Margaret's, Westminster, on April 21st. Hardy's signature, with those of Lord Morley of Blackburn (the biographer of Gladstone), and Sir James Bryce, all three of whom had received the Order of Merit, is to be found in the register of marriages.

On June 2nd, 1920, Hardy attained his eightieth year, and a deputation was sent from the Society of Authors, composed of John Galsworthy, Sir Anthony Hope Hawkins, and Augustine Birrell. The present writer also travelled down to Dorchester, and had the opportunity of a word with Mr. Hardy, and in the late afternoon returned to London as did Sir Anthony Hope Hawkins and the other members of the delegation.

On the Dorchester platform Anthony Hope, as we prefer to call him, who was well known to us, and whom we had met on many occasions, remarked on the extraordinary vitality Hardy had shown, and the lively conversation in which he had engaged during the lunch. He also told us of the scores of telegrams that had been received, including messages from the King, the Lord Mayor of London, the Prime Minister, and the Cambridge Vice-Chancellor.

The following note is of particular interest when one recalls the great delight Hardy had, which might almost be described as being a passion, in visiting cathedrals. He said : " We have visited two cathedrals during the last month [Exeter was one of these, of which he was

"Winchester." "Winton Cester."

particularly fond], and could not help feeling that if men could get a little more of the reposefulness and peace of these buildings into their lives, how much better it would be for them."

He also makes observations of interesting character regarding the question, which has troubled many people, as to whether the present age is any improvement upon the age which he had known in his youth. Most people will agree with the view he held, namely, that although the world has advanced enormously in materialistic things, real civilization has in no measure kept pace with this, and that people are not so humane nor is disinterested kindness so frequent.

On November 11th one of the best poems that Hardy ever wrote, entitled "And there Was a Great Calm," appeared in the Armistice supplement of *The Times*, and it is interesting to know, in relation to this poem, the following fact : So important did the great national newspaper consider a contribution from Hardy, that one of the editorial staff was sent to Dorchester to see him, and convey to him the request. He appears to have had considerable difficulty in bringing his mind to contemplate the work. But we are told, as sometimes happens with writers, the idea came to him in the middle of the night, and he got out of bed and set to work upon the verses which were duly published.

A dramatic version of *The Return of the Native* was staged by the members of the Debating and Dramatic Society on November 15th, and their well-known skill of presentation appears to have pleased Hardy on this occasion as on most others, for he told the producer that " the dancing was just as it used to be at Higher Bockhampton, in my childhood."

Hardy's life was bound by reason of his own temperament to be one of controversy, and it was perhaps his fate that he should be often misinterpreted by critics, and misunderstood by many of those who were amongst his greatest admirers. At the end of 1920 Alfred Noyes, the poet, delivered a lecture on " Poetry and Religion," and made a statement, according to the report in the *Morning Post* and other papers, that Hardy's philosophy was one which held " that the power behind the Universe was an imbecile jester."

On Hardy's attention being drawn to this report, he wrote to Alfred Noyes saying that he held no such philosophy, and to the best of his recollection never had held it, and asked the lecturer to give him references to where in his writings he had expressed any such opinion. Alfred Noyes replied, saying that he thought it was unfortunate that the abbreviated report of his address excluded the warm tribute he had paid Hardy as a writer, and as standing at the head of living authors, but that he did dissent from his (Hardy's) pessimistic philosophy, one which, in his (Noyes's) opinion, could only lead to the conclusion that the power behind the Universe was malign. In support of this conclusion, he quoted various passages from Hardy's poems that he held to bear out his contention that Hardy held the views that he attributed to him.

Hardy defended himself in a long letter to his critic, dated December 19th, and pleaded that the extracts and references that Noyes had quoted in his writings, which seemed to support the contention, should never have been taken for anything but fancies and the opinion of the moment.

Hardy added that he had often in prefaces to various volumes warned readers to consider his views in that light, and went on to say : " But it has always been my misfortune to presuppose a too intelligent reading public."

The fact, however, remains that the critic after all stands excused if the writings of poets or novelists convey an impression to his mind which the said poet or novelist had no definite intention to convey, but which view is in a measure supported by the actual words. Nevertheless, Hardy was constantly being fiercely criticized and misrepresented, often by obviously unintelligent critics, and sometimes by pained but friendly ones.

P

Hardy's philosophy at any rate was of the nature that led him always to give sympathetic support to efforts to promote international peace, and he sent to the *New York World* on December 23rd the following message in response to the request from that paper for an expression of his own : " Yes, I approve of international disarmament on the lines indicated by the *New York World*."

The year drew to a close and on the night of Christmas, carol singers and mummers came to Max Gate, and the latter performed especially for Hardy the play of *St. George*, in the manner in which he had witnessed its performance in his childhood.

On December 31st the *Athenæum* published a poem by Hardy called " At the Entering of the New Year."

Although during the earlier part of the year, Hardy was engaged in research work in connection with a family connected by marriage with his own, he as a general rule passed his time quietly and uneventfully.   On May 11th, Sir J. M. Barrie was at Max Gate on a brief visit, and on the following day went over to Upper Bockhampton and visited the picturesque thatched cottage in which Hardy had been born.

A month later an address was presented to Hardy from a group of the young writers of the day with, to him, a delightful birthday present in the shape of a fine copy of the first edition of *Isabella, Lamia, The Eve of St. Agnes, and other Poems* by Keats, as originally printed, including the often missing pages of advertisements.   St. John Irvine, well-known critic, was the originator of this idea, and also of the address, which was signed and sent to Hardy by 106 writers.

Hardy, though failing in strength, was able during June to go motoring, and to visit Sturminster Newton in company with Mrs. Hardy and his friend Cecil Hanbury to witness a performance by " The Hardy Players " of *The Mellstock Quire*, given in the castle ruins.

He afterwards went into the house, Riverside, in which he had written *The Return of the Native*, and where he had lived some time with the first Mrs. Hardy.   Very appropriately the company of players were given tea at this house. Hardy was still physically able, notwithstanding his advanced age, to take walking exercise, and in the month of June, when his friend Walter de la Mare, the poet, was at Dorchester, walked with him to Stinsford, and examined many of the tombstones of those whom Hardy had known in his youth. Perhaps one may quote as an example of the often self-centred nature of the life of people in the country at that time, the fact that when in July a company of film actors came down and set to work filming the principal scenes of *The Mayor of Casterbridge*, no notice was taken of them by passers-by or the country folk, or that they were dressed up in costumes of some eighty years before.

Hardy met the actors outside the King's Arms, in which one of the most dramatic scenes in the novel is laid, and he then went with them to Maiden Castle, the ancient earthworks on the outskirts of the town, where another important scene of the story was filmed.

Hardy's life from this time was not only a quiet one, but was in a measure chiefly concerned with the more peaceful things in life. We find that he was present at a morning service in St. Peter's Church, Dorchester, when " Awake my soul and with the dawn " was sung by the choir to Barthélémon's setting, a rendering of the well-known hymn which had been especially arranged so that Hardy should hear it by the rector of the church. Perhaps as a result of this his poem " Barthélémon at Vauxhall " was published in *The Times* on July 23rd, a few days after.

Hardy was able, at the end of July, to open a bazaar, held in aid of the Dorchester County Hospital, and returned to the town in the evening to see some dancing in the Borough Gardens. At the beginning of September he was present at the christening of the infant daughter of his friends, Mr. and Mrs. Cecil Hanbury, at Kingston Maurward. His little godchild received a unique and charming gift in the shape of the manuscript of a short poem contained in a silver box, to be found reprinted in the volume

Human Shows, Far Fantasies, Songs and Trifles, inscribed to " C.F.H."

It was during this month that Hardy gave sittings to his friend Ouless, R.A., the well-known portrait painter, for a picture which now hangs in the National Portrait Gallery, Trafalgar Square, London. The poet, John Masefield, and his wife, came on a short visit on October 14th, bringing with them as a present a full-rigged ship which Masefield himself had made and named the *Triumph.*

CHAPTER X

DURING JANUARY, 1922, Hardy was busily engaged in writing the preface to his volume of poems, *Late Lyrics and Earlier, with many other Verses*, which he had collected together, and the manuscript of which was forwarded to the publishers at the end of the month. The preface was in fact a very strong protest against some of the criticisms from which Hardy had suffered, and it is well known that, although he gave very few verbal expressions of his feelings, he was of the very sensitive type of which most poets have almost invariably been.

In April, Hardy had the pleasure of a visit from Sir J. M. Barrie, and in the middle of May his *Late Lyrics and Earlier* appeared.

About this period he seemed to be clinging especially to old memories of past times, for towards the end of May he once again visited Sturminster Newton especially to call at Riverside, where he had spent several happy years soon after his first marriage. Only a few days later we find him also visiting Stinsford and Upper Bockhampton, where he found the garden of his old home overgrown with weeds. He recalls that he went up to the heath and plantation at the top of the garden, where he used to spend so much time in his childhood and early boyhood reading and communing with Nature in all her varied moods.

During July he appears to have been somewhat better in health, and although he was then eighty-two, he took excursions in the car to Blackmoor Vale and to Sherborne, the " Sherton Abbas " of *The Woodlanders*. He also had visits from Edmund Morgan Forster, the writer, and the two poets Siegfried Sassoon and Edmund Charles Blunden, and witnessed an outdoor performance of *A Midsummer Night's Dream* on the lawn of Trinity Rectory.

To show how vigorous was Hardy, almost up to the end of his life, one may recall that early in August he cycled with Mrs. Hardy to see his brother and sister, who were living at Talbothays. A little later in the month he was motoring with his friend Newman Flower, who held an important post in the publishing house of Cassells, and has since become the chief proprietor of that old-established firm, and walked to the top of High Stoy. Even in November he was able to be out motoring with friends, and he much enjoyed seeing the country in this way. In the third week of November he received a letter from the Pro-Provost of Queen's College, Oxford, to say that it had been decided to elect him as an Honorary Fellow, and this honour he wrote and accepted.

In April, Hardy finished the draft of *The Famous Tragedy of the Queen of Cornwall at Tintagel in Lyonesse*, the idea for which had germinated in his mind for a considerable period. He states in the sub-title that it is arranged as a play for mummers, and it did not require any theatre or scenery.

One can scarcely, indeed, conceive that the drawing of Tintagel Castle, used as the frontispiece of this romantic poem, was the work of a man who had passed his eighty-second year, and it is of great interest in that we believe it was the last finished sketch he ever made.

In April, in a letter to the late John Galsworthy, he speaks of his belief in the exchange of international thought as the only possible salvation for the world. One wonders a little whether Hardy would have had this view shattered by the failures of the numbers of Conferences which have, during the last few years, been held for the purpose of the exchange of international views upon many exacting and perplexing problems.

In June, Mr. and Mrs. Hardy were both again at Oxford, to stay at Queen's College of which he was now an Honorary Fellow, and remained there for two nights. This proved to be the last occasion on which he slept away from home, or took so long a journey. They motored by way of Salisbury, where they paid a visit to the cathedral, which it was Hardy's practice to do whenever the opportunity offered. He also went to the Training College described in considerable detail in *Jude the Obscure*, where, many years before, his two sisters, Mary and Kate, had been students.

Fawley, in Berkshire, which appears under the disguise of " Marygreen " in the same novel, had always an interest for Hardy, quite apart from the fact that he found it a suitable place in which to lay some of the scenes of his most discussed work. This was by reason of the fact that his grandmother, on his father's side, who had exercised considerable influence on the novelist's early years at the home in Upper Bockhampton, had, as an orphan, spent some years of her early life in the little village.

Hardy and his wife were present, on the day following their arrival at Oxford, at a lunch in the Common Room of Queen's College, and had the opportunity of meeting many of the Fellows and their wives, after which Hardy posed in his Doctor's gown for a souvenir portrait in the garden.

Notwithstanding his age, there is a record kept by Mr. Godfrey Elton, who acted as the Hardys' guide while at Oxford, that he showed few signs of his many years, and was an untiring sightseer, having insisted upon seeing many interesting places in the city. While there, he took the opportunity of visiting John Masefield and his wife, who had taken up their home some time before in the literary and artistic colony that had been established at Boars Hill, just outside Oxford.

A month later, and Hardy had the distinguished honour of a visit from the Prince of Wales, which was, perhaps from the fact of the informal nature of the visit and the friendliness shown him by His Royal Highness, the greatest and most pleasing event in his life. The Prince was in Dorchester for the purpose of opening the then newly erected Drill Hall for the Dorchester Territorials. Hardy was naturally invited to meet him, and then to drive back to Max Gate, where the Prince and those accompanying him were to have lunch.

What might have been a very trying ordeal for Hardy, was rendered, owing to the tactful sympathy of the Prince, a very pleasant experience. In addition to His Royal Highness, and his host and hostess, there were at the lunch, Lord Shaftesbury, Admiral Sir Lionel Halsey, Sir Godfrey Thomas, Bart., the Prince's private secretary, and the two stewards of the Duchy of Cornwall, upon the ground of which Max Gate was built.

After lunch the Prince and Hardy had a long talk in the garden, and the latter often afterwards referred to the friendly and charming character of his royal guest.

To the Year Book of the Society of Dorset Men in London for 1922 Hardy contributed a charming poem, entitled " News for Her Mother," which, however, had been written some years previously.

It tells of the fear of a young girl lest her marriage should make a difference in her relations of affection with her mother.   She muses in one verse :

" Yet I wonder,
Will it sunder
Her from me ?
Will she guess that
I said ' Yes '—that
His I'd be,
I thought she might not see him as I see ! "

The poem is notable as exhibiting the extreme care with which Hardy was accustomed to search for, and ultimately track down, the exact word. In the first verse of the poem he wrote originally :

" One mile more is
Where your door is,
Mother mine—
Harvest's coming,
Mills are strumming,
Apples fine,
And the cider made to year will be as wine."

THOMAS HARDY O.M.
WAS BORN IN THIS ADJACENT
COTTAGE 2ⁿᵈ JUNE 1840
AND IN IT WROTE
UNDER THE GREENWOOD TREE
AND
FAR FROM THE MADDING CROWD

THIS MONUMENT IS ERECTED
HIS MEMORY BY A FEW OF
HIS AMERICAN ADMIRERS
1931.

The AMERICAN MEMORIAL
to THOMAS HARDY. 1931.

UPPER BOCKHAMPTON.
(Egdon Heath.)

Douglas SNOWDON

On the proof, which we have been shown, Hardy altered the word " made " to " wrung," so that in the published version the line read :

" And the cider wrung to-year will be as wine."

It was a slight, but wonderfully illuminating alteration.

On November 15th, *The Famous Tragedy of the Queen of Cornwall* was published, and aroused a considerable amount of attention.   Within a few days of the publication of the book " The Hardy Players " produced it at the Corn Exchange in Dorchester, and the performance, particularly the rehearsals, at some of which Hardy was present, evidently gave the author great pleasure.

In the large council chamber upstairs, on the walls of which were inscribed the names of the mayors of Dorchester for many generations, there was a cheerful gathering of the players and their friends for refreshments.   Hardy, though often present at rehearsals, as well as at the actual performances, seldom, we know, offered suggestions to the stage-manager, Mr. T. H. Tilley, or did more than sit silently watching.

Early in December, to be exact, December 9th, another of Hardy's oldest friends passed away in the person of Sir Frederick Treves, the famous surgeon, who was not only a Dorchester man, but as a child attended the same school as Hardy's sister Mary.   Sir Frederick's father had kept a shop in Dorchester, at which it is said Hardy bought his first writing-desk, which he showed us on one of our visits, placed on a table in his library, which appears in a photograph that we took at the time.

Sir Frederick Treves also had in common with Hardy a great love of Dorset, and was the author of one of the most charming books, *Highways and Byways in Dorset*, ever written concerning the country.

On January 5th, 1924, three or four days after the delayed burial of Treves in the Dorchester cemetery, Hardy's poem, " In Memoriam, F.T.," appeared in *The Times*.

In June of that year Hardy had been approached by Mr.

Rutland Boughton, the musician, with a view to the setting of *The Famous Tragedy of the Queen of Cornwall* to music, and had paid Hardy a visit at Max Gate to discuss the matter. In August, the version that Rutland Boughton had prepared was produced at Glastonbury, and on August 28th, Hardy motored over with his wife to attend a performance.

We have more than once referred to Hardy's love of animals and humanitarian instincts. On June 16th a poem entitled " Compassion," written to mark the centenary of the Royal Society for the Prevention of Cruelty to Animals, appeared in *The Times*. Hardy had always disliked writing anything to order or in haste, and more than once expressed the view that " the artist cannot be hurried in his stride." He, doubtless, used the word in the widest sense.

A very interesting event took place in July of 1924, when Hardy was visited at Max Gate by a party of Oxford undergraduates, who were touring the West of England, giving performances of *Orestea*, called by them *The Curse of the House of Atreus*. Hardy, whose love for Greek tragedy is well known, was delighted with the performance, and regarded it as a delicate compliment to him that it should have been given. Among the players, with whom he chatted animatedly, were Mr. A. L. Cliffe and Mr. Anthony Asquith, son of Lord Oxford and Asquith, who has since distinguished himself as a producer of films. We gather from the report of the visit that the players were touring on their bicycles, their properties following them or preceding them in a motor lorry.

The members of the Dorchester Debating and Dramatic Society, the dramatic members of which had become known as " The Hardy Players," had long wanted to produce *Tess of the D'Urbervilles* as a play, but Hardy had by this time very settled views concerning the desirability or otherwise of dramatized novels. Indeed, he had come to the conclusion that it was a mistake ; but notwithstanding this, after a great deal of hesitation, Hardy sent to Mr. A. J. Gillam, the secretary of the Society, his own dramatization of the story of *Tess*, and it was produced not only at

Dorchester in the Corn Exchange, on Wednesday, November 26th, 1924, and three following nights, but also at Weymouth.

It was in four acts, with an after scene. The title role was played by Mrs. Gertrude Bugler, who, indeed, made for herself a very considerable reputation in several of the "Hardy" productions by the company of amateur players, of which she became a prominent member. The production met with such a success that it was staged in London the following year, with Miss Gwen Ffrangçon-Davies playing the title role.

The New Year saw Hardy sitting up again to see it in, and listen to the bells, as was formerly his custom, but which had been discontinued. And we believe that it was on this occasion he heard for the first time Big Ben strike and London church bells ringing on the wireless.

During January, 1925, Hardy sent to the *Nineteenth Century and After* a poem entitled "The Absolute Explains," which was printed in the February number.

In the summer of this year Hardy was given the distinction of the Honorary Degree of a Doctor of Literature by the Bristol University, and a deputation waited upon him at Max Gate to confer the degree upon him. He had already, it will be remembered, received such honours from Aberdeen, Cambridge, Oxford and St. Andrews Universities in the order named.

A manuscript of a volume of poems, to be called *Human Shows, Far Fantasies, Songs and Trifles*, was sent to his publisher in July, and appeared in the autumn.

Tess of the D'Urbervilles, meanwhile, had been produced at the Barnes Theatre, and owing to the great success that it had met with was, after about two months' run, transferred on November 2nd to the Garrick Theatre in Town. In December it was arranged that the cast should go down to Max Gate and give a performance of *Tess* in the drawing-room, and on December 6th the company arrived for this purpose.

From one of those present we gather that Hardy betrayed no excitement on the arrival of the actors, but met them in the hall as though such an invasion of his quietude was a common occurrence, and that he chatted animatedly with the members of the company while they took tea. The " audience," it is interesting to note, consisted of only five people—Mr. and Mrs. Hardy, one of their friends, and two other people. We are also told that Hardy, after the performance, talked of his heroine as if she were a real person, with whom he had been acquainted and greatly liked. As a matter of fact he told the present writer that Tess represented the type of girl he had once, and once only, seen, driving in a cart on the outskirts of " Egdon " Heath many years before.

In January of the following year, 1926, Hardy reluctantly gave up his governorship of the Dorchester Grammar School, as he had felt for some time that his advancing age prevented him filling the office even in an honorary capacity. Of a retiring nature, he had always reluctantly consented to join the various bodies which were anxious to enlist his influence, or for the use of his distinguished name. This is not to be wondered at, for he was of a temperament—almost invariable with poets and artistic geniuses—which made dull routine work of committees distasteful.

He led a very quiet life during the year 1926, going about very little. One of the chief events of the year was undoubtedly the production of John Drinkwater's version of *The Mayor of Casterbridge* at the Barnes Theatre on September 8th. Twelve days later the play came down to Weymouth, where Hardy went to see it. He met with a wonderful reception in the theatre, the people rising and cheering and clapping their hands and waving handkerchiefs, and very much the same reception outside the Pavilion Theatre on the pier at the close of the performance.

The end of the year was destined to bring a great sorrow to Hardy in the death of his dog, his faithful companion for thirteen years, to which had been given the historic name of " Wessex." In the shrubbery on the west side of Max Gate, where in fact there is a small cemetery, owing to the fact that also here lie buried several pet cats, " Wessex " was laid to rest.

Hardy wrote the inscription which is found cut on the headstone.   It runs :

THE
FAMOUS " WESSEX "
Aug. 1913 to Dec. 27, 1926
Faithful.   Unflinching.

Many of Hardy's friends have said that they thought that the death of this dog, which had been so faithful and constant a companion, had a very detrimental effect upon Hardy's health, and that he grieved deeply over his loss.

He enshrined memories of " Wessex" in a poem which was called " Dead Wessex, the dog to the Household," in which the animal soliloquizes regarding his human friends, and in the verses mentions the incidents which occurred so regularly in his life, especially the walk which he often took with Mr. and Mrs. Hardy across the field which lay in front of Max Gate and led to the Came Plantation.

In the January number of the *Fortnightly Review* in 1927, a poem appeared entitled " Philosophical Phantasies."   It was a practice of Hardy's for many years to publish a poem early in January.

Then he had another visit to Max Gate from the Players of Balliol College, Oxford, who on this occasion gave a performance of *Iphigenia in Aulis*.   Indeed, such happenings as this formed the chief distractions of his increasingly secluded life.

On July 21st he laid the foundation stone of the new building of the Dorchester Grammar School, although the day was cold and windy.   The block now forms a prominent landmark, and is within sight of the entrance of Max Gate, almost in a line with the tower erected to the memory of Nelson's Hardy, which stands nearly 800 feet above sea-level, on the crest of Blagdon Hill, above Portisham, the village where the Admiral was born.

Hardy gave a most interesting address, which was clearly heard by the audience.   He touched particularly in it upon the historical connection of the old school, founded by his namesake in Elizabethan times, now used as an office, and the new, in due course, to rise in evidence of modern progress. Although little is known of Hardy's namesake, who was such a generous friend to the ancient borough, Hardy was able to tell his hearers that he was one of the Le Hardys or Le Hardis, who had come from Jersey in the 15th century, and purchased small estates in the valley of the Frome, and many of whose descendants are known to have stayed in the neighbourhood for centuries. It is worthy to note, the speaker said, that the Christian name of Thomas appeared to have been a much favoured one in the family since those early times.

Notwithstanding the vigour which Hardy had shown in his speech, and in the actual stone-laying, a fact recorded by the local Press, he was naturally considerably fatigued by the strain that had been put upon him, and in afterwards chatting to friends, to whom, indeed, he expressed a fear that this might be his last public appearance.

Early in August, Gustav Holst, the well-known London musician and composer and the Music Master of St. Paul's Girls' School, Hammersmith, came to Dorchester, and they motored across " Egdon " Heath, which is, at this time, a beautiful sight on account of the miles and miles of purple heather. They then returned by way of Puddle-town Church to inspect the old Jacobean Musicians' Gallery, and the Athelhampton Chapel.

It is interesting to note in relation to the enormous popularity as a novelist, which has, the last few years, been attained by Mr. J. B. Priestley, the author of *The Good Companions*, that Hardy, about this time, in acknowledging the present of a copy of Priestley's book upon " George Meredith," in the English Men of Letters Series, said : " I . . . have been much interested in the bright writing of one in whom I have already discerned a coming force in letters."

The late summer and autumn of this year was spent very quietly. Mr. and Mrs. Hardy, however, motored to several places, including Bath, where he walked about for a considerable time visiting places which had been familiar to him in earlier days.

One of the chief external interests of Hardy's life at this time was the progress he was able to note made with the building of the new Grammar School, and on several occasions to enable him to see this he visited the site with Mrs. Hardy.

A new edition was called for of the small volume entitled *Selected Poems of Thomas Hardy* in the "Golden Treasury Series," which Macmillans had first published in the autumn of 1915. Hardy spent some time in revising and rearranging the contents for the new edition, and this was the last literary work of the kind upon which he was ever engaged.

Towards the end of September, a rather curious thing occurred, for Hardy motored over to Charborough Park which, it will be remembered, was the scene of his novel *Two on a Tower*, and it is recorded that this occasion was the first on which he had entered the house that he had described in his novel.

During November, Hardy paid a visit to his brother, Henry Hardy, at Talbothays, and this proved to be the last time that he was to go there. Hardy, who was very clannish and affectionate at heart, had during the life of his parents when he was in Dorchester gone over to Upper Bockhampton to see them almost every Sunday afternoon, and after his mother's death he continued his visits to his old home, where his two sisters and we believe also his brother were then living.

Ernest Rhys in his *Everyman Remembers* refers to a visit that he paid about this time to Max Gate in company with Mrs. Rhys.

They were staying at Abbotsbury, near Weymouth, at the time, and he thus describes the visit to Hardy: "There was a good fire burning of Wessex logs, which made the room cheerful as we entered. Hardy did not appear at once, and we were beginning to fear that he was not well enough to see visitors, when his wife said he was just back from a walk and would join us presently.

"Meanwhile, a round table was being spread for an old-fashioned tea, and next moment the door opened, a flame sprang up on the hearth, and in its gleam we saw

Hardy stepping in with nothing of an old man's deliberation. . . . He was the life of that tea party."

Hardy was at this time over eighty.

Ernest Rhys, during the conversation which followed, asked Hardy if he knew the old Exmoor prayer, which runs as follows :

> " God bless me and my wife,
>   My son Jan and his wife——
>   Us four.
>   No more."

Hardy had not heard this " most exclusive prayer in the Christian repertory," and was much amused by it. It had, too, the effect of starting him off on some quaint reminiscences of Wessex life and character which equally interested and entertained his visitors.

Hardy was now slowly but definitely failing, and seemed to be given a great deal to introspection and depression at times. Strangely enough, although he had won worldwide fame in two very distinct fields of literature—those of prose fiction and poetry—he right up to the end of his life expressed the view that had he to live it over again, he would prefer to be an architect in a small way in a country town, as was his first employer, Mr. John Hicks, to whom he had been articled.

It was about this time that he found and revised the poem called "He Resolves to Say No More," which appears in the volume *Winter Words : In Various Moods and Metres*, published in 1927, and the last verse of which runs :

> " And if my vision range beyond
>   The blinkered sight of souls in bond,
>   —By Truth made free—
>   I'll let all be,
>   And show to no man what I see."

It was on December 11th of the following year that Hardy was so far from well that, although, we are told, he

Q

sat at his writing table in his study, he was obviously unfit for work. His condition, however, did not for the moment cause those in his household any serious anxiety.

Just before Christmas, a poem that he had written, entitled "Christmas in the Elgin Room," referring, of course, to the Elgin Marbles in the British Museum, was sent to *The Times*, and duly appeared in its columns.

It was said at the time that Hardy, on this occasion, as was his practice, forwarded a stamp to cover the return of the manuscript if unsuitable. This story, or tradition, whichever it may be thought to be, was quoted after his death as evidence of his unfailing modesty regarding the value of his work. We do not know whether there was any reliable foundation for it.

On the day after Christmas, it was quite clear that he was seriously ill and perhaps even dying, chiefly from gradually failing strength rather than from any definite illness.

His own doctor wished for a second opinion, and Sir Henry Head, who was living in the neighbourhood and was a personal friend, was called in.

On January 10th he rallied somewhat, and filled in and wrote his signature on what was to become an historical document, namely the cheque for four guineas—his subscription to the Pension Fund of the Society of Authors. This he insisted upon doing, although entreated not to exert himself even to the extent of signing his name.

On the evening of January 11th, although in the morning he had seemed a little better, the watchers over him were alarmed by a serious heart attack. The local doctor was hastily summoned and arrived very shortly, but could do nothing. Hardy, who remained conscious until a few minutes before his death, died at a few minutes after nine the same evening.

Thus passed away peacefully, at a great age and full of honours, one of the last great figures in the literature of the Victorian and Edwardian eras.

It was recorded in the newspapers that the dawn of Thursday, January 12th, was, in Wessex, one of marvellous

"Overcombe"

SWORDON

SUTTON POYNTZ

beauty, the splendour of the red sky bringing to one's
mind the old saying of " a red sky in the morning is the
shepherd's warning."

On the same day, the Dean of Westminster gave his
assent that Hardy should be buried in the Abbey. A
suggestion that had been made in many of the morning
papers.

It was understood, however, and generally known
among his friends that it had been Hardy's wish to be
buried at Stinsford, where his parents, many of his ancestors, and his first wife lay. A compromise was at last
arrived at, and on Friday morning the heart was taken out
of his body and placed in a casket.

When this fact became known, it must be recorded that
a feeling of regret that such a thing should have been done
was very prevalent among many of Hardy's friends and
admirers.

On the following day the body was taken to Woking,
and there cremated, and a few hours later the ashes were
taken to Westminster Abbey in an urn, and placed in the
Chapel of St. Faith until the memorial service could be
held. On Sunday, January 15th, Hardy's heart was conveyed to the church at Stinsford and placed on the altar
steps, where it remained until the following day.

On Monday, January 16th, 1928, Hardy's ashes were
interred in Westminster Abbey in the Poets' Corner, and
with most of those gathered in the Abbey there was the
common feeling that Hardy's place was indeed by the side
of Charles Dickens, and surrounded by the poets Tennyson,
Browning, and by Macaulay, Thackeray and Johnson.

There had gathered together to do him honour a large
and very representative congregation. The King was
represented by Lord Herschell, lord-in-waiting ; the Prince
of Wales by Sir Walter Peacock, secretary to the Duchy of
Cornwall ; and the Duke of York by Mr. P. K. Hodgson.
Literature and the Drama, Music and Art and Science had
official and a large unofficial representation, and doubtless
many of Hardy's readers, who joined in mourning the
dead poet, and were drawn from all classes.

People began to assemble not only in the nave, which was open to all who cared to attend, but in the north and south transepts long before the time fixed for the service. Among those invited was the present writer.

Rain was falling outside, and but little light was able to penetrate through the windows into the Abbey, which, but for the electric lamps, would have been a temple wrapped, indeed, in gloom.

Mrs. Hardy was accompanied by Miss Kate Hardy, the dead novelist's surviving sister, and Mr. Sydney C. Cockerell, M.A., and occupied seats near the catafalque.

The small bronze urn containing Hardy's ashes had been placed on a bier, and covered with the official pall of white brocade, embroidered with the crest and arms of the Abbey, crowned Tudor Rose and the crowned Portcullis of Westminster.

On either side of the pall walked the ten pall-bearers : the Prime Minister, the Right Hon. Stanley Baldwin and Mr. Ramsay MacDonald, these representing the Government and Parliament ; Sir J. M. Barrie, Bart. ; Mr. John Galsworthy ; Sir Edmund Gosse ; Professor A. E. Housman ; Mr. Rudyard Kipling ; and Mr. Bernard Shaw, representing literature ; with the Master of Magdalene College, Cambridge, Mr. Arthur Stanley Ramsey ; and the Pro-Provost of Queen's College, Oxford, Dr. E. M. Walker, representing the Colleges, of both of which Hardy had been an Honorary Fellow.

The casket was placed on the catafalque of plain dark wood, around which were grouped six tall candles of golden brown wax, the flames of which threw a soft light on the bier, and the set faces of the mourners in the immediate vicinity.

The service commenced with the 23rd Psalm, followed by the passage from Ecclesiasticus, which begins with the very appropriate words : " Let us now praise famous men." The Precentor read the lesson, which must have been heard, so clear was his voice, by all of the congregation.

Particularly appropriate seemed the call for praise : " Leaders of the people by their counsels, and by their

knowledge of learning meet for the people, wise and eloquent in their instructions ; Such as found out musical
tunes, and recited verses in writing."

At the close of the reading a procession of clergy was
formed, which moved slowly away with the ashes to the
Poets' Corner, while the choir who remained in their
stalls sang Wesley's anthem : " Thou wilt keep me in
perfect peace."

Sir James Barrie, who walked beside the pall, carried
Mrs. Hardy's sheaf of lilies.

When the group on the purple dais, which had been
placed in the Poets' Corner, had assembled, the Dean
stood at the side of the small cavity made in the pavement,
and continued the recital of the burial service. When he
reached the committal, the casket was taken from beneath
the pall and laid in the space prepared for it. Then the
Dean scattered on the grave the earth which had been
brought from Hardy's Wessex home, dug and sent by a
labourer. While he was doing this the choir was singing
Goss's setting of : " I heard a voice from Heaven saying
unto me, write ; From henceforth blessed are the dead
which die in the Lord."

In the hushed silence by the tomb, the music and its
message, coming from unseen singers in the distance, had
a strange and appealing beauty. After the Lord's Prayer
and the Collects, the congregation joined in the hymn
" Lead Kindly Light," which was a favourite one with
Hardy. Then the service closed with the " Nunc dimittis "
and the blessing, after which the congregation stood silent
and motionless while the organ pealed forth " The Dead
March " in Saul.

Before leaving the grave, Mrs. Hardy took her lilies
from Sir J. M. Barrie and laid them by the opening where
the casket rested. Temporary barriers were immediately
placed around the spot, and in a few minutes a long line of
those who wished to pay honour to the dead poet filed
slowly by.

As one passed in front of the cavity, the top of the urn
was just visible, and it was possible, where the light struck

it, to read the simple inscription : " Thomas Hardy, O.M., born June 2nd, 1840—died January 11th, 1928."

Down in Dorset, at the same hour, at the little church at Stinsford, which Hardy so often visited, where he frequently attended the services, and in which he had been baptized, his aged brother, Mr. Henry Hardy, was the chief mourner. There was a simple service. Not less impressive, perhaps, from its surroundings and association with the dead writer than the one of pomp and ceremony in London.

It is probable that many who were present had only heard the rumour of Hardy's greatness and were unacquainted with his works. It could be seen at a glance that they were chiefly simple folk, dairymen, woodmen, ploughmen and their wives and daughters too, whose daily lives, and whose dramas of love and jealousy, revenge and disillusionment, Hardy had so vividly chronicled. So they came as though to mourn one of themselves.

They had known him and seen him bicycling about the countryside, strolling in the market-place in Dorchester, or along the streets of the little towns and villages he knew so well, or walking in later times beside the trout stream which runs through the meadows around Max Gate to the churchyard at Stinsford.

They knew him not as one of the most human of writers, but many of them as one of the simplest and most understanding of fellow-mortals. They certainly knew him also as one who cared more than most for the common needs of the countryside, which was their home and formed the boundaries of their lives.

But some of the throng at Stinsford were the landowners and farmers, some fellow-townsmen from Dorchester, and a few mourners who had come from distant parts of the county. But after the casket containing Hardy's heart had been carried in solemn procession by the Vicar of Stinsford, the Rev. H. G. B. Cowley, accompanied by Mr. Henry Hardy, and placed at the graveside, as they stood in the sloping graveyard, some of them, beneath the shade of the great yew tree, must have felt that they were present on a memorable occasion, and were marking the passing of a great and famous man.   Before the committal prayer was read the casket containing Hardy's heart was handed to a man standing down, and was slowly lowered to the place prepared for it in the Wessex soil, and in the grave of his first wife, among the ancestral tombs in the shade of the great yew tree which stands in a corner of the churchyard.

Many of those who had gathered there and had failed to gain admittance to the little Church bore flowers, and when the service ended they and many others filed past the grave, and when all had passed the casket lay hidden under a mass of wild and other flowers and bunches of evergreen.

The third, and memorial, service was held in the Church of St. Peter, Dorchester, outside which stands the bronze figure of Hardy's great and almost lifelong friend, the Rev. William Barnes, the Dorset poet.   It was attended by the Mayor and Corporation, a number of Mayors of neighbouring towns, the county and borough magistrates, representatives of various local societies and organizations with which Hardy had been connected, and a large number of his fellow-townsfolk.

The service, which followed closely that taking place at the same hour in the Abbey at Westminster, was conducted by the Rural Dean, Dr. G. C. Niven, who was a personal friend of Hardy.   A touching feature of the service was the reading at the close of the Rector's address of Hardy's poem "Afterwards," in which he foreshadowed his own passing away, and marvellously summed up what his friends and neighbours would feel about that event.

Here are two of the verses.

AFTERWARDS

When the present has latched its postern behind my
    tremulous stay,
    And the May month flaps its glad green leaves like wings,
Delicate-filmed as new-spun silk, will the neighbours say,
" He was a man who used to notice such things " ?

If, when hearing that I have been stilled at last, they stand
    at the door,
Watching the full-starred heavens that winter sees,
Will this thought rise on those who will meet my face no
    more,
  " He was one who had an eye for such mysteries " ?

We well remember reading in the columns of the
Dorchester paper how the news of Hardy's death travelled
through the countryside from village to village. The
cottagers stood at their doors in the early morning ere
the stars had time to pale in the red sky, discussing his
passing. To many of them he was in former years little
known, but his fame had at last penetrated to the most
isolated hamlet of the Wessex he had created, and
aroused an interest that was indeed wide-spread.

It was a remarkable dawn, and people as they watched
it marvelled and wondered what the flame-coloured sky
portended.

Hardy had lived to a great age owing not a little, one
may imagine, to a sound constitution—for he had few
serious ailments in his long life—to the placid existence he
led when once he had settled down in his native county,
and also to the unremitting care of his second wife, who
not only gave him the sympathy and intelligent appreciation of his great gifts that the artist needs, but warded off
from him in his later years many of the ' frets and fumes
from which poor humanity is prone to suffer,' and often
kept from him too insistent callers.

Indeed, we heard a mutual friend of the Hardys declare,
after he had passed away, that he owed ten years of his life
to his wife's care and attention.

Inasmuch that Hardy produced memorable poetic work,
or was able to look out and revise and repolish such verses
as he had years before written, during the last fifteen years
of his life, posterity will owe her a debt of gratitude.

Hardy, though one may doubt that he had much sympathy for the modern ' insurgent ' type of womanhood—
with which indeed he did not, of course, come much in

contact—had a very clear opinion of the perfect marriage as a complement of two differing natures and complex spiritualities.

In several of his books this idea is clearly indicated. One can, however, only quote two or three most striking examples in support of our contention. He states that two beings intended to love each other are two halves of a single whole. This idea is indicated in his most famous novel *Tess of the D'Urbervilles* where he writes of " two halves of an approximately perfect whole." In *A Few Crusted Characters* one has the same idea expressed in the phrase " The two halves by nature intended to form a perfect whole." And in *Time's Laughing Stocks and Other Verses*—" Since the first two sighing half-hearts made a whole." While Eustasia Vye (a real Dorset name—Vye) expresses herself as thinking that she has discovered " her perfect complement in attainments, appearance and age."

But whereas one has every reason to believe that in his second wife, as in his first, he found that " complement " to himself in a more or less degree, Hardy's couples in his novels invariably have a sense of isolation. They are usually two creatures, indeed, who have become suddenly as Adam and Eve, and in a world of their own.

In one of his phrases, which are so pregnant with descriptive beauty, Hardy writes : " The spectral, half-compounded aqueous light which pervaded the open mead impressed them with a feeling of isolation, as if they were Adam and Eve."

And the innermost art of Hardy is never better displayed than in his invariable practice of heightening this idea of isolation by giving his couples a scenic environment that suggests it and primitive surroundings where rustic love-making finds conditions in which it can develop an elementary force, and in which the lovers are stripped of all artificialities, if with them such could, indeed, exist.

*　　*　　*　　*　　*　　*

Among the most notable memorials to Hardy with which his native town and vicinity have been enriched is the stained-glass window in Stinsford Church, a mile or two outside Dorchester, in the churchyard of which his heart lies buried.

It was unveiled by the Countess of Ilchester on Friday, November 21st, 1930.

The window, which is one of three lights, is from the design of Mr. Douglas Strachan, and the subject is that of the prophet Elijah listening to the " still, small voice ! " A brass tablet records that the window was given by public subscription " to the glory of God, and in memory of Thomas Hardy, O.M. 1840–1928."

Both Mrs. Thomas Hardy and the novelist's sister, Miss Kate Hardy, were present at the unveiling, the service connected with which was conducted by the then vicar, the Rev. H. G. B. Cowley.

Bishop Joscelyne, Archdeacon of Sherborne, said, in dedicating the window, that the service called to remembrance one who was " a master in letters, the window being a sacred memorial to a great intellect, a great genius and a great lover of Nature, especially that of his own countryside."

The speaker quoted a saying of Hardy that " In spite of myself I cannot help noting countenances and tempers in objects of scenery, for instance trees, hills, houses," and drew attention to one of the dead writer's characteristics which set him apart from so many of his contemporaries—his love of introducing old customs, quaint superstitious practices and traditions which were characteristic of the Wessex of half a century or more ago.

One may add that this fondness of Hardy for introducing these is very marked in his novel *The Return of the Native*, where it will be remembered Susan Nonsuch by these means sought to break the evil spell which she believed Eustacia Yeobright had cast upon her child.

Soon after Hardy's death a proposal to provide a statue as a memorial to him in his native town was mooted. It was not, however, till nearly four years after that this was done, when, on Wednesday, September 2nd, 1931,

Sir James Barrie, an old friend of Hardy's, came to Dorchester to unveil the statue, which now stands on a Portland stone plinth at Top o' the Town, Dorchester.

The seated and life-like figure is the work of Mr. Eric Kennington, and the statue was formally presented to the town by the Countess of Ilchester, Chairman of the Memorial Committee, and was accepted on behalf of the town by the then Mayor, Mr. W. J. Fare, J.P.

Sir James Barrie, in a whimsical speech, defended Hardy (though we do not think successfully) against the charge of pessimism that was undoubtedly often brought against him as a writer. The speaker admitted that "there were years, certainly, when I thought him the most unhappy man I had ever known ; but if he had escaped his weird we could not have had our Hardy. And after all can one be altogether unhappy even when ridden by the Furies, if he is producing a masterpiece ? May we not suspect that he has moments of exultation which are denied to other mortals. I daresay the shades of the departed Great gathered in that room at Max Gate to watch their brother write the last page of *The Dynasts*. Happily after that he was to pass into a long evening of serenity," adding, in paraphrase of Hardy's own words at the closing scene in *Tess of the D'Urbervilles*: "The President of the Immortals had ended his sport with Hardy."

Hardy had been dead rather more than three years when the striking and appropriate memorial from American admirers, consisting of a roughly hewn stone obelisk standing upon a stone plinth was erected and unveiled.

It stands near a group of trees on the edge of the "Egdon" Heath so closely associated with his life, which by his wonderful descriptions of that far-extending expanse of moorland, he may be said peculiarly to have made his own. The cottage in which he was born lies not far away, and, indeed, from the window of the bedroom in which he was born the memorial is the outstanding object.

Douglas Snowdon.
Salisbury. Chichester.

This was unveiled on Thursday, April 16th, 1931, in the presence of Mrs. Hardy, Miss Kate Hardy, the novelist-poet's surviving sister, and a large gathering of officials of the Town Council of Dorchester, including the Mayor (Councillor W. J. Fare, J.P.); the Rev. Andrew Legatt, the Mayor's Chaplain ; the Deputy Mayor (Councillor T. H. H. Wheeler); the Borough Treasurer ; the Borough Surveyor, and many members of the Corporation. A number of the Hardy Players also attended the unveiling, including Alderman T. H. Tilley, the producer of the Hardy Plays, Mrs. Gertrude Bugler, who made a name for herself by her sympathetic and able presentation of several of Hardy's leading characters far beyond the limits of Dorchester.

Among others present were Lady Pinney, who with her husband, Major-General Sir Reginald Pinney, K.C.B., entertained Professor John Livingston Lowes, of Harvard and Oxford Universities, at their seat, Raiedown, near Crewkerne—because of his great admiration for Hardy and for his own distinguished scholarship, he had been chosen to unveil the memorial—Mr. Alfred Pope, long a friend of Hardy's, Lady Grogan, the Rev. and Mrs. R. G. Bartelot, Mr. Charles Lacey, a former school-fellow of Hardy, Major H. R. Kindersley, Dr. E. J. Day, and many others who had known Hardy in former or later years.

The time of the unveiling was fixed for three o'clock, but long before the hour struck and came from the church tower across the meads, a large gathering from all parts of the county and the outer borders of Wessex, with not a few Londoners, had gathered on the slopes of " Egdon " Heath, and the narrow roads leading to the nearest point were blocked with car traffic.

To Mr. St. John Hornby had been given the honour of introducing Professor Lowes. He referred in a brief speech to the fact that the spot on which the memorial had been erected might be said to be, for Hardy lovers in all lands, sacred ground, for it was so closely identified with him almost throughout his life. Mr. St. John

Hornby, continuing, said that the occasion was not one on which merely to sing Hardy's praises, but rather one by means of which honour could be done to a man who was born and dwelt among them, and was one of the great ones of his generation, and notwithstanding he belonged to the world through his genius, was also in a very special and intimate sense identified with the town of Dorchester and with the county of Dorset.

The speaker also expressed the source of pleasure and satisfaction that the monument should have been placed where it stood by Hardy admirers in the United States of America. He referred to Professor Lowes's reputation as a man of learning and culture, than whom no better representative of their kindred across the sea could have been chosen for the unveiling ceremony. Professor Lowes had already written with sympathy and understanding of Hardy as a poet and writer of prose, and held, in common with the speaker and those who were gathered there and were Hardy's admirers, the opinion that he had written not only for the generation in which he lived, but for all time, because his themes were the eternal verities of life, and that he had in him the elements of immortality.

Before unveiling the memorial Professor Lowes said : " It is fitting that this memorial should have its base in the soil of this heath. For ' Egdon ' Heath is in a sense the heart and centre of Hardy's world. And so this monument commemorates what needs, save as an act of piety, no remembrance—the spot which will always remain, above others, the symbol of Hardy's peculiar power. For no other English novelist or poet has been so profoundly conscious of the roots of England, deep in its immemorial, prehistoric Roman and Saxon past. Nor has any other," the speaker continued in an eloquent address, " so imbued his landscape (and who does not recognize the truth of this plea), roads and moors and barrows with a strange sentience, as though they had become, through centuries of human contacts, participants in that unending life. And in this heath, as in no other spot, that sense of an enduring past and of the indissoluble oneness of humanity with the earth from which it sprang, found its supreme impression. Hardy himself once wrote of this in one of his finest passages of prose : ' The place ["Egdon" Heath] became full of a watchful intentness now ; for when other things sank brooding to sleep the heath appeared slowly to awake and listen.'

" And, as it has dealt with man's memorials for centuries, that aged watchful heath will in time incorporate this trespasser upon its solitude with itself."

In concluding the speaker said : " And as one passes— and I know whereof I speak—along the roads and through the villages of Hardy's kingdom it is his folk who are still one with the heaths and woodlands, whose steps one traces, and who still are more vividly alive than we or our fellow-mortals whom we meet. Not since the older Greek poets—and then in a different fashion—has the imagination so merged in each other, without identifying, earth and its denizens. And nowhere can that essential quality of Hardy's genius be more deeply felt than here.

"But it is not here alone on ' Egdon' that it is felt. Three hundred and thirty-two years ago, in 1599, twenty-one years before the English Pilgrims landed on a shore which, even with a prefixed ' New,' they called England, Samuel Daniel wrote, in his ' Musophilus,' of the English tongue :

' And who, in time, knows whither we may vent
    The treasures of our tongue, to what strange shores
This gaine of our best glory shall be sent.
    T' inrich unknowing nations with our stores ?
What worlds in th' yet unformed Occident
    May come refined with accents that are ours ? '

" And the donors of this monolith, who are beyond the Atlantic, when they would be here, are but acknowledging in their memorial one of the deepest debts which we of that world which Daniel with a seer's vision saw, owe to the land from which our fathers came. More than thirty years ago Hardy received an invitation to visit the United States, which for various reasons he felt obliged to decline.

" In doing so he wrote some lines of self-revelation :

> " For, wonning in these ancient lands,
>   Enchased and lettered as a tomb,
> And scored with prints of perished hands,
>   And chronicled with dates of doom,
>   Though my own sowing bear no bloom,
>   I trace the lives such scenes enshrine,
>   Give past exemplars present room,
>   And their experience count as mine."

" But in the records of these lives, and in these scenes, and in the experiences which he made immortally his own, he *did* come to us, to remain, I must believe, *ours*, as he is yours. And it is as a symbol of that devotion that this memorial stands.

" And only on those terms would he accept it, could he know."

Professor Lowes closed with an apt quotation from one of Hardy's own poems :

> " My spirit will not haunt the mound
>   Above my breast,
> But travel, memory possessed,
> To where my tremulous being found
>   Life largest, best.
>
> My phantom-footed shape will go
>   When nightfall greys,
> Hither and thither along the ways
> I and another used to know
>   In backward days.
>
> And there you'll find me, if a jot
>   You still should care
> For me, and for my curious air ;
> If otherwise, then I shall not,
>   For you, be there."

R

In some well-chosen words the Mayor of Dorchester thanked the donors of the memorial, and especially referred to Mr. A. Edward Newton, of Philadelphia, Pennsylvania, for the active part he had taken in promoting the gift.   He thanked Professor Lowes in the name of Dorset, for his presence there and the eloquent address he had given.

The inscription on the monolith reads :

THOMAS HARDY, O.M.
was born in the adjacent cottage
2nd June, 1840,
and in it wrote *Under the Greenwood Tree,*
and *Far from the Madding Crowd.*

This monument is erected to his
memory by a few of his American Admirers
1931.

CHAPTER XI

Hardy, as we know him in his greatest novels, is un-likely to ever be very popular with the average reader ; because for all his directness and clearness of expression, he is far too inclined to melancholy, and definitely too preoccupied with the greater and more fateful problems of life. The side of his work which has most appealed to readers is his vivid portrayal of rustic humour, and the picturesqueness of rustic occupations, and his sketches of nature as he uses these as a background to life.

This is certainly a noticeable fact. Other writers have laid the ages under contribution and travelled to various climes in search of romance. Hardy contented himself with fellow countrymen of the obscure and until then almost unknown district of southern England, which he made famous ; and of the humour of the common people, and the details of their occupations, wove a series of romances, the originality and strength of which dwarfed those of all of his contemporaries.

Hardy found that indisputably the people of Dorset possessed a character of their own, and he was fortunate not only in growing up during a particularly interesting epoch in English history, but was racially and temperamentally a representative man to whom the experiences, bitter struggles, disillusionments, stoical sufferings of wrongs, and primitive passions of the peasantry, who formed the bulk of his characters, were well and intimately known.

Consequently his peasants are not those made familiar by comic operas, or of the other imaginative writers, but realities, and his studies of them naturally affronted and, as we know, shocked the sentimental reader at almost every turn, and the townsman, out of his preconceived ideas regarding them, by reason of their frank truth and fidelity to type. They are, indeed, only romantic figures because truth is, at the bottom, more romantic than imagination.

Hardy too, possessed a most wonderful descriptive gift. He knew Nature from the inside, had studied her various moods from childhood, and, therefore, was able on paper to describe the dawn, the sunset, a smiling summer morning, the bleak winter night, the rich land of his " Vale of the Great Dairies," the grimness of a desolate moorland like that of " Egdon " Heath, and in fact these things are found permeating his books, with a classical restraint but indubitable finality.

Future historians, indeed, will owe a debt to Hardy for the wonderful and accurate pictures he has left behind him of many agricultural operations as these things were in the times of which he wrote.

It is, perhaps, a little strange that Hardy in literature should have ended practically where he began, that is to say, by poetry, and after the publication of *The Well-Beloved*, he devoted himself exclusively to verse.

It is true, however, that much of the poetry which appeared in his various volumes of collected poems represented work that had gone on over the whole period of his adult life, and the critical and intelligent reader of his poems should notice their dates, as by them he can trace a distinct link between those of the various romances and short stories.

Many critics of Hardy's verse have been prone to say that the poems show in many places defective technique ; but this criticism is only true in so far that he was manifestly seeking by experiment to create a new technique, and it should be remembered that the essential poet has always revealed himself by his quest for new metres and new stanzas.

Hardy's are far removed from the literary and artistic

ballads, and it is doubtful if any other English poet has come so near to the secret of the ballad as a natural growth, but it is obviously that of a changed world.

Hardy has left behind him a full harvest of verse, considering the amazing and important contribution that he also made to English literature by the more important of his novels. But critics will probably all agree that *The Dynasts*, that great epic drama in three volumes dealing with the life history of Napoleon, forms his crowning work, and that it really represents the whole of his emotional philosophy of life.

Just as he had found in the lives of the peasants around him many incidents which seemed to suggest the sheer fatalism which Hardy portrays in imaginative form in his ironic and tragic tales, he discovered also the same elements in the meteoric and fateful career of Napoleon.

In *The Dynasts* Hardy reads into history the influence of an unknown and irresistible power, to which men and nations were and are subject, just as pieces are on a chessboard subject to the controlling hand of the players.

Into this, his greatest poetic work, he crowded the knowledge, thought and information that he had gathered during a lifetime.

As a work of art *The Dynasts* has been severely criticized, and to say that it was a perfect one would, of course, be ridiculous. Nevertheless, it seems doubtful if any poem of equal importance, or any so full of descriptive and historical detail, was ever more deeply characterized with emotional power, or rendered so impressive by the domination of one central idea. We think it can now be safely claimed for it, that it made Hardy's position as a poet unassailable, and that he may be considered one of the few great poets of the century in which he lived.

Another interesting aspect of Hardy is the fact that, the last of the great Victorians, he lived to become the first of the Georgians, linking up the two epochs, both by his catholicity of subject and his independence of expression.

Indeed, one of the most remarkable phases of Hardy's life and character is that he should have been able to keep abreast of times which in the last two decades of his life showed such violent changes. Hardy will certainly rank in English literature not only as a novelist of great distinction, but as one who attained almost equal fame as a poet.

Indeed, from 1914 onward his standing as a poet became more and more universally recognized.

His work as a novelist can be decisively summed up; the English novel before Hardy's time was, with a few exceptions, of a discursive type, and it remained for him to first endow it with structural cohesion and make it a work of art. Doubtless this gift was largely due to his early training, and his love for the study of architecture, and his liking for introducing architectural details into his novels. Other writers, many of them, pursue their course at will, depicting the varied comedy and tragedy of life, discursively if well, but Hardy, even, as is the case sometimes, when he seems to be discursive, is nevertheless charting his way deliberately and relentlessly to the goal to which he has set his face; and so the grip of tragedy invariably increases until the end. That end, however, although some people read into it mere fatality, is not actually merely that, but also often tinged by pity.

While some of Hardy's novels leave their mark upon one because of their brilliant descriptions and variety of the life described, it is works like *The Mayor of Casterbridge*, *The Return of the Native*, *Tess of the D'Urbervilles* and *Jude the Obscure* which have secured for him his place in literature, and for them admission that they are works of both power and art.

There are some critics who consider Meredith, one of Hardy's valued friends, occupies the first place among English novelists of the last quarter of the 19th century. But whereas Hardy is still widely read, and by classes of the community to whom one might, perhaps, imagine he would be caviare, Meredith is very little heard of, or read, to-day, and for this reason one would allot to Hardy the premier position.

Both these writers, however, being contemporaries, and both of such distinction that it is difficult to separate

Church Hope Cove.
Portland. "Isle of Slingers".

Douglas Snowgar

them in one's mind, had some qualities in common, and even the points in which they differed were chiefly those to challenge comparison. Both men possessed critical intellects, always challenging things that were. Meredith, we must admit, is the more finished artist, and more possessed with the spirit of art, so that he watched the various phases of life and character in men and women with the more detached vision.

Hardy, in his wonderful instinct for picturing the Dorsetshire peasants in their true environment, resembles, in some measure, a fellow-poet, Wordsworth, and indeed achieved far more effectively than Wordsworth what the latter intended. And certainly one can find nothing greater in English literature in the description of scenery than is found in the pages of *The Return of the Native*, in which Hardy makes of " Egdon " Heath a living thing.

It must not, however, be supposed that Hardy was entirely dependent on the district which his genius ultimately made so thoroughly his own. It has been pointed out over and over again in relation to genius in Art, Music and Letters that it is greater than the rules or the confines that may apparently be arbitrarily set about it. Had Hardy been born in Devon, Cornwall or, say, Yorkshire, we make no doubt that he would have accomplished for these counties something of the kind that he has for his loved Dorset, and the wider area of Wessex.

It is, nevertheless, probably true that he is in one sense one of the most local of all distinguished writers of fiction : but it is equally true that his great gifts would have enabled him to break any county boundaries, and that in adopting Wessex for his field of study and of literary expression he is not one whit the more circumscribed than was Scott, Dickens, Fielding or other great masters of the English novel.

In our view Hardy excels in selecting, from portions of the Wessex that he loved, backgrounds suitable to the characters which he describes so vividly. We think it will be agreed that his men characters, with a few exceptions, far excel in lifelikeness and in vitality his women. In describing his women one is led to think that Hardy's interest and regard for them was habitually coloured by his masculine amusement or contempt, and for this reason on the whole they are inferior to and less vital than his men.

The women in his books seem to have charmed him, or touched his sense of tragic futility or of comic caprice, but they very rarely stirred his deeper sympathies and more fertile imagination.

Hardy certainly understood little of, or cared little, in a literary sense for, conscience, or of passion, and in his books grave wrongs are condoned with an amazing ease, and love is usually depicted as a placid type of emotion, or merely shallow philandering.

But underlying his undoubted sense of the futility of life, there lay a perception of its even humorous aspects. No writer has linked the humour and tragedy of life together with more skilful and powerful effect than he.

What little of the modern side of life and modern civilization that is to be found in Hardy's prose works appears to us rather to injure them than otherwise to act as a complement of the whole. This was but natural, for to a large extent Hardy stood aloof from modern life, although mingling with it more frequently than he was commonly supposed to do, and mixing in society in London and elsewhere to a considerable extent.

As we once heard a very old friend of his say : " Hardy is essentially of the soil of Wessex, he is almost lost in a crowd of ordinary modern society people, and he always strikes me, when I have met him in London, as having left more than half of himself in his country home."

But, perhaps, this noticeable detachment from surroundings so foreign to his tastes and nature chiefly arose from the fact that he was undoubtedly all the time meditating deeply on the problems of life, the scene presented to him, and contrasting them with other scenes of a purely rustic character.

CHAPTER XII

WESSEX IN THE FOUR SEASONS

To one who has known Wessex, has lingered lovingly amid its lanes and valleys, has climbed the steep sides of natural downs and of British and Roman camps, has seen early dawn and gorgeous and almost Venetian sunsets gradually illumine or flood the landscape with almost indescribable beauty, it is difficult indeed to determine in which of the four seasons of the year Wessex is fairest—in spring, when new life is coursing through the countryside and there is a freshness of greenery pleasant alike to the eye and the heart ; in summer, when white roads stretch past broad fields of ripening corn, the shady coppices resound with the songs of birds, and the promise of harvest greets one on every side ; in autumn, when the days begin to draw in and shadows to lengthen on moor and hillside, and the woods and lanes to take upon themselves the glorious mantle of the dying year ; or in winter, when grey mists and tempered sunlight, hoar-frost and sparkling rime, give a beauty of their own to moorland pool, placid river, and naked hedgerows. " Each season has a beauty of its own," we are told, and of the four seasons in Wessex this axiom is singularly true.

Spring in Wessex ! In the lanes which creep sinuously, as though indifferent of purpose, below the swart expanse of Bere Heath, part of the famous " Egdon " Heath of *The Return of the Native*, or lead the traveller by easy gradients into the leafy boscage of Cranborne Chase, or from the larger towns to scattered hamlets, Nature is astir.

Green jewels of buds are gemming the long bare branches overhead, and on the latter throstle and blackbird carol a full-throated welcome to spring. Beneath the hedgerows the flowers are springing—bright-eyed primroses, tender-hued violets, and silvery anemones ; and later on masses of may and blackthorn blossom give the hedges a bridal robe of white fragrance.

The tiny rivulet, freed from icy bonds, sings its song over the pebbles, and here and there flashes with light as the sunshine strikes its fretted surface through the hedgerow or overhanging branches of trees. As Shelley sings :

> "The brightest hour of unborn spring
> Through the winter wandering,
> Found, it seems, the halcyon morn
> To hoar February born ;
> Bending from Heaven, in azure mirth,
> It kissed the forehead of the earth,
> And smiled upon the silent sea,
> And bade the frozen streams be free,
> And waked to music all their fountains."

The spirit of new life has commenced to strew flowers upon the barren way, and in Wessex the joy of spring is in the air—the ambient sunshine, the blue sky with banked clouds white and impressive as Alpine peaks, and the sense of Nature's awakening.

In the coppices which lie over the hedges are wonderful carpets of vernal green diapered with the yellow blazonry of primroses and deep-blue patches of hyacinths. And as the sun sinks westward at close of day, the fretted tracery of twigs and branches, as yet but partially delivered from the starkness of winter, lies upon the mossy and flower-bedecked undergrowth.

In the vale, through which a placid river flows past willow-clad banks and rush-grown pools, at early dawn diaphanous mists have hung—mists out of which Titania's robe might have been woven ; swirling vapours in fantastic shapes, at first grey and sombre, and then, as the sun creeps up over the environing hills, tinted with all the exquisite colours of nacre and of the rainbow.   Upon the steel-grey pools and in the shallow backwaters coots dart to and fro like ebon shuttles, eager for the work of rough architecture which forms their nests, and leave a furrowed wake of ripples behind to mark their courses.

On the downs of Wessex shepherds are busy, and flocks once more appear to roam at large.   And amid the gorse of moorland, and the stunted heather of the outer wild, birds are building to an accompaniment of twittered music and fluttered wings.

On the coast the sea breaks in gentler music, and seems to say : "Winter is gone and spring is here."   And in the caves and on the rocks of deserted shores the deep organ-note of winter seas gives place to the softer lullaby of spring ; and the crying of gulls and seabirds seems softened in the mating time.

But it is in the orchards of north and north-western Wessex that spring is most exquisite.   The rugged trees, which, but a few months ago, in their nakedness and grotesquenesses of aged growth, appeared even in the light of day impossible of beauty, and at night alarmingly distorted, are decked with a beautiful garment of pink and white blossom, transfiguring them and rendering them lovely beyond all other springtide visions.   And beneath them, as the soft breeze from off the uplands blows, comes a white and pink carpet more exquisite of tint than any yet woven for the palace of a queen—a carpeting of green and white ghostly at dawn, and fairy-like at sundown. Surely it is on such a one that the " little, wise folk " of legend and story hold their revels.

> " This is the time when bit by bit
>   The days begin to lengthen sweet,
>   And every minute gained is joy——"

has sung a poetess.   And of such is the springtide of Wessex when, as Francis Bacon says, " the breath of flowers is far sweeter in the air, where it comes and goes like the warbling of music," and Nature, as yet untired by the labours of a year, is fresh from winter's sleep, and eager to do her best to rejoice the wayfarer, and bring hope anew into the heart of man.

The summer comes, with its wealth of blossom and harvest; the pilgrims in Wessex will find a new interest in its scenery and its life. Lanes and by-ways, which a few months before held but the promise of rich foliage, now have that promise fulfilled. The overarching trees make a royal canopy of shade for sun-weary eyes, and provide many a pleasant wayside nook for tired bodies a-tramp.

Now the hedges are gay with blackberry, clematis, dog roses, and bell-flowered convolvulus. The little brook which trickles along below them sings a sharper song than in spring, for its volume is less, and its notes, as it passes over the pebbles, are attuned to a different key. Beside it now are kingcups, orange-yellow and athirst for dew, in place of the paler primroses, and the shy violets have given place to azure-eyed forget-me-nots, whilst in the banks bloom the purple cranebill, pink mallows, and crimson-tipped daisies, all half-hidden 'neath the lush grass and fronds of hartstongue and " basket " ferns.

In the hedges are heard the querulous twitterings of the nestlings, and the anxious calls of parent-birds who have returned to find their fledgelings gone. There is not the joyous, full-throated carolling of the year when young, save perhaps at early dawn and when at last the shadows come after the long summer's day.

But to the hedgerow and the field have come new inhabitants—many-hued butterflies hovering and flitting from daisy to thistle and hedgerow to hedgerow—dainty, fragile things fit only for summer's breezes and summer's sun; and gauze-winged dragon-flies, with steel-blue and grey-green bodies, flashing hither and thither in the sun-shine.

In the sunlit vales the cattle are lowing, standing knee-deep in the meadow grass, or in some shallow, tree-shaded pool at a river bend. And in the pasture the grass is falling beneath the rhythmic swing of the scythe, and to the mower's song.

The river itself has cast the silver of its surface into Nature's melting-pot, and now, in the summer sunshine, shows long stretches of dazzling gold. In the shallows the current plays against the rushes and pours forth a humming melody like that of a slowly driven spinning-wheel. The coot has built her nest and hatched her young, and now she sails across the quiet reaches of the river with a flotilla of fledgelings in her wake.

Sometimes yet in Wessex, if the wanderer is fortunate, he may catch a glimpse of a sheeny kingfisher, watching from a willow trunk with bright eye, or flashing like a ray of amethyst and emerald downward into the shimmering water.

In the farther woods which lie amid the hills there is a shade for the weary—the deep shade and the silence of the eternal. Underneath is the carpet of flowers which love the coolness and the filtered lights of the woods—tall foxgloves mottled pink and white, purple-flowered wood betony and yellow toad-flax, and the emerald-green mosses and colour-enriched lichen, which few fabrics woven by human hands have succeeded in imitating in colour or rivalling in beauty. Whilst hidden in the upper branches of the overshadowing foliage the song-bird's note, hushed in the sun-stricken open, makes melody.

In the silence of the summer's day—

> " The time so tranquil is and clear,
>   That nowhere shall ye find,
> Save on a high and barren hill,
>   An air of passing wind.
>
> All trees and simples, great and small,
>   That balmy leaf do bear,
> Than they were painted on a wall,
>   No more they move or stir."

On the high chalk downs, whose rounded bosses, in the springtime green as emerald, now have taken upon them somewhat of the tan of summer's sun, the great flocks are wandering, and the tinkle of sheepbells (the music loved of shepherds) floats faintly down into the vales. On these uplands, the soft summer's breeze sings at early morn and at even in the gorse, but at noon is silent, made dumb by the ambient sunshine.

But when the night-wind blows, it is scented with the perfume of gorse and upland flowers—wild thyme and brier and pinks—and the shadows thrown by the silver moonlight chase each other across the hill-slopes, and the conies frisk and scuttle from the warren to the gorse, and from the shade to twilight patches.

Over the valleys beneath comes the pall of a starlit night, the scattered hamlets in the vale gradually fading from view ; and then yellow star-like lights blink at one from the windows of scattered farm-houses for a time, and then all is wrapt in the blue darkness of a summer's night.

At summer's dawn on the coast the grey waves break with a lazy music along the sandy shores, and with a more silvery song against the rocks and crags. And out at sea " the white-sailed ships dream on their silent way."

At the edge of the sea, white-winged gulls hover like un-quiet spirits ; but the beat of their wings is slower than at other seasons, and when they contend against the gale. By noon, the lazy summer sea has written its rippled story on the strand, which none human can read, for the wave-characters have a place in no language ; they are the lettered notes of sea music, sad or gay, as its mood may be.

Summer, the time of flowers and ripening corn, brings to Wessex gardens a blaze of colour, a riot of blossom which speaks of a rich soil and pure air. Over the thatch of cottages climb roses red and white ; along the tiny paths leading to porch and cottage door nod campanulas and roses, and the mingled scent of stocks, sweet peas, and lavender perfumes the air ; whilst on either hand are wide-faced yellow sunflowers and upstanding spikes of red and white hollyhocks.

In such gardens, instinct with colour, perfume, and beauty, is the concentrated joy of summer life, with the underlying song of bees and the twittered accompaniment of sparrows in the thatch. Many a Wessex garden such as we have known is indeed a quiet bower, far from the noise of town—a spot full of sweet dreams, and health, and gently breathing peace.

Autumn brings many beauties to Wessex—exquisite tints of foliage, beauty of cloud and shadows, glories of the lingering summer days. Along the winding lanes there is new charm. Overhead the green canopy has changed to one of yellow, russet, crimson, and browns of many shades, and underfoot the carpet of the dying year is thickening day by day. In the hedges the same story is told. Lingering blackberries give a sombre or a crimson note to the hedgerows, and the scarlet of the wild rose's fruit flashes upon the wayfarer on every side. Creepers are " turning," and exquisite autumn tints are veining all leaves, Nature's rich pencilling for mortal's admiration. Summer flowers yet linger in the hedges, loth to go with the rest of summer's joys, and the pale forget-me-nots seem to be frailer still beside the brook and river.

In the orchards golden leaves are falling, to rival in their carpeting of greensward underneath the trees the beauty of that of spring ; and boughs which bent with blossom are bending 'neath the russet and the sun-kissed crimson of the fruit.

In the wide fields the nodding corn, yellow-brown, is falling in the track of the reaping machine ; but here and there comes still in Wessex the music of the scythe and sickle being sharpened, and the rustle of falling swathes of heavy-headed grain. And amid the corn and behind the sweep of scythe are Wessex maids, busy to bind the fallen stalks, on whose cheeks, as Tom Hood wrote :

> "An Autumn flush
> Deeply ripened ; such a blush
> In the midst of brown was born,
> Like red poppies grown with corn."

Wareham. "Anglebury."

Douglas-Snowdon

S

In the well-watered vales of Wessex the cattle roam at will amid the grass which is a rich aftermath. The river flows along less noisily than in the drought of summer days, now once more silvery grey, and green where the weeds grow thick, in place of golden with the summer sunshine. The reeds are high along the banks, and they bend reluctantly beneath the flow of water, and the velvety brown spearheads of rushes nod gravely in the autumn breeze. The silvery green of the willows is now changed to pale gold, and at sundown, in this season of mists and mellow fruitfulness, diaphanous vapours enshroud the landscape.

On the uplands the breath of autumn has come ; the bracken has put on its exquisite tints of brown, the gorse's golden glow is slowly fading, and the wild thyme no longer gives out its full perfume. At nights the flocks herd in the shelter of the gorse, for the night-wind blows chill. Below the downs the woodlands stretch, a blaze of orange, purple and brown foliage, slowly thinning in the autumn wind—

> "The year grows still again, the surging wake
> Of full-sailed summer folds its furrows up ;
> As after passing of an argosy
> Old silence settles back upon the sea,
> And ocean grows as placid as a cup.
> Spring the young morn, and Summer the strong noon,
> Have dreamed and done and died for Autumn's sake ;
> Autumn that finds not for a loss so dear
> Solace in stack and garner here too soon
> Autumn, the faithful widow of the year."

In the coppice the nuts are falling earthward from their husks, and the industrious and provident squirrels are already laying up their winter stores.

Here and there in cottage gardens under the hills roses linger amid autumn flowers—reminders of the summer that has gone into the past ; and from the cottage chimneys the blue smoke of wood-fires curls—another signal that autumn is here.

William Barnes, the true poet of Wessex life, has pictured
Wessex autumn nights thus :

"Now the light o'rhe west is a-turn'd to gloom,
   An' the men be at hwome vrom ground ;
   An' the bells be a-zenden all down the Coombe
From tower their mwoansome sound.
   An' the wind is still,
   An' the house-dogs do bark,
   An' the rooks be a-vled to the elems high an' dark,
   An' the water do roar at mill."

The sea, too, which now surges on the Wessex shore
o' nights with a dirge for the summer which has gone, has
taken on its autumn tints. Now at dawn it is grey as a
Puritan maiden's gown ; at noon, grey-green as chrysoprase,
not a wedding of amethyst and emerald ; and at sunset a
slaty blue, ominous of coming storms. Its voice upon the
shore has altered too, and the listener for its music hears the
low booming as of minute-guns—the diapason of the sea,
or the harsh rattle of the shingle like " reeds " out of tune.
Under the moon it is sullen and cold, and the unbroken
fairy moon-track of summer has vanished.

But in autumn Wessex has a rare beauty both of foliage
and of atmosphere, and Nature paints her clouds at sunset
with no niggardly hand. In the western sky is often a
blaze of glory, a heightened echoing of that in woodland
glade and hedgerow of the earth.

When winter comes, it is but to give another season to a
year full of varied beauties. The dawn breaks red and
flushes the hills for a brief space, ere permeating the sheltered vales beneath them with its roseate hue ; and seaward
it turns the pale and ghostly chalk cliffs into things of
pearly beauty.

Along the lanes, erstwhile a blaze of autumn glory overhead and leaf-carpeted beneath the feet, bare trees point
skyward—their branches a black tracery against the pale
winter firmament at dawn ; at eventide a weird tangle of
half-lost shapes. Over the fields almost from sunrise to

sunset hang blue-grey mists, torn now and again into fantastic forms as the winter's breeze comes across the hills or down the vale.

On the uplands is the great silence of winter.

From the heights one can see fairy valleys emerging for the moment from their enveloping mists, to disclose the steel-grey ribbon which marks the course of the river. But all around is silence. Bullfinches no longer sing from the gorse bushes ; larks no longer pierce the clouds and drop their strings of melody down to earth. Even the conies seem to have retired to their burrows from the chill of winter's dawn and winter's day.

In the vales the rush-grown river flows, swollen by rains and the inpourings of new-made brooks and rivulets, under a sullen sky ; the rushes, olive-green and withered-brown, forming a thicket along its banks. In the meadows and in the pools, where the river has overflowed its banks or formed backwaters around the sharp curves, the birds of winter give the only element of life—agate-hued wild duck, dun-coloured plover, and long-billed snipe.

On the moors, not long ago ablaze with purple heather and gloriously golden with late-flowering gorse, there is a sombre beauty which Hardy so often referred to—a beauty which pervades the heart of the wayfarer, and grips him with an emotion finely tuned to the vast silence of those lonely wastes. In winter, whether in daylight or in darkness, these illimitable moors are the abode of mists and tempests ; at night becoming "the home of strange phantoms . . . the hitherto unrecognized original of those wild regions of obscurity which are vaguely felt to be compassing us about in midnight dreams of flight and disaster, and are never thought of after the dream till revived by scenes like this."

Amid the stretches of olive-brown heather and whins, and stark and stunted trees, the tiny pools stare up at the grey and heavy sky like the dull, glazed eyes of mammoth beings stretched dead upon the wild.

Along the Wessex coast huge waves are surging—winter waves, hungry and sonorous. And in the sea-washed caves there is the booming organ-note of storm, carried miles inland by the rising gale. From the rocks, lashed by white crest of surges broken in their attacks upon the immovable, comes the sharper music of a wailing note, half wind and half seething foam.

Winter has touched the sea with her darkling spell, and come are

"The strong, shouting days and nights that run,
  All white with stars, across the labouring ways
  Of billows warm with storm, instead of sun.

And as one stands upon the sea-girt heights

  By some tempestuous bay,
What time the great sea waxes warm and white,
And beats and blinds the following wind with spray——"

the watcher feels the spell of winter's rude magnificence.

But its most beautiful aspect is when hoar-frost and snow come, turning the bare into the clothed with its bridal garment of white, and its sparkling jewels of rime ; making the hedgerows, though stripped of foliage, one exquisite fairy-like tracery of soft whiteness.

Each blade of grass in the meadow is now a gemmed spear, brighter in the winter sunshine than any polished lance of knight of old. Along the roadside withered thistles and upstanding teasels are transformed into exquisite clusters of sparkling gems and fairy diadems. On the uplands the gorse is rime-laden and beautiful, with the fretted webs of spiders like the exquisite tracery of rose-windows set in the shining walls of some fairy palace.

In the valleys, white and glistening beneath its mantle of hoar-frost, the little brooks are silent, and the river flows slowly, and looking the blacker for its environing fringe of rime. Reeds and rushes, sedge and weed, are jewelled by Nature's generous hand, and winter's beautiful garment enshrouds the land, vale and coppice and sloping pasture.

On the great stretches of moor, which lie beneath the

winter's sun glistening with the exquisite sheen of frosted silver, the pools which lay dull under the lowering sky now glint like blinking eyes at the wayfarer, at night becoming steely mirrors under the pale-faced moon. Here and there a ruddy-breasted robin, " Christ's bird," carols on a gorse twig, or from the naked branch of some storm-beaten tree ; but all the other voices of Nature are still.

But there is yet a fairer, purer beauty sometimes, when on moor and vale and coppice and hillside white snow-flakes have floated, blotting out all ugly things, all angles of Nature's architecture. Then it is a white world, indeed, that lies under the red winter sun—a world of snowy imagery beneath a mantle of unsullied purity.

> " Then at even
>   Burning logs, drawn from near-by copse and ancient wood,
>   Smoulder ruddy on the hearth,
>   And the flames send shadows dancing,
>   Keeping time to upward-flying sparks.
>   Whilst outside the winter wind is voicing
>   Dirge-like music of the dying day."

This the Wessex that Hardy loved, mused in, painted in poems and word-pictures.

CHAPTER XIII

SCENES FROM FIVE TYPICAL NOVELS

No book upon Hardy could be considered to approach completeness without some reference to the towns and villages which, many of them of little importance in themselves, and some situated in counties other than Dorset, have yet gained considerable interest and fame from the fact of their having been made the locale of Hardy's novels, tales and poems.

The term " Wessex " in his works conforms with a fair degree of accuracy to its historical area, but on occasion extends somewhat beyond those borders. It comprises the whole of Dorset, portions of Hants, Wilts, Somerset, Devon and Oxfordshire, with occasional reference to places in Berks and Cornwall. Hardy himself divides " Wessex " into North Wessex, South Wessex, Mid-Wessex, Outer Wessex, Lower Wessex and Upper Wessex, which area, it may be said, comprises what may be roughly called the greater part of the South and West of England.

A very large number of the towns, and even villages of importance, and some hamlets in the counties of Hants, Wilts, Dorset and Somerset are mentioned by name or have been thinly disguised in the novels and volumes of short stories and poems which, numbering nearly a score, bear his name. But it is to Dorset, after all, with its sharp contrasts in scenery and character, that Hardy devoted loving and unremitting care and study. Indeed, it may almost be said that Dorset is " Wessex," so comparatively seldom does he in his descriptive work wander even for a brief period of time outside its confines.

It is with the identification of some of the more famous scenes depicted in the various stories, and the description of the actual places, we now seek to deal.

Dorchester, from which centre the scenes of the various novels may almost be said to radiate, is a typical West Country town of some eight thousand inhabitants. Its importance, however, in the past has at various times been great, and now in the present day it is still greater than its size would imply. A Roman military base, it was anciently known as Durnovaria. The vicissitudes which overtook it during the period of the Danish occupation were numerous and disastrous. Just after the dawn of the 11th century the town, then flourishing, and one of the chief places in the West of England, was totally destroyed by fire, and for some two hundred years its history is rather of a recuperative than of an advancing character. The disquieting times following the Norman Conquest had much to do with the slow advance the town made towards regaining the position the calamities that had at various times overtaken it caused it to lose. But eventually a rich priory was established, a castle erected and the town walls enlarged, repaired and strengthened.

Dorchester, however, had not yet done with misfortune. For half-way through the last decade of the 16th century it was stricken with the plague, and the population of the town was, according to the chroniclers, reduced by one-half. Eighteen years later it was once more the scene of conflagration, which laid two-thirds of the town in ruins. During the great Civil War the town was loyal to the Parliament; it was captured, however, by the King's forces under the Earl of Carnarvon, and during the rest of the war played an important part in the struggle for supremacy in the West, being alternately occupied by the Cavaliers and Roundhead forces.

Not quite half a century later the ancient town, with its dismantled defences, became the scene of one of the bloodiest farces of justice staining the pages of history. It was here that the infamous Jeffreys, judicial in nothing save name, in September, 1685, held his "Bloody Assize." He lodged in the High West Street ; where the window, which in those days commanded a view of the gaol, and out of which he gazed at the execution of his victims, is still shown.   There were over three hundred prisoners to be tried, and Jeffreys, in whose hands their fate lay, let it be understood that the only hope of mercy was a plea of guilty.   Scores of the unfortunate people, who had been directly or indirectly implicated in the Duke of Monmouth's attempt to seize the English throne, on pleading guilty, were without trial ordered to be executed forthwith—two hundred and ninety-two receiving sentence of death out of about three hundred and twenty prisoners.

Jeffreys's chair is still to be seen at the Town Hall.

Dorchester, by reason of the magnitude of its misfortunes, almost from time immemorial up to the commencement of the 18th century, deserved well of Fate, and from the termination of the period embraced by the Monmouth Rebellion its history has down to the present day been uneventful.

As is perhaps natural, Dorchester, the " Casterbridge " of the novels, plays an important part in a considerable number of the novelist's stories.   The immediately sur-rounding country, indeed, lends itself admirably to the descriptive gifts which Hardy possessed in so marked a degree.

It is not possible to describe in detail the locale of the whole series of twenty-three volumes into which the novels and short tales and poems have been published in the handsome " Wessex " uniform edition.   We are compelled from consideration of space to make a selection as repre-sentative as possible, not laying claim, however, either to the selection or the inclusion of necessarily the most excellent of the novelist's works in every case.

For the purposes of this choice the novels (excluding the three collections of short stories, *A Group of Noble Dames*, *Life's Little Ironies* and *Wessex Tales*) may be classified in three divisions with some attempt at exactness—namely, the Idyllic, the Tragic, and the Miscellaneous, in which latter division are included the tales having a romantic, comic, ironic or extravagant note.

Under the first head may be placed *The Trumpet Major*, and Mr. Hardy's second novel, as regards sequence of publication, *Under the Greenwood Tree*. Of these two we have selected the first-named as being the more powerful book, and as providing a better example of "action." The second classification includes, in order of their publication—*Desperate Remedies, Far from the Madding Crowd, The Return of the Native, The Mayor of Casterbridge, The Woodlanders, Tess of the D'Urbervilles* and *Jude the Obscure*. Of these *Far from the Madding Crowd* and *Tess of the D'Urbervilles* have been selected. In the remaining class may be placed *The Hand of Ethelberta, A Laodicean, Two on a Tower* and *The Well-Beloved*, from which *Two on a Tower* and *The Well-Beloved* have been selected—the latter more especially because of its elusiveness, a quality which makes it distinctive and fantastical.

Although Hardy has studied his characters and their background so closely that identification of the places and scenes used becomes a matter of no great difficulty to one well acquainted with the counties in which they are laid, he has on occasion availed himself of the novelist's privilege to idealize, and sometimes even to combine two or more places under one description. For example, the "Welland House"—Lady Constantine's home of *Two on a Tower*—is partly Charborough House, near Winterborne, and partly an old mansion (now a farm-house), near Milborne St. Andrew. In like manner the column (the tower of the story) which plays so important a part in the novel is, as regards situation and surroundings, that standing within half a mile of the house, in the midst of a tree-clad hill, called Weatherbury Castle ; while, as regards its architectural character and accessibility, the column is rather that placed on the rising ground amid the trees near Charborough. The same may be said of Talbothays, the dairy in *Tess of the D'Urbervilles*.

Referring to the identification of this, Mr. Hardy said

Lulworth Cove. "Lulsted"

Douglas Snelgrove

in a letter to the writer that Talbothays represents " two
or three dairies in the Frome Valley . . . any existing house
of that name has been so called since the novel was written
and has no claim to be the scene."* And, indeed, he
was most careful always to suggest that most of the
places he described were of a "composite" character
and not to be taken as photographically or geographically
correct.

Dorset, it may truly be said, is like no other county of
England. It gives a general impression of age, and yet
not merely age as a modern world would understand it,
but rather that of the true Dorset phrase—"an old, ancient
county." Time—one is almost tempted to write civilization—has affected it probably far less than any other
district in the South and South-West of England. Each
great period of history seems to have affected it deeply,
but instead of being obliterated by succeeding periods, it
blends with them while still retaining much of its own
individuality.

Dorset has a trace of the Roman occupation still left in
its idioms and in the faces of its peasantry ; of the ecclesi-
astic of Saxon times in its buildings and traditions ; of the
Norman period in many of its customs, and of the Middle
Ages in much of its placidity and " behind the times " air.
Many of the old towns are still Roman in character as
regards their plan, while many examples of Elizabethan
and early Georgian architecture are still to be found
throughout the county in manor houses (many singularly
well preserved), and in the townlets and villages. Dorchester is rich in all these echoes of the past. And whenever the foundations of a new house are being dug, or a
field is turned up more deeply than usual with the plough,
it is always with the chance that some Roman spear-head,
coin, fibula, urn or pin will be unearthed.

From time to time in the chalk-pits skeletons of the
Roman soldiery are discovered, lying on their sides

* Hardy's brother, Mr. Henry Hardy, in after years named his home,
not far from Dorchester, " Talbothays."

in a roughly hollowed-out coffin, carved in the chalk itself.

Outside Dorchester, along the road trending southward, is the huge amphitheatre, round which several legends have been woven, the most circumstantial of which is that in summer-time persons sitting in the arena even in broad daylight have at times, on lifting their eyes from the book they were reading, or on first opening them after a doze, been startled to see the green slopes lined with the Roman legion of Hadrian, apparently intent upon some equally spectral gladiatorial show going on in the arena below them ! Even, it is said, the hoarse murmur of the voices of these long-dead Romans has been heard ere the whole vision of phantasms disappeared as swiftly as it was conjured up !

It is not, however, in these legends alone that the England of the past seems almost still the England of the present to the traveller and wayfarer who journeys through Dorset and other parts of Wessex with open eyes and in a romantic spirit. On all sides—in the names of the villages and hamlets scattered in the fertile vales or perched on some hill which, from its configuration, suggests the " earthworks " of the ancient Briton or those of the period of Roman occupation rather than hillocks of Nature's formation : in the ruins of monastic institutions scattered thickly throughout the countryside ; in the churches, Saxon and otherwise, such as that of Saint Cuthberga at Wimborne (the " Warborne " of the novels), in which, at least, one Saxon king has found sepulture, and the old Saxon church at Shaftesbury (" Shaston ") where King Edward the Martyr lies, and in the slow, old-time speech of the peasantry—the same almost medieval spirit seems still to exist.

"Dorset has stood still for several hundred years" is not the exaggerated statement of the antiquarian who made it, but a, perhaps, singular but scarcely deniable truth.

The Trumpet Major deals with an older period of Dorset life than any other of Thomas Hardy's novels—if we exclude the shorter stories—and yet the speech of the characters in the comparatively modern *Tess of the D'Urbervilles*, which cannot be post-dated more than half a century, probably considerably less, is that of those in the other story dealing with events in the early days of the 19th century, when the south of England was under arms awaiting the threatened Napoleonic invasion, and children, if not their elders, lay a-bed of nights trembling at the thoughts of the redoubtable " Boney." And, doubtless, had there been a novelist of Wessex life in the century before, the talk of his types would have been but little different from that of the Wessex novelist of to-day.

In each of Hardy's novels the reader is kept within a definite sphere of interest. In *The Trumpet Major* the sphere is practically that of a radius of ten or fifteen miles from Weymouth—" Budmouth." In his preface the novelist states that this particular " tale is founded more largely on testimony—oral and written—than any other in this series." And the relics in the way of trenches dug on the summits of the downs, old pike heads found in lofts, and volunteer uniforms preserved in clothes-presses of old-fashioned folk, are by no means a thing entirely of the past in Dorset.

In comparatively recent times during the repairs of a warehouse on the Quay Poole (" Havenpool "), the upper shutters of the loft were discovered to be drilled for musketry, and in a chest were found the sabre-taches, uniforms and hats of the Poole volunteers of the time when Napoleon Bonaparte was hourly expected by the inhabitants of the coasts of Sussex, Hants, Dorset and Devon more especially. The fisher lads and townsmen who put these moth-eaten trappings on for periodic drills little realized the romance that attached to each brass button and each inch of cloth.

The Weymouth of the present day differs, no doubt, materially from the watering-place at which George III disported himself to the wonder, astonishment and admiration of the inhabitants of the countryside round about, but the outlying villages of " Overcombe " (Upwey and Sutton Poyntz), "King's Bere" (Bere Regis), "Oxwell" (Poxwell), are now very much what they were then, and have altered quite unappreciably since fair Anne Garland threw down her work on that fine summer morning to watch the soldiers assembling on the top of the down above Overcombe Mill.

Indeed, after reading the story on the spot one can realize to the full the consternation of the villagers lest these unlooked-for soldiers should indicate that Bonaparte had outwitted the fleet cruising in the Channel, and had attacked timorous " Budmouth " on the flank. The stolid villagers of to-day make one feel instinctively that they would act in just the same wonder-struck wide-open-mouthed way were such an event possible at the present time—just, in fact, as they did in the pages of *The Trumpet Major*. Overcombe Mill—in reality from its description that at Upwey—still grinds (like those of the gods) slowly if exceeding small ; and the miller, if not a Loveday by descent, might well pass for one. " The Look-out," to which several of the characters in the story made anxious pilgrimage, in search of signs of the French invaders, is still known as such locally, and the troublous times which gave rise to such things are permanently recorded by the name of Kimmeridge Look-out, a few miles farther down the coast.

A succession of not the least humorous and successful scenes in the story are those in Chapter XII, in which is recorded, " how everybody, great and small, climbed to the top of the downs." We are told that it was on " a clear day, with little wind stirring, and the view from the downs, one of the most extensive in the county, was unclouded. The eye of the observer who cared for such things swept over the wave-washed town, and the bay beyond, and the isle, with its pebble bank, lying on the sea to the left of these like a great crouching animal tethered to the mainland."

It is a scene like this, which, happily, in many instances yet remains immutable in Wessex. The isle " crouches " to-day as it did then : " the wave-washed town " still preserves something at least of its early-in-the-century air, and when once away, out of sight of present-day fashions and the ubiquitous motor car, one can well imagine that the soldiers of the German legion and York Hussars in "white buckskin pantaloons, three-quarter boots, scarlet shakos set off with lace, mustachios waxed to a needle point, and, above all, those richly-ornamented blue jackets mantled with the historic pelisse " are still patrolling the street of the distant town, or guarding the matutinal bathing of His Majesty King George the Third.

"At twelve o'clock," we are told in the story, " the review was over, and the king and his family left the hill." The troops then cleared off the field, the spectators followed, and by one o'clock the downs were again bare. The white horse and rider, one of the several cut in the chalk downs and uplands of England, and now an object of curiosity to tourists and visitors to "Budmouth," and a landmark for those who go down to the sea in ships, was, as regards the horse, supposed to be of considerable antiquity. The figure of the horseman, said to represent George III, was probably cut by the soldiers encamped there during that monarch's visit to Weymouth, as described in *The Trumpet Major*.

The harbour, too, has scarcely altered since sailor Bob Loveday, on the morning of September 3rd, long ago, after his renunciation of the girl he loved in favour of Soldier John, returned from the barracks to " Budmouth," " passed on to the harbour, where he remained awhile, looking at the busy scene of loading and unloading craft, and swabbing the decks of yachts ; at the boats and barges rubbing against the quay wall, and at the houses of the merchants, some ancient structures of solid stone, some green-shuttered with heavy wooden bow-windows, which appeared as if about to drop into the harbour by their own weight."

The chief difference is the presence of steam, which has, doubtless, driven most of the barges away ; and a new bridge connecting Weymouth with new Melcombe Regis.

But the houses, the quay and the stores are still there, as in Loveday's time. The town itself has, of course, altered much since George III was king.

The Isle of Portland—no true island now or then, but a peninsula—has altered even less. Anne Garland might still set out, as is related of her in *The Trumpet Major*, from " Overcombe " by carrier, and after finishing her shopping in " Budmouth " itself, take her way to Portland through the old town along the coast road. To-day she would be, as then, confronted before reaching the base of Portland Hill by the steep incline, dotted with houses, raised tier upon tier, so that the doorstep of one man is sometimes almost on a level with the chimney of his neighbour immediately below.

From the bare promontory of the " Bill " she would look upon the same prospect as when she watched Nelson's flagship, the *Victory*, with Bob Loveday aboard her, and the *Euryalus* frigate in her wake, sail clean out of sight down Channel.

This desolate isle, with the wonderful pebble beach linking it to the mainland and stretching for ten miles in an unbroken curve towards Bridport to the west, and encircling the famous West Bay, is much the same as when Anne Garland, watching the last topmast of the *Victory* sink below the distant horizon, murmured, without removing her wet eyes from the vacant and solemn horizon : " They that go down to the sea in ships, that do business in great waters——" and turned, at the sound of another voice completing the verse, to find the vanished Bob Loveday's brother John at her elbow.

In *Far from the Madding Crowd* Hardy has written a story almost exclusively of the farm. And it is no small tribute to his genius that he can enlist his readers' sympathies so completely in this everyday life, which is bounded, one might, with tolerable accuracy, say, by the lambing season in the spring and the getting in of root crops in the autumn. The contrasts of character in the book are sharper than in several of the Wessex novels. A more clean-cut divergence than that afforded by the vicious adventurer,

T

Sergeant Troy, and the unselfish, plodding, dog-faithful
Gabriel Oak, the shepherd, it would not be easy to imagine
—the one with his cheap gallantry and echo of town ways,
his power over women with whom he came in contact by
both physical and mental means (as an example of the
former there is the wonderful sword-play bewitchment of
Bathsheba in the ferny hollow, when he severs a lock
of hair from her head, and of the latter his veneer of
education and flattering talk) ; the other with his stolid
life and countryman's ways and sympathies. And the
same applies to the women characters also. Fanny Robin,
the dazzled and deceived, serving as a foil to the trust-
ful, ignorant Bathsheba, equally dazzled, but at first
cautious.

Though tragedy and comedy jostle each other in the
pages of the novel, the tragic consequences of Sergeant
Troy's amours being in a measure set off by the excellent
rustics and their delicious, humorous talk, it is the tragic
note which predominates. For the fate of Fanny is not
less insistent than the pen of the artist would have it, and
the marriage of the long-suffering Gabriel Oak with Bathsheba in the last few pages does not succeed in effacing
from the memory the tragic doing to death of Troy by
Boldwood in the hall of his own house.

The scene of the story is circumscribed, as in so many
of Thomas Hardy's books. It centres in Puddletown,
" Weatherbury " (a village a few miles from Dorchester),
and within a radius of a few miles of this Wessex hamlet
the whole action of the tale takes place.

Many of the descriptions of rural life are charming, and
conjure up as accurate an idea of the locale as would be
afforded by an etching. One of the most important rural
scenes in the book—the sheep-washing—affords an instance
of this. It is a good example of the care and accuracy
with which Hardy literally built up his descriptions of even
unimportant places and events. The true artistic economy
of words is evident in every phrase. Boldwood, Shepherd
Oak, Jan Coggan and the other farm-hands were there, and
Bathsheba was looking on. " The river," we are told,

" slid along noiselessly as a shade, the swelling reeds and sedge forming a flexible palisade along its moist bank. To the north of the mead were trees. . . ." Though this might serve as a general description of numberless Wessex meads, and the streams running silently through them, yet a distinct vision of this particular mead on Bathsheba's farm is brought before the reader's eyes.

Nowhere, probably, do fairs survive with more pertinacity in the South and South-West of England than in Dorset. And if one may believe the word of the country folk, who have attended them from days of childhood to those of hoary old age, the surviving fairs differ little or not at all from those of five decades or more ago. Ever on the alert to make use of existing circumstances in his novels indicative of the placidity of life, disturbed only occasionally by such things, it is little to be wondered at that Hardy should have fixed upon one of the most noted of these gatherings for description. " Greenhill " (Woodbury Hill) Fair, held in September, is known throughout the countryside. To it come shepherds with their flocks of South Downs, Leicesters, old West of England horned breeds, and even Exmoors, with parti-coloured faces and legs—in the vale below lies Bere Regis (" King's Bere "), in the church of which are laid the bones of the ancestors of " Tess of the D'Urbervilles." Antiquarians are of the opinion that the hill, up whose crumbling sides the two main roads leading to the top wind, is the site of an ancient British encampment ; for at the summit there is a huge rampart and entrenchment, oval in form, and within the confines of this the fair takes place. There are a few hovels and cottages of a permanent character on the crest of Greenhill ; but most of those who forgather for the fairing are content to be under canvas, or in the gipsy caravans which are still a leading feature. Down the centre of this temporary encampment, running almost north and south, the main street of the fair is made, on either side of which stand the booths and stalls—the abodes of dancers and other performers, and of thin men, fat women, two-headed calves, gingerbread and cheap, gaily-coloured china ornaments, with which shooting-galleries, " cokernut shies " and ninepins contest popularity.

The old drovers, commoner ten years ago than now throughout Wessex, are another survival of Greenhill. Early on the morning of the first day of the fair, Hardy tells us, "nebulous clouds of dust (were) to be seen floating between the pairs of hedges in all directions. These gradually converged upon the base of the hill, and the flocks became individually visible, climbing the serpentine way which led to the top. Thus, in slow procession, they entered the openings to which the roads wended."

This is almost as true of Greenhill now as of the fair sixty years or so ago, when Thomas Hardy wrote the novel. Even the circus which plays so important a part in Troy's reappearance, and in his wife Bathsheba's subsequent history, was there last autumn, and was almost exactly like its prototype of the story, and one could well imagine that Troy was giving his sensational performance of Dick Turpin inside. Now, as then, everybody for miles round goes to Greenhill, the gentry and better-class farmers patronizing the first day, and the second day being more or less given over to the labourers, their wives, sweethearts, sons and daughters. It is true that it has not the vogue of ancient times, nor are the gigs and wagonettes to be seen in any number as of yore, their places being taken by motor cars, and motor coaches.

From the time of Greenhill Fair and Troy's reappearance the story moves with rapidity to its close. The gaol, in which Boldwood, the farmer, one of Bathsheba's most pertinacious suitors, was confined, waiting under sentence of death for execution, has since that time been pulled down and rebuilt after more modern ideas, but the gateway is much the same as ever. And it is easy enough to enter into Gabriel Oak's feelings as he turned to look back (after saying good-bye to the condemned man, who was also his rival) at the gaol, and saw " the upper part of the entrance . . . and some moving figures "—these last

Corfe Castle "Corvesgate"

lifting into position the post of the gibbet to be used on the morrow.

One cannot help feeling that the true end of the story comes with the scene at midnight on the Casterbridge road, when Laban brought to Oak, Coggan and the rest of the waiting villagers, who had walked towards Casterbridge from Weatherbury to meet him, the news of the murderer's reprieve. The conventional ending, with "the most private, secret, plainest wedding that it is possible to have," comes, indeed, almost as a dangerous anticlimax.

Few, if any of the Wessex novels attain to the supremacy of interest which *Tess of the D'Urbervilles* has for the general reader—vastly human, tragically idyllic as it is ; compact of the impulses of a woman of the soil, and a weak man's vacillations. At the time of its first appearance the story, as is well known, aroused much discussion and comment, one critic at least regarding it—erroneously, we should say —as a "manifestation of a new Hardy" rather than as a usually marked and stronger development along one particular line of the novelist's preferences in his art. Although the novel is rather of the nature of a brief for the inexorableness of Fate than a story teaching any one particular moral idea (as might, perhaps, be inferred, was the novelist's intention from the sub-title, *A Pure Woman Faithfully Presented*), it is painful with the stern reality of recorded facts rather than with that of so-called realism clumsily introduced. But with all its onward march towards the end—at times one obtains a glimpse, as it were, of the inevitableness—the story fails to carry absolute conviction. The reader is tempted in reading the last few pages of the book to ask why, when Tess has once more succumbed to the evil influence of Alec D'Urberville, the murder is committed. This may appear hypercriticism, but for not the first time in Tess's history does the motive assume an apparently shadowy and insufficient character.

With the main incidents of the story most of our readers will doubtless be familiar; with the feckless, ne'er-do-well Durbeyfield and his haphazard wife and family ; with the incident of Alec D'Urberville's treachery (with which the real history of Tess may be said to commence) ; with Angel Clare and the life at Talbothays ; with the love of Tess for Angel and her ultimate marriage with him ; with their almost immediate separation on the latter's discovery of his wife's former declension from virtue ; with Tess's struggle for subsistence (one of the finest parts of the novel) and faithfulness to her absent and non-communicating husband, till the villain of the piece—Tess's " bad angel " —reappears in the person of Alec D'Urberville ; with the murder of the latter by Tess in the " Sandbourne " (Bournemouth) apartments ; with the coming of Clare, too late, as so often happens with men of his type in real life as well as in fiction ; with the flight of the reunited husband and wife into Wessex ; with the capture of Tess at Stonehenge ; with the last scene, when Angel Clare and 'Liza-Lu watch with pain-contracted hearts the black emblem denoting Tess's sudden plunge into eternity flutter slowly, almost on the stroke of eight, up the bare staff on the tower of " Wintoncester " (Winchester) Gaol.

Once or twice during the progress of the story the novelist seems to suggest—it is little more—that Tess's misfortunes and predilections are the outcome of heredity and what are usually known as " the sins of the fathers." But it is scarcely possible to consider the book in the light of a study of hereditary consequences. There is too little indication of the life of her ancestors to allow one to trace heredity as clearly as one should to enable one to accept the conclusion of the book as in the first place inevitable, and in the second as accounted for by the theory of heredity.

The story opens with what may be described as the undoing of John Durbeyfield (D'Urberville). Always lazy, he is destined to become more so by reason of the antiquarian Parson Tringham's indiscretion in telling him he was in reality a descendant of the D'Urbervilles, and the possessor of grand and noble " skillentons " laid to rest in the family vault of " King's Bere " (Bere Regis) Church—information which turns lazy John into a dreamer of dreams, and a man disposed to make heavy drafts on the bank of former greatness to meet current expenses brought about by a large family and slender resources.

The scene where the parson meets John Durbeyfield on the road to Marlott as the latter is returning from the hill town of " Shaston " (Shaftesbury), is in true Hardy vein ; a blend of the humorous, the pathetic and the ridiculous.

It is towards " Shaston " that Tess eventually takes her way in search of the grand relatives, of whom Mrs. Durbey-field (her mother) hopes so much, and the town is still so denominated on the ancient milestones which stand on the road to it from Sturminster Newton. The more modern and usual name is Shaftesbury. The town itself stands perched on a hill overlooking the beautiful Blackmoor Vale in which Tess had lived all her life ; it is, if one may believe tradition, the site of more than one skirmish between King Alfred the Great and the Danes, and is, therefore, at least a thousand years old. It still contains many houses of ancient date, and the church tower goes back well into the Norman period.

Along " Shaston " High Street Tess must have passed on her way from Marlott to " Chaseborough " (Cranborne), which lay to the south-east, on that early morning following the loss of the Durbeyfield horse, which proved the last straw, and broke up the huckstering business, by which her father sought to gain a precarious livelihood when sober, and precipitated the disorganization of the family finances. One can almost believe that the street has not altered a stone since Tess trod it on her way to seek aid of her supposititious relatives in their grand house, " The Slopes," where she was destined to suffer so much.

The third phase of Tess's story provides us with some of the best of the rural scenes contained in the novel. It is the second setting-out of the girl to relieve the pressure upon her family's ever-slender resources. The motive is the same as the first ; but the inspiration—how different ! Not any more were there fine ancestors or grand relatives

in Tess's simple calculations; " there should be no more
D'Urberville air castles in the dreams and deeds of her
new life" which she was adopting. " She would be
dairymaid Tess, and nothing more." And so it was that
" on a thyme-scented, bird-hatching morning in May "
Tess set out, in a hired trap, " luggage and all," for " Stourcastle" (Sturminster Newton), through which it was necessary to pass on her journey to Talbothays. " She went,"
we are told, " through Stourcastle without pausing,"
passing, doubtless, over the old bridge which lies at the
bottom of the hill at the foot of the main street of the old-
fashioned town, past the remains of the cross, along the
street which has a wide commencement and a narrow
ending. " Egdon" Heath, beloved of the novelist, is afterwards crossed, and Tess, " after sundry wrong turnings . . .
found herself on the summit commanding the long-sought-
for vale, the Valley of the Great Dairies," in which the
most purely romantic phase of her chequered life was
afterwards passed.

The courting of Tess by Angel Clare after they had met
as fellow-workers at Talbothays Dairy is the least convincing portion of the vivid picture of the life led on this
typical Wessex dairy farm. But the drive in the thirtieth
chapter is an excellent example of the skill with which the
novelist contrives to suggest atmosphere and the effect of
atmospheric conditions on his characters. In the first few
lines a description of the " Egdon" Heath occurs, which,
to those who have traversed its wide waste of broken moorland, conjures up a picture with a wonderful economy of
words at once convincing and suggestive. It was likewise " in the diminishing daylight that (we) went along
the level roadway through the meads, which stretched
away into grey miles, and were backed in the extreme
edge of the distance by the swarthy and abrupt slopes
of ' Egdon ' Heath. On its summit stood clumps and
stretches of fir-trees, whose notched tips appeared like
battlemented towers crowning black-fronted castles of
enchantment."

The railway station towards which Angel Clare and Tess

were bound with the full milk cans in the cart on this particular evening is still as then a friction point in the iron
chain which serves to link Wessex and its dairy farms with
the outer world, of which the inhabitants then knew comparatively so little. And the holly bush under which
Tess sheltered is still there, and has doubtless since afforded
a like scant comfort to other dairymaids who made similar
journeys in the rain.

It was during this memorable ride that Tess attempted
the thankless task of confessing to her lover her previous
misfortune—a task made difficult by her own sense of dis-
grace and fear of losing him, and rendered impossible by
the spirit of raillery with which Angel Clare received her
opening sentences. The spirit of aloofness—we can find
no better word—which characterized all Clare's and
Tess's love-making still seems to exist as " they drove on
through the gloom, forming one bundle inside the sail
cloth, the horse going as he would, and the rain driving
against them." And notwithstanding the suggestion conveyed by the words " the appetite for joy," which may be
held to hint a reason for Tess's consenting to marry Clare,
the motive other than that afforded by an almost furtive
expression of affection remains to the general reader
shadowy.

Tess is soon afterwards married. And Clare, who
has decided to make himself acquainted with milling,
carries her off to " Wellbridge " (Wool) at which
place is the flour mill where he had elected to gain his
experience.

By a singular coincidence the house in which he had
taken rooms is a portion of a fine old manorial residence,
once belonging to the D'Urberville family, now, since its
partial demolition, a farm-house. To travellers by rail
from Wareham to Dorchester it is a familiar object just
before, as well as just after, Wool station is reached—a
grey-reddish pile standing amid the meads, with modern
excrescences in the way of outbuildings and a cottage or
two attached to its own fading glories, and with the weed-
grown Frome almost washing its garden wall.

We are told that the newly-married pair, after the ceremony, " drove by the level road along the valley to a distance of a few miles, and reaching Wellbridge, turned away from the village to the left, and over the great Elizabethan bridge which gives the place half its name."

It needs no very great stretch of the imagination, when one stands on the bridge, to conjure up the scene as the broken-down conveyance, a relic of post-chaise days, with its juvenile postillion of sixty odd years, lumbered up to the little wicket which would admit them to the bare patch of garden surrounding the house. We can see these two walk along the narrow path to the porched doorway, with its bench recessed on either side, and enter the house, which was to become the scene of the wrecking of Tess's happiness.

On the landing the portraits of the two " horrid women " which so alarmed poor Tess were still staring at the casual visitor when last we visited the house ; and the bridal chamber, large, uneven of floor and lighted by narrow stone-mullioned windows, remains as it was then, except for the addition of a garish modern wall-paper.

In this gloomy house, with its mouldy greatness, Hardy truly found a fitting and a singularly appropriate setting for the mutual confessions of Angel Clare and his wife. The different values that society was pleased to set upon the sin as between man and woman at the time Hardy wrote the book is not insisted upon, but, with consummate art, it becomes the inevitable value in this particular case.

The weakness of the man's character, his one-sided logic, and the piteous trust and weakness of the woman stand out, clear cut and convincing. We feel Tess's loneliness as Clare, closing the door softly behind him, goes out into the blackness of the night, well matching in its sinister gloom his own thoughts. The dog-faithfulness of Tess, who follows Clare at a distance, dumb with pain on becoming aware momentarily of that " cruelty of fooled honesty (which) is often great after enlightenment," and that such feeling was indeed overwhelming in her husband now, is brought clearly to the reader's mind.

The immense folly of the man is brought out subtly, but with ever-increasing clearness, during every yard of that night's walk, and in the conversation and attitude of Clare on his return to the house.

Their life during the few succeeding days before they part, Clare to go abroad and Tess to return to her old home, is described in detail. The man takes his way daily to Wellbridge Mill and the woman waits in the gloomy house, eating her heart out in sorrow, and devising wild schemes by which she might put an end to herself, or by which her husband might rid himself of her.

At midnight, before they are to part, Tess, asleep in the upper chamber, awakes on hearing the noise of footsteps in the darkened farm-house.

Her door opens, and she sees Angel Clare entering the room in the moonlight.

At first a throb of joy possesses her, emanating from the thought that flashes into her brain—that he has come to her with forgiveness. But it is not so. She soon realizes that he is asleep, and that he thinks her dead. But when he stoops over her and, taking her in his arms, creeps down the creaking staircase, and after leaving the house proceeds in the direction of the mill and the ruins of the Cistercian abbey, away to the south amid the trees, she makes no resistance, half hoping, indeed, that she and he will find an end to all their troubles while crossing the river on the slender and now railless footbridge by a heedless step on his part, which would plunge them into the swirling, foaming, weed-grown stream below.

At length we read that " they reached the ruined choir of the abbey-church. Against the north wall was the empty stone coffin of an abbot. . . . In this Clare carefully laid Tess."

While standing looking into the strange stone coffin, furnished as it is with a slight access of breadth at the shoulders, and a scooped-out hollow for the head, the traveller in Wessex can easily reconstruct the midnight scene as Clare, stooping beneath the boughs of the over-hanging trees, laid white-robed Tess in the leaf-strewn resting-place. On the day we last visited it the environing trees were rich in autumn tints, and the thick canopy of foliage made the spot little less gloomy than on the moonlit night of Tess's adventure.

And it was the day after this midnight scene, so graphic-ally described by the novelist, that she and Clare parted—he to make his way into the wide world outside the confines of Wessex, and she to return to her home once more, and then to her struggle for existence at field work on the farm at Flintcomb Ash (Nettlecombe Tout).

The story proceeds with the narration of her life on the farm ; her fruitless visit to her husband's home ; the re-appearance of Alec D'Urberville ; the death of feckless John Durbeyfield ; the breaking up of the old home ; the journey to " King's Bere " in search of lodging, and the temptation which Alec D'Urberville placed in her way, to which after a struggle she succumbed.

The Durbeyfield household, with their furniture, set out almost immediately after the father's death for " King's Bere," " the spot of all spots in the world which could be considered the D'Urbervilles' home."

" Though they had started so early it was quite late in the afternoon when they turned the flank of an eminence which formed part of the upland called Greenhill—just ahead of them was the half-dead townlet of their pilgrim-age, King's Bere, where lay those ancestors of whom her father had spoken and sung to painfulness "—the " skillen-tons " of those whose departed glories had so prejudicial an influence on the Durbeyfield family in general. The rooms they wanted were let ! This wandering family was therefore suddenly and unexpectedly confronted with the problem as to where they could repose for the night. " Her (Tess's) mother looked hopelessly at fault. ' What shall we do now, Tess ? ' " she said bitterly. And then she summed up her stricken faith in these ancestors, who had never brought them any luck, but bad, in the sentence, " Here's a welcome to your ancestors' lands ! "

The wagon eventually pulled up under the churchyard wall, and the homeless ones camped out under the four-post bedstead placed near the D'Urberville window, on the south wall of the church. Inside the window " were the tombs of the family, covering in their dates several centuries. They were canopied, altar-shaped and plain ; their carvings being defaced and broken, their brasses torn from the matrices, the rivet-holes remaining like marten-holes in a sand cliff. . . ."

It is while Tess, who had crept in at the open door of the church, is gazing at and meditating upon this evidence of the fallen greatness of her family, that Alec D'Urberville makes his reappearance. It is the beginning of the end. Shortly afterwards the story finds Tess in apartments at Sandbourne (Bournemouth) as his mistress.

The murder of Alec by Tess ; her flight with Angel Clare, her returned husband, who has relented and come to her assistance too late, occupy a very few pages, although every detail of the pitiful business is clearly indicated.

Like a hunted creature, Tess, in company with Clare, for some days eludes justice, which at last finds them on the Great Plain (Salisbury Plain), amid the weird circle of Stonehenge. It is here, early in the morning, that the officers of the law capture her as she is sleeping—a veritable Hardy touch this—on one of the immense stones of this sacrificial temple of the past ages. As the police officers close in upon her " the eastward pillars and their archi-traves stood up . . . against the light."

The actual end of the story is very rapid. Two pages or little more suffice. Tess is condemned to death and is confined in Wintoncester (Winchester) Gaol. Angel and Tess's sister, 'Liza-Lu, journey to the city to see what of the end was vouchsafed to them. It was not much. They climbed the upward slope of the High Street, and passed to the top of the great Western Hill, whence they gazed at the distant building, with the ugly, flat-topped octagonal tower, in which the few remaining minutes of Tess's life are speeding away.

" Upon the cornice of the tower," we are told, " there was a tall staff. Their eyes were riveted on it. A few minutes after the hour had struck something moved slowly up the staff and extended itself upon the breeze. It was a black flag."

" The two speechless gazers bent themselves down to the earth, as if in prayer . . . the flag continued to wave silently.

" ' Justice ' was done, and the President of the Immortals (in Æschylean phrase) had ended his sport with Tess."

In *Two on a Tower* we have a romance ; a book of a different calibre and importance from *Tess*. Here Hardy crosses the borders of Wessex somewhat, and in the character of Lady Constantine he gives us a woman of the world in place of the rustic maidens " with primeval passions," in which the novelist took especial delight. Swithin St. Cleeve, the young astronomer, in whom Viviette, Lady Constantine, takes so deep an interest, is essentially a dreamer, and it speaks well for the skill of the narrator that he arouses in the reader so satisfactory a curiosity concerning his doings. Lady Constantine herself is one more of those indiscreet subtly emotional women among the feminine portraits of Hardy's gallery. A woman at first so æsthetically interested in the beauty of the astronomical youth, whom she accidentally found in possession of the " tower " on her estate, as to stimulate an enthusiasm which she did not feel for a science which she could not comprehend, and afterwards to commit the indiscretion of allowing herself to fall in love with the lad, and seek to cover her *faux pas* and legitimatize her and Swithin's child, with true Hardyesque irony, by her marriage with a bishop !

The story opens with Lady Constantine's arrival, on a clear wintry afternoon, at the entrance of her domain, Welland House situated a little off the old Melchester (Salisbury) road at Milborne St. Andrew. She gazes at the surrounding country through the field gate, and her attention is riveted by " the central feature of the middle distance . . . a circular isolated hill, of no great elevation . . . covered with fir-trees." This hill " was yet further marked out from the general landscape by having on its summit a tower in the form of a classical column, which, though partly immersed in the plantation, rose about the tree-tops to a considerable height." It was this tower (compounded of two such memorials, the other being situated near Charborough) that was destined to play so important a part in the history of Lady Constantine and Swithin St. Cleeve. It is now, owing to the growth of the surrounding trees, only possible to catch a glimpse of the column from a few stated points.

This " fir-shrouded hill-top," we are told, " was (according to some antiquaries) . . . an old Roman camp . . . with the remains of an outer and inner vallum, a winding path leading up between their overlapping ends by an easy ascent. . . ."

It was up this ascent that the writer climbed to find, as so frequently happened during his pilgrimages in Wessex, the description of the book accurately fitting the actuality of nature. As Hardy phrases it in his novel : " The gloom and solitude which prevailed round the base were remarkable . . . some boughs and twigs rubbed the pillar's sides or occasionally clicked in catching each other. The sob of the environing trees was here expressly manifest. Below the level of their summits the masonry was lichen-stained and mildewed, for the sun never pierced the moaning cloud of blue-black vegetation. . . ."

It was not for some months that Lady Constantine found an opportunity of visiting the spot which had aroused her curiosity on the afternoon of her home-coming.

However, one day in February she drove out and directed that the carriage should enter the gate of one of the fields surrounding the hill, and put her down as close to the base of the hill as possible. She climbed the outer slope of the old earthworks and entered the wood, prompted partially by curiosity and partially by a desire to vary the monotony, by even so mild an adventuring, of her curiously lonely and uninteresting life. She discovered the door-way at the foot of the column, and finding it unfastened, pushed it open, and ascended the staircase. On the top she was brought face to face with the youthful astronomer, who at first is too occupied with the cyclone, which he states is taking place in the sun, to pay any attention to her presence, even when she addressed him.

When he at length looks up, it is to be mutually enamoured, and it is with the history of these two persons so strangely thrown together that the story is concerned.

The main interest of the tale it is somewhat difficult to locate with exactness, the whole plot turning upon Lady Constantine's matrimonial experiment with Swithin—which proves to be a bigamous one, as her husband, Sir Blount, was still alive at the time—and her singular method of adjusting matters and of saving her reputation by her marriage with the Bishop of Melchester.

Her death from heart failure on the day when she again meets Swithin, on his return from South Africa, whence he had gone to pursue astronomical studies, is the method of disposal of a character as whimsical and elusive as any the novelist has used.

The scene of the final novel of our quintette of selected stories is to all intents and purposes laid in the extreme south of Wessex (Portland), with an occasional trans-ference of that scene to London. *The Well-Beloved*, which has the illuminating sub-title of *A Sketch of a Temperament*, is chiefly concerned with the doings of one Jocelyn Pierston, a successful artist, son of a quarry owner, and three generations of Avices—the first of whom was Avice Caro, the girl playmate of his childhood's days on the island, and the last the granddaughter, and one Marcia Bencombe, with whom the vacillating Jocelyn philanders and eventually marries.

The novelist in the preface to the standard edition of the book gives this explanation of the elusive character of the story, which without it would appear scarcely more than a shadowy puppet-show, and a peg on which

to hang some fine and unsurpassed descriptions of
the island scenery and atmospheric conditions in South
Wessex.

" The peninsula, carved by time out of a single stone,
we are told . . . has been for centuries immemorial the
home of a curious and almost distinctive people, cherishing
strange beliefs and singular customs, now for the most part
obsolescent. Fancies, like certain soft-wooded plants
which cannot bear the silent inland frosts, but thrive by
the sea in the roughest of weather, seem to grow up
naturally here, in particular among those natives who have
no active concern in the labours of the ' isle.' Hence, it
is a spot apt to generate a type of personage like the character imperfectly sketched in these pages—a native of
natives—whom some may choose to call a fantast . . . but
whom others may see only as one that gave objective
continuity and a name to a delicate dream."

This dream is, it may be remarked, the feminine
alter ego of the man, but, after all, not merely that.
The *Well-Beloved* is not only the other self, which
even less often materializes to reward the most earnest of
seekers.

The village of Portland lies on the landward side of the
" Isle of Slingers," as it is named in the novel, facing
almost north-west, a conglomeration of houses and stone
sheds built in tiers one above the other up the steep hillside.
Above the highest towers the green and then grey slope
marking the summit. The main street of the townlet,
which " is connected with the mainland by a long thin
neck of pebbles—unparalleled in its kind in Europe," is
exceedingly steep, and leads into the centre of the once
island, now peninsula, " that stretches out like the head
of a bird into the English Channel."

It was up this Street of Wells (as it is called in the story)
that Jocelyn Pierston on a summer afternoon climbed on
his way to the eastern village. He was paying one of his
periodical visits to his birthplace, which he had left in
youth to become a sculptor. He felt warm and sat down
opposite a cottage to rest. The whirr and see-saw of the

quarry-men and stone sawyers at work came to him
as he sat, a sound familiar enough in his boyhood,
but now strange and familiar at one and the same
time.   In the cottage lived a Mrs. Caro and her
daughter Avice, the latter having been the playmate of
his childhood.

He enters the cottage, and while talking to her mother
Avice herself makes her appearance ; and notwithstanding
that she has grown up (her age is about eighteen) and he
has attained almost to man's estate, greets her returned
playfellow with a kiss.   Jocelyn gives a start of surprise,
which escapes the girl, but not the eyes of her mother, who
reproves her : "Avice—my dear Avice !   Why—what
are you doing?   Don't you know that you've grown up
to be a woman since Jocelyn—Mr. Pierston—was last down
here?   Of course, you mustn't do now as you used to do
three or four years ago ! "

When Jocelyn, who protests somewhat ineffectively that
he expected the form of greeting he had received, has gone,
her mother pursues her lecture on Avice's impropriety.
The girl herself, with the simplicity of manners which runs
like a thread through this story of primitive folk, who, till
at all events recently, had several curious customs altogether out of keeping with the age in which they live, said
simply enough : "I—I didn't think about how I was
altered . . . I used to kiss him, and he used to kiss me before
he went away."

The girl goes out into the garden at the back of her
mother's dwelling to expiate her impropriety and to celebrate her newly-acquired sense of womanhood and shame
and grief with tears.   Jocelyn, not finding his father at
home, also goes out into his garden, which abuts on that
of the Caros.   He hears Avice sobbing and moaning out,
" Oh, what shall I do, what shall I do ! . . .   So bold as it
was—so shameless ! . . .   He will never forgive me—
never, never like me again !   He'll think me a forward
hussy——"

Jocelyn after hearing this retreats as quickly as he can,
but he is conscious that he is not displeased either by the

girl's difficulty in seeing anything out of the way in her
action, or by the fact that she is distressed lest she should
by it have lost his good opinion.

But with the difficulty he labours under all through his
life he is unable to feel that love has come rather than the
mere elusive fancy of the ideal, which already has on
several occasions caused him trouble.

During the month of his holiday he sees much of Avice
and for a time is deluded into thinking that she is, after all,
the " well-beloved " of his errant search.   The night before
he is to leave again for London he has a tryst with Avice
at King Henry VIII's Castle, which Hardy calls
" Sandsfoots Castle," which lies on a sandstone promontory almost straight across from the townlet of Portland on the mainland, behind which is Budmouth (Weymouth).   He is on his way thither when he is overtaken
by a boy with a note.

It is from Avice, who, doubtless from the newly-awakened
sense of the alteration which has taken place in them both
since his last visit, declines to keep the tryst, saying, after
an explanation which shows the subtlety of the novelist's
characterization : " On the whole, therefore, it is best that
I should not come—if only for appearances—and meet you
at the time and place suggesting the custom, to others than
ourselves, at least if known."

The " custom " referred to, it may be remarked,
being one involving privileges as a rule coincident
only with marriage, but given freely before the actual
ceremony—till a comparatively recent period—by the
primitive inhabitants of the Isle of Slingers.   One is
left somewhat in doubt as to how much this revolt is
caused by Avice's half-cultivated refinement, and how
much by a latent fear that Jocelyn would despise her
for yielding to it.

Jocelyn, disappointed at Avice's failure to meet him—
not, however, angry with her ; which serves to show how
fleeting and unsubstantial was her assumption of the role
of the " well-beloved " in his eyes—goes on towards Budmouth.

While walking along the shore road he meets a woman
almost overpowered by the wind, which has risen to the
force-of a gale. This woman, the daughter of a Mr.
Bencombe, he assists. She is running away in a fit of
anger at her father's treatment of her. Her destination
is also London. They shelter for some hours under
one of the lerrets (a large, stoutly built boat) and then
proceed to a hotel at Budmouth, and next morning to
London.

Meanwhile, the " well-beloved " has assumed with the
rapidity which is so elusive and startling both to Jocelyn
himself and to the reader, the form of this woman, Marcia
Bencombe.

They live at a hotel together for some days while waiting
to be married, and then eventually quarrel (before the
ceremony can be performed) over their respective parents,
and the merits of a feud which had existed for many years
between them. They part ; and Jocelyn suffers from
several incursions of the " well-beloved " into the temple
he had prepared for *the* " well-beloved." Twenty years
pass, and he again finds himself in the isle, present at the
funeral of his Avice, who had married and left behind her
a daughter, also called Avice, who, in time, becomes
another of the elusive visions of Jocelyn Pierston's " well-
beloved."

This Ann Avice haunts him after his return to London,
and he takes a lease of Sylvania Castle, the Pennsylvania
castle built early in the last century by John Penn, a
grandson of William Penn, the founder of the State of
Pennsylvania, one of the few important residences of the
island, and settles there in the hope of his ideal ultimately
materializing in the form of this second Avice.

Some of the finest pictures of local scenery and atmospheric conditions are found in this portion of the narrative.
Avice the Second's temperament, Jocelyn discovers, is
affected strangely by the weather. " Among other things,"
we are told, " he observed that she is often anxious when
it rains. If, after a wet day, a golden streak appeared in
the sky over Deadman's Bay, under a lid of cloud (as it

frequently does), her manner was joyous and her tread light." Avice, at Jocelyn's behest, returns with him to London as a servant.

But the " well-beloved " in the case of Avice the Second proves as elusive as that of Avice the First, and when Pierston confesses to the former that he was the " false young man" of whom her mother had spoken, she refuses to have anything more to do with him. Pressed for a reason why she will not accept his offer of marriage, she confesses that she is already married, having fallen a victim to the " island custom," the fear of which had probably lost Pierston to her mother as a husband.

This revelation causes the return of Pierston and Avice to Portland. After inspecting the register of marriages, and finding that Avice's story of marriage is true, Jocelyn leaves her.

Another period of twenty years passes, and the wanderer once more returns to his birthplace, having lived during the time elapsed mostly in Rome and abroad. He finds Avice the Second a widow, and her daughter, a young woman of about eighteen, a modernized and educated edition of her own mother and grandmother.

Avice the Third enters upon the scene of Pierston's life as her two former namesakes had done in the past. Of this third incarnation the novelist says : " He (Pierston) was subject to gigantic fantasies still. In spite of himself, the sight of the new moon, as representing one who, by her so-called inconstancy, acted up to his own idea of a migratory well-beloved made him feel as if his wraith in a changed sex had suddenly looked over the horizon at him."

In some respects the third Avice has more of her grandmother's temperament than of her mother's, for we are told that she possessed " the flippant, harmless freedom of the watering-place ' Miss,' " acquired during her life at a a boarding-school at " Sandbourne " (Bournemouth). Taught by past experiences, Jocelyn carefully guarded the secret that he had aforetime courted her mother and even grandmother !

" Like her granny, she was too inexperienced to be

reserved," and the strange courtship, on account of this, proceeds apace. Pierston takes lodgings at Budmouth ; but finds many opportunities to come over to the island and take evening walks, sometimes with Avice the Third alone, sometimes with her mother as chaperon.

With true Hardy selectiveness, Sandsfoot or Henry VIII's Castle, which might have turned the course of events in her grandmother's day, is made the scene of Avice's enlightenment as regards Jocelyn's intentions. In this castle, open to the sky, placed on the very verge of the rag-stone cliff, Pierston consults with the mother as to her daughter's feelings, to discover that the former, at least, would not be adverse to an alliance which had just eluded her and her own mother.

Pierston somewhat neglects his courtship after this moon-light excursion to the castle, but returns to the island to bid Avice's mother good-bye. Mrs. Pierston, for such is her married name, is ill, and Avice the Third agrees on her mother's representations to marry Jocelyn. After Mrs. Pierston's recovery she and Avice visit London ; during which visit the final arrangements for the marriage are made. They then return to the island, where Jocelyn was to follow them for the event. He does so in due course, only to find his future mother-in-law again seriously ill, and while she lies abed, on what was to have been the wedding morn, Avice, her daughter, steals from the house in the company of a young Jersey man named Leverre— the son of Marcia Bencombe, whose image had supplanted that of Avice the First for a brief period in Jocelyn Pierston's errant fancy.

Thus, to some extent, was justice done to the memory of that first Avice, whom Jocelyn had jilted.

Jocelyn in the end marries Marcia, but makes it per-fectly plain to her that she is not, after all, the " well-beloved " of his life-long search. She marries him, apparently, because she ought to have done so some forty years before.

Avice the Third by this arrangement becomes Pierston's daughter-in-law by marriage ; she is forgiven and provided with a house at Sandbourne, where she had secretly met her future husband, while still a girl at the finishing school.

The novel thus ended is so unlike any other of the writer's works, that it must be classed by itself as a more than slightly fantastic study of an unusual temperament. The story probably interests the general reader chiefly because of its very elusiveness, and those who know the " Isle of Slingers," and its ways, because of the fidelity of its descriptive portions. But it is one of the few novels of Thomas Hardy of which it is possible to give a synopsis without robbing the story of its chief charm.

The other larger towns and villages, other than those we have mentioned, which appear in Hardy's works are numerous. Among them may be briefly mentioned Bridport, the " Port Bredy " of the tale *Fellow Townsmen* ; Wareham, the " Anglebury " of *The Return of the Native* and *The Hand of Ethelberta* ; Poole, the " Havenpool " of *To Please his Wife* ; Wimborne, the " Warborne " of *Two on a Tower* ; Corfe Castle, the " Corvsgate Castle " of *The Hand of Ethelberta* ; Sherborne, the " Sherton Abbas " of *Tess of the D'Urbervilles* and of *The Woodlanders*; Blandford, the " Shotsford Forum " of *Far from the Madding Crowd*; and Winchester, the " Wintoncester " of the tale *Lady Mottisfont*, and mentioned, of course, in the tragic ending of *Tess of the D'Urbervilles*.

In the wider " Wessex " of the smaller villages, many of which lie hid in the heart of this fertile land, Hardy has found fitting and singularly effective backgrounds— as in the other places we have mentioned or described— for the action of his tragic and humorous stories. He never recklessly tears a character from out of its native environment. And here, too, he has not only found opportunity for the exercise of his unrivalled powers of brilliant and picturesque description, but it is also from them that he has drawn many of his most convincing and interesting characters.

The small portion of the county of Somerset which has come within the confines of the Wessex of romance, by reason of the excursions of several of Hardy's characters into it, is a beautiful stretch of country, amid which are scattered picturesque cottages and farm-houses, many of them substantially built of yellowish stone.   The country-side, too, is noted for its beautiful churches, and scarcely a village of any size without its own and venerable sanc-tuary.   In many of Hardy's characters who happen to be Somerset folk we can almost catch the softer accent than prevails with their immediate neighbours over the border in Dorset.   The " a " is less broad, while the " s " has been softened into " z "   On the margin of the two counties one finds the form of speech still obtaining among the peasant and working-classes which has been woven into the fabric of several of Fielding's novels.

Among the Somerset towns and villages which appear in the " Wessex " novels or tales, Yeovil, the " Ivell " appear-ing in several of the collection, *A Group of Noble Dames*, and in two of *Life's Little Ironies*, *The Tragedy of Two Ambitions*, and *For Conscience' Sake*, is a town of importance.   It possesses a fine church of the Perpendicular period, and is picturesquely situated on the hillside above the River Yeo, from which, indeed, its name is derived.

From Langport north-eastwards from Frome lies a beautiful stretch of country, with the Mendip Hills sending their eastward spurs within ten miles or so of the latter town, busy with its cloth manufactures and standing on a steep slope, with its main streets climbing the hill.   The church is rather florid in type, and it was not only restored by the former Ritualistic Vicar, the Rev. W. J. E. Bennett, but possesses a remarkable Calvary, also set up by him.

Hard by is Melbury Park, the principal scene of the short story *The First Countess of Wessex*, therein disguised by Hardy under the name of " King's Hintock Court." Close to Falls Park, mentioned in the same story, are the beautifully situated ruins of Nunney Castle, once besieged by Fairfax himself during the Civil War.   Under the slopes of High Stoy lies Melbury Osmund, the " Little Hintock " of *The Woodlanders*, which the novelist so tersely, but adequately, describes as " one of those sequestered spots outside the gate of the world, where may usually be found more meditation than action, and more listlessness than meditation." This little village lies amid hills and deep hollows, which, though adding to its picturesqueness, serve to shut it in closely from the outside world.

Of other villages worth the attention of the lovers of Hardy's books, and of Hardy students, there are quite a number southward from Yeovil. Many of them, as can be well understood, are in the immediate neighbourhood of Dorchester, and can be easily reached from that ancient and historic town.

THE END

INDEX